The Business Value of Developer Relations

How and Why Technical Communities Are Key To Your Success

Mary Thengvall

With a Foreword by Jono Bacon

Apress®

The Business Value of Developer Relations

Mary Thengvall
San Francisco, California, USA

ISBN-13 (pbk): 978-1-4842-3747-2
https://doi.org/10.1007/978-1-4842-3748-9

ISBN-13 (electronic): 978-1-4842-3748-9

Library of Congress Control Number: 2018958879

Managing Director, Apress Media LLC: Welmoed Spahr
Acquisitions Editor: Louise Corrigan
Development Editor: James Markham
Coordinating Editor: Nancy Chen

Cover image designed by Erick Zelaya

Distributed to the book trade worldwide by Springer Science+Business Media New York, 233 Spring Street, 6th Floor, New York, NY 10013. Phone 1-800-SPRINGER, fax (201) 348-4505, e-mail orders-ny@springer-sbm.com, or visit www.springeronline.com. Apress Media, LLC is a California LLC and the sole member (owner) is Springer Science + Business Media Finance Inc (SSBM Finance Inc). SSBM Finance Inc is a **Delaware** corporation.

For information on translations, please e-mail rights@apress.com, or visit www.apress.com/rights-permissions.

Apress titles may be purchased in bulk for academic, corporate, or promotional use. eBook versions and licenses are also available for most titles. For more information, reference our Print and eBook Bulk Sales web page at www.apress.com/bulk-sales.

Any other supplementary material referenced by the author in this book is available to readers at https://www.marythengvall.com/devrelbook.

Printed on acid-free paper

To all the community builders and Developer Relations professionals who have been by my side for the last decade as we've built this industry from the ground up . . . this is for you

Table of Contents

TABLE OF CONTENTS

About the Author

Mary Thengvall is a connector of people at heart, both personally and professionally. She loves digging into the strategy of how to build and foster developer communities and has been doing so for more than ten years. After building community programs at O'Reilly Media, Chef Software, and SparkPost, she's now consulting for companies looking to build out a Developer Relations strategy. In addition to her work, she's known for being "the one with the dog," thanks to her ever-present medical alert service dog Ember.

Mary is founder and cohost of *Community Pulse*, a podcast for community managers and developer evangelists who are looking for information on community building. She curates *DevRel Weekly*, a weekly newsletter that provides a curated list of articles, job postings, and events every Thursday. She's also a founding member and "Benevolent Queen" of the DevRel Collective Slack team.

She is also a member of Prompt, a nonprofit that encourages people to openly talk about mental illness in tech. She speaks at various conferences and events about building and fostering technical communities, as well as how technology professionals and teams can prevent burnout.

About the Technical Reviewer

Jono Bacon is a leading community manager, speaker, author, and podcaster. He is the founder of Jono Bacon Consulting, which provides community strategy/execution, developer workflow, and other services. He also previously served as director of community at GitHub, Canonical, XPRIZE, and OpenAdvantage and has consulted and advised a range of organizations.

Bacon is a prominent author and speaker on community management and best practice, and wrote the best-selling *The Art of Community* (O'Reilly Media, 2012). He is the founder of the Community Leadership Summit, the primary annual conference for community managers and leaders, as well as the Open Collaboration Conference. Bacon is a regular keynote speaker at events on community management, organizational leadership, and best practice.

Bacon has provided community management consultancy, for both internal and external communities, for a range of organizations. These include Deutsche Bank, Huawei, GitLab, Intel, SAP, HackerOne, data.world, Sony Mobile, Samsung, Open Compute Project, IBM, Dyson, Mozilla, FINOS Foundation, Executive Centre, AlienVault, and others. He holds advisory positions at AlienVault, Moltin, data, world, Open Networking Foundation, and Open Cloud Consortium.

In addition to writing *The Art of Community*, Bacon is a columnist for *Forbes* and opensource.com, author of *Dealing with Disrespect*, and coauthored *Linux Desktop Hacks* (O'Reilly Media, 2005), and *The Official Ubuntu Book*, 2nd Edition (Prentice Hall, 2007). Bacon has published more than 500 articles in 12 different publications. He writes regularly for a range of magazines.

Bacon was cofounder of the popular *LugRadio* podcast, which ran for four years with more than 2 million downloads and 15,000 listeners, and which spawned five live events in both the UK and the United States. He also cofounded the *Shot Of Jaq* podcast and the *Bad Voltage* podcast, a popular show about technology, open source, politics, and more.

He lives in the San Francisco Bay Area with his wife, Erica, and their son, Jack.

Acknowledgments

This book was not a solitary activity. Like most things in my life, it took a community. I can't possibly thank them all, but I'd like to shine a spotlight on a few particular people.

First and foremost, my partner Jeremy Price—thank you for giving me your blessing to write this book (perhaps against your better judgement ;-)) and for standing by me through it all, even when the amount of work increased dramatically. Your support and encouragement have meant the world to me, and there's no one I'd rather share this journey with.

To my parents, thanks for your belief in my writing ability. Your encouragement over the years, from my elementary school days when I was publishing a neighborhood newspaper to your willingness to take a first pass at this book even though it's out of your element, has pushed me to where I am today.

To my sister Sarah, thank you for your pride in my work despite not understanding what it is exactly that I do ;-), and to my brother-in-law Dan, for being my virtual writing partner as you worked on your dissertation. Thanks to both of you for creating the three most amazing nieces and nephew in the whole world. Emily, Ethan, and Hannah: I love you to the very edge of the universe and back.

To my "brother" Tim—thank you for being a constant in my life, no matter how busy I am or how many times I miss your phone calls. I know you'll always be there for me, which means more than I can say.

To Aydrian, Avi, and Danielle: the original (and dare I say the best) Developer Avocados, and to Daeyon Griffin, for the slip of the tongue that has led to my professional brand. We learned a lot of lessons along the way (many of which wound up in this book!) and, more importantly, have formed friendships that I wouldn't trade for the world. You'll always be my favorite Developer Avocado team. Rest assured that I'm wearing my avocado socks for good luck as I'm writing these words.

To Louise, my amazing editor, who put forth the idea of this book and has supported and encouraged me along the way, as well as kicking my butt into gear when I needed it. You have talked me down from more than one cliff through this process, and I'll always be grateful for the friendship that we've built along the way!

ACKNOWLEDGMENTS

To Julie Gunderson, Jason Yee, and Nathen Harvey, who volunteered me to be the fourth and final author. You may not be with me at the finish line, but you successfully passed the baton to me to finish the marathon, and that's no easy task. I wouldn't be here without you, and this book wouldn't be the same without your insights and experiences.

To Laura Baldwin, president of O'Reilly Media, who gave a fresh-faced 20-something the chance of a lifetime. You jump-started my journey and opened me up to opportunities I couldn't have even dreamed of when I first asked to have conversations *with* our audience instead of just talking to them. To you and all the rest of my O'Reilly family: Sara and Sara, Courtney, Brady, Marsee, Jon, Betsy, Keith, Simon, Tony, and so many others . . . thank you for the eight years we shared!

To Carol Adams—the teacher of a lifetime. You nurtured my love for learning in ways that few others have been able to do. I still have your note from my third-grade yearbook, and I'm finally making good on sending you an autographed copy of my first book. Keep an eye on your mailbox!

Jodi, Pete, Matt, and Caryn—the four of you are some of the best friends I could ever ask for. Your encouragement, laughter, prayers, and reminders that this too shall pass got me through these last few months with (most of) my sanity in check.

And Paul—for not only listening to my explanation of why Developer Relations is like avocados with bemusement, but coming up with a brilliant name for Persea Consulting as a result. To say that your patience as I've finished this book while simultaneously planning REdeploy has been greatly appreciated is a huge understatement.

Last but certainly not least, thanks be to God, who gave me the strength to finish this book and the talent and opportunity to do it in the first place. Thank you for the continual reminder that no matter how others see me or what religious edicts are in place, I am, and always will be, yours.

Foreword

I am deeply passionate about communities. I have been ever since my earlier involvement in open source and when I started experimenting with building my first few communities back when I lived in the UK.

This early interest really culminated when I strapped on my goggles and nose-dived into a new project called Ubuntu, tasked with building a global movement around an open source operating system. Eight years later I came up for air, and we had built a community comprised of hundreds of developers around the world, millions of users, local Ubuntu groups littered across the globe, and people actively shaping Ubuntu every day by producing documentation, translations, marketing initiatives, testing, and more.

This early experience in my career showed me the true potential for harnessing groups of engineering talent and availability, particularly when wrapped around a clearly articulated mission.

I didn't fully appreciate this, though, until I worked at XPRIZE, an organization that coordinates and leads major incentive competitions. My first XPRIZE, the Global Learning XPRIZE, challenged teams to build an Android app that taught kids how to read, write, and perform arithmetic within 18 months without the aid of a teacher. It was designed to bring education to the more than 250 million kids who don't currently get it around the world. The prize purse was a whopping $15 million, underwritten in part by everyone's favorite science-reality entrepreneur, Elon Musk.

Working at XPRIZE was at times bizarre. It was an environment where over lunch we would talk about how we could solve water sanitization issues, produce vehicles to improve goods and services in rural third-world areas, use 3D printing to print houses for low-cost widespread housing initiatives, and more. This is what I loved about XPRIZE: genuine "moonshot" thinking underlined by the question "How do we incentivize people enough to make this reality?"

Unsurprisingly, the Global Learning XPRIZE attracted a wide range of people, from educators to startup founders, artists, translators, and more.

Many developers joined, but due to the competitive nature of the prize, their ideas and talent were . . . well, rather private. Competitors formed into their own teams and attacked the challenge with steel smiles and open minds, but this innovation occurred largely in a private setting, with the exception of some shared foundational projects.

As such, one element that was so compelling and familiar to me about the open source developer experience was curiously missing: problem-solving and collaboration around tractable solutions, out in the open.

This was entirely to be expected and no fault of XPRIZE. The organization was not an open source project, and the whole point of the incentive prize model is that people actually compete with each other. However, as Eleanor Roosevelt once mused, "Absence makes the heart grow stronger," and I started to miss the culture of collaborative engineering communities, with the broader open source community being one such prime example.

This realization was not merely a cultural one. It got me thinking about the psychology and driving forces behind developers. What really makes great engineers tick? Throughout my career at that point, there were clear differences in engineering cultures—such as the difference between a "GitHub generation" startup and an enterprise Windows shop—but there were a remarkable amount of consistency and common themes too.

This is something that would illustrate itself in droves over the following years. As a consultant, I build community strategy and execution for a wide range of industries, including technology, financial services, consumer products, entertainment, security, professional services, and others. A significant chunk of my work is focused on building developer communities and ecosystems where developers either build on top of a platform or contribute to a core platform itself.

Across these widely varying clients, it has been fascinating to see these consistent themes emerge among these different types of developers, even when the scope, focus, culture, and norms of these different organizations vary so significantly. Of these commonalities, though, I see one of the most significant as being a desire for *mastery*.

With any discipline—carpentry, mechanical engineering, chemical engineering, biomedicine, robotics, and others—there is a journey from *learning* to *optimization* and then *mastery*.

A fundamental principle in converting learning to mastery is not just that we can furnish ourselves with the education to deliver good work, but—importantly—that we can construct hypotheses for how to execute this work well, and then something or or someone validates or rejects our hypothesis. In other words, we need to be able to experiment and see whether our experiments work out.

For many of these other disciplines, this experimentation is limited. If you are learning bioengineering, you probably lack the equipment, certifications, and budget to do it in your home office. If you are learning chemical engineering, I doubt you have a refinery in your backyard. For many software developers, though, these limitations largely don't apply: a computer, an Internet connection, a curious mind, and a giant bucket of coffee will get you most of the way there.

There is another critical component in this developer soup du jour, though. Unlike many other institutions, code can be shared, improved, refined, and iterated at little to no cost. A global patchwork of GitHub and GitLab repositories don't just contain software—they contain our shared understanding and collaboration around common interests and problem solving.

With this common tooling, readily available (and normative) peer review, and a self-starter culture of learning and collaboration, this has jump-started millions of initial curiosities about programming into well-compensated, rewarding, in-demand careers.

The impact of all this has been profound. We have seen entire industries "disrupted" and reconstructed by talented developers with the aforementioned, not-entirely-insignificant bucket of coffee and a bundle of self-motivation. We have seen developers able to apply their talents to not just reshaping the world we live in, but to how we effect change at both a professional and social level. It is all really quite remarkable.

Tapping into this machine, though, can be a challenge for many, and this is where community engagement and Developer Relations play such critical roles. This isn't as simple as marketing and broadcasting targeted messages to developers. Great Developer Relations requires someone to not just understand the needs and goals of a developer, but to fundamentally understand the fabric of their culture—where it differs and where it is the same. Doing this well can result in remarkable results; doing it poorly can manifest in developers awkwardly shoeing away such Developer Relations like an unwanted fly at a picnic.

Before you delve into Mary's book, I will leave you with one piece of advice. Developer Relations, and more broadly how we engage and build culture in communities, is a remarkably nuanced, complex, and context-specific discipline. There simply isn't a one-shot recipe that works well for everyone. You can benefit from others, such as the insight from Mary in this book, but consider this guidance as a starting point to get you going and then evolve your own approach.

I tell this to my clients all the time: every community is different, and although many methods and techniques work well and reliably, the most critical skill of all to learn is observing what is happening in your community and being able to react and optimize it. Just like with software engineering: learn, optimize—and then true mastery of your own can be accomplished.

This is an exciting journey. Good luck!

Jono Bacon

Jono Bacon Consulting

www.jonobacon.com | jono@jonobacon.com

May 2018

Introduction

This book is for anyone who's trying to figure out what a technical community is and why it's essential for the success of certain companies. It's for Developer Relations and Community Manager professionals, as well as directors, VPs, and C-suite folks who are trying to manage those teams within an ever-changing landscape of company goals and priorities. It's for those who are discouraged by the misconceptions of community building as well as those who are encouraged by the influx of companies trying to hire someone who understands the developer audience. It's for those who have yet to discover the true value of Developer Relations, as well as those who know that it has inherent value but struggle to put it into words.

But first, what is Developer Relations? At its foundation, the purpose of Developer Relations (or DevRel) is to *build relationships with the developer community*. DevRel professionals act as a liaison between their company and the developer audience, who are typically the end users of the product. Whereas most professionals have the best interests of the business at their front of their minds driving their day-to-day decisions, DevRel professionals have the best interests of the community as their driving factor. They, of course, care about the success of the business as well—it is, after all, what pays their bills—but they understand that if the community is happy and successful as a result of using the product, the business is far more likely to succeed as well.

In order for the DevRel team to succeed, however, they must be fully supported by the company. From having a clear set of business goals and expectations to having the right tools for the job, they need to know that their work is seen as valuable and is therefore not only allowed but actively encouraged by the stakeholders in their company.[1]

Many companies are realizing that it's not enough to simply have a Developer Relations team. The stakeholders must understand the true value such a team provides, and the team must be set up for success.

---

[1]You can read more on the items that every company needs to have a successful DevRel team in Anil Dash's post "A Developer Relations Bill of Rights": https://medium.com/glitch/a-developer-relations-bill-of-rights-21381920e273

As such, this book is divided into two distinct sections. These sections, while applicable for both groups I've mentioned, are geared toward different audiences. Part I (Chapters 1–5) is directed toward the decision makers in the company who are trying to understand the value of a technical community. Their questions likely revolve around whether or not they need to foster their community, what the appropriate metrics are, what the difference is between Developer Relations and community building, and how to create a successful team.

In Chapter 1, I address the key questions you want to ask before investing in a technical community: why do you want one, what do you hope to accomplish, and who actually makes up your community?

Chapters 2–4 speak to creating a business case for building a technical community. How do you convince the business owners and decision makers that connecting with the developer community is an important investment, and how do you agree on metrics to ensure alignment and success?

Once we've discussed how to build this business case for including Developer Relations in your success strategy, it's time to figure out who's going to help fill that role. Chapter 5 walks through who your first hire should be, what the differences are between a community manager, Developer Advocate, and technical evangelist, and where your newly founded Developer Relations team should be placed within your organization.

Part II (Chapters 6–10) is geared toward the Developer Relations practitioners— those who are involved in community building on a daily basis. Their questions focus more on the day-to-day tactics, including finding the right audience, walking the tightrope between representing the company and building a personal brand (which also benefits the company), and doing in-person events.

Chapters 6–8 dive into what you can accomplish now that you actually have a team in place, from finding your particular segment of developers to interacting with them, both online and in person.

Lastly, I wrap things up by talking about some common issues that can pop up and how to prevent them (Chapter 9), as well as what it means to build your personal brand alongside the company and community (Chapter 10).

Throughout the chapters, I'm joined by other Developer Relations professionals who share their stories and give specific, real-world examples so that you can see a practical application of the principles I put forth. It should be noted that there is no "magic bullet" to building a community or being successful with a particular developer audience, and following the example of another company just because it was successful for them isn't always the best solution.[2] But by using the principles I've laid out to walk through your company goals and discover where Developer Relations fits within that framework, you can formulate a plan tailored to your specific community.

For some, it will make sense to read straight through, following the process from start to finish and building out your documents, resolutions, and goals as you go. Others should feel free to jump around to solve any problems you're having right now. I often refer back to topics addressed in a previous chapter, so you'll know whether there's relevant material you should reference.

If you're reading this in print format, don't worry about trying to type in all the URLs. I've created an online resource to make your life a little easier—just navigate to marythengvall.com/devrelbook.

I embarked on this writing adventure largely because the essence of the word *community* has impacted me greatly. From launching my career and enabling adventures to facilitating lifelong friendships and making my daily job something that I love, I am deeply committed to communities both personally and professionally: building, fostering, engaging, and loving them. As such, my viewpoint may be a little unique and different from the typical "put the company first" mentality. But I truly believe that if you put the community first, the company will succeed. On the other hand, if we choose to value the product over the community that uses it, we harm both ourselves and the company as a whole, setting us up for potential failure at worst, or at best, keeping the company from reaching its full potential. It's my hope that this book will not only prove the intrinsic value that exists within developer communities, but it will encourage you to place relationship- and community-building at the core of your business.

Let's begin, shall we?

---

[2]https://twitter.com/matthewrevell/status/1003477945707462656

PART I

What Is the Value of a Technical Community?

CHAPTER 1

An Introduction to Community

If you run a Google search for "community" you'll find a wide variety of results, from the hit TV sitcom of that name to three different online dictionary definitions, to a handful of developer community websites for particular brands, to a company that sells loudspeakers. With almost five billion search results, it's no wonder people in the technology industry have such a hard time agreeing on what a community actually is, who it's comprised of, and how to work with them.

BusinessDictionary.com[1] says community is defined as a "Self-organized network of people with common agenda, cause, or interest, who collaborate by sharing ideas, information, and other resources". Merriam-Webster says[2] it's everything from a unified body of individuals to society as a whole, or even a social state of condition. Dictionary.com[3] defines community as "a social, religious, occupational, or other group sharing common characteristics or interests and perceived or perceiving itself as distinct in some respect from the larger society within which it exists". But even this implies that everyone within the group holds largely the same beliefs and comes from a similar background.

Nothing could be further from the truth when you're talking about technical communities. The only thing that by definition should bring us together is a common use of or interest in a particular technology, role, tool, or programming language. Yet in my experience, although the starting place may be the use of a particular piece of software, that's not what makes technical communities special. What starts out as a simple response to a question can lead to a mentorship opportunity, a collaborative project, or the overwhelming success of a product.

---

[1] http://www.businessdictionary.com/definition/community.html
[2] https://www.merriam-webster.com/dictionary/community
[3] http://www.dictionary.com/browse/community

© Mary Thengvall 2018
M. Thengvall, *The Business Value of Developer Relations*, https://doi.org/10.1007/978-1-4842-3748-9_1

Leveraging these definitions and my own professional experience, the definition that I propose for community as it relates to a technical audience is the following:

A group of people who not only share common principles, but also develop and share practices that help individuals in the group thrive

It's important to keep this definition in mind as you work your way through the topics in this book—it will come into play in how you define your departmental goals, what direction you decide to go in with your team, and how you interact with your community.

Establish the (Flexible) Boundaries

Generally speaking, you'll want your community to be inclusive—not limiting yourself to free or paid customers, or even, for that matter, to only those who are actively using your products. You'll want it to be inclusive in other ways as well: accepting of all (respectful) opinions and insights, no matter who they come from or how they challenge the current standards. This isn't always easy! Creating a welcoming, safe environment where everyone feels included is a difficult task that requires a lot of empathy, forethought, and humility to admit when you're wrong. But it's been proven that a more diverse workplace results in better products as well as a healthier work environment,[4] and this is true in communities as well.

We'll talk later about the importance of getting feedback from a wide variety of customers—paid as well as free accounts, end users as well as buyers, and an assortment of company sizes, as well as gender and geographic demographics. Without a diverse group of customers, you'll wind up with biased feedback, which at best can result in a product that doesn't meet the needs of particular customers and at worst can actively offend the community you're trying to interact with.

That said, though being inclusive is important, you also need to define whom you want to actively engage with as a part of your community, and where the role of Developer Relations (DevRel) comes into play. Are you looking to engage new customers who may not have fully bought into the product yet? Is your priority to work

---

[4]https://www.mckinsey.com/business-functions/organization/our-insights/why-diversity-matters
https://hbr.org/2018/03/5-things-we-learned-about-creating-a-successful-workplace-diversity-program

with customers who are already actively engaged, gaining feedback and working with the product and engineering teams to improve your product based on said feedback? Perhaps you want to build up a community of external advocates who will in turn help increase your community support and awareness as you move into new geographic locations. Or maybe you're trying to find folks within the larger developer community who may not be using your product but who have the potential to do so.

Each of these questions ties into a concrete business value that aligns with a company goal: reducing churn, having a better product roadmap, reducing customer acquisition cost, recruiting employees, and more. The real question isn't whether DevRel is capable of contributing value, but which particular value it should focus on at this point in time.

Establishing your overarching goals for community engagement helps you define what your community looks like and what areas you should focus on. Giving yourself an all-inclusive view of community is great, but it can cause problems when your team is suddenly tasked with reaching "anyone and everyone who could possibly use or is already using our product." That's too broad of a task and has too many stakeholders in the company, resulting in an overwhelmed DevRel team with too many tasks on their plates, struggling to figure out what their priorities are. Suddenly, no matter what department DevRel falls under, they've got marketing, product, engineering, customer support, and sales clamoring for their attention. By understanding the specific value this team brings to the company and which segment of the community they should focus on, you can prioritize and delegate these overwhelming and sometimes conflicting requests.

So, first things first: it's essential that you understand your company goals. Once those are clear, think about whether or how fostering an active community can help your company achieve those goals. Here are some questions you'll want to ask:

- Why do you want a community?

- What do you hope to accomplish with a community?

- Who makes up your community?

- Which segment of that community do you want to focus on first?

And perhaps most relevant to our conversations throughout this book:

- Do you actually need a Developer Relations team to accomplish those goals? (Hint: the answer isn't always yes!)

Why Do You Want a Community?

To begin with, you have to establish the *why* behind your community. This is also a question you'll ask every time you contemplate a new community initiative. Why is this question a top priority? Because your *why* drives how you will interact with your community. It will also drive the structure of who handles and is responsible for which aspects of the community, as well as where you send people for more resources.

Let me be clear: the question isn't whether you're choosing to create a community or not, but whether you choose to be an active participant in fostering the community that already exists. Whether you've spent the time to build up a community, every product has a community of customers, both current and potential. But as I said earlier, your *why* determines how you choose to interact with this community.

The *why* doesn't have to be quantitative metrics—it can be abstract—but it should be aligned with the organization's goals and explain the purpose behind each community-related endeavor at the company. You'll also want to make sure your *why* is driven by a reason, not by a result. For example, *to make a profit* is a *result* of growing relationships, nurturing leads, and having a great product, not a *reason* to do what you're doing. Your reason for establishing a community might be generating engagement, making a better product, or improving customer retention.

PAGERDUTY'S GOAL IS TO IMPROVE THE ENTIRE INDUSTRY

Matt Stratton is a DevOps evangelist at PagerDuty, a digital operations management platform that allows organizations to access data in real time, resolve and prevent business-impacting incidents, and automate workflows with machine learning. Part of his role as an evangelist is to assist PagerDuty's innovation in the incident response and prevention space and help the entire industry improve as a result of combining machine and human data for better outcomes.

"Our philosophies about incident response and prevention are baked into the very DNA of our product. The workshops that we do around incident command training don't have anything to do with PagerDuty explicitly, except for the fact that those theories and principles are the foundation of the company. In other words, while using PagerDuty technology isn't required to be effective at incident response, the principles and the product have a natural symbiotic relationship, as it's the default path that we lay out for you.

"Part of what attracted me to PagerDuty in the first place was the amount of data that we've collected around incident response over the last nine years. We're now starting to analyze that data and draw conclusions from it that can begin to help the ops community as a whole. As the team gathers information and tests it internally, I can then take that information out to the larger community and share the insights that we're gaining, which helps to drive the entire industry forward. I also gather data and feedback from the community, and then relay that to our product groups. They use that information to continue growing and shaping the product so that it's more useful for our end-users.

"This becomes a virtuous cycle that brings value back to the company as well, as we use this data and feedback to build out further training sessions and materials to show how we're using these principles internally. We're setting ourselves up to be the experts in the field, and at the same time, directly impacting the community by enabling them to drive these practices forward.

"We do this because we want to help other people's lives be easier when it comes to incident response and prevention. But at the end of the day, when the way that we think about doing things and the principles that we follow are seen as 'state of the art,' then that becomes the natural glide path that leads you to PagerDuty."

Your company goals should make the reason for your community clear. Once you've got your *why* solidified, you can figure out what the result might be, which leads us to our next question.

What Do You Hope to Accomplish with a Community?

This question is arguably similar to "Why do you want a community?" but it can help determine whether you're trying to create a community of customers or simply define a market. This answer is going to be different for every segment of the technology industry. For example, companies working on cloud infrastructure will be looking to a different audience than those working with programming frameworks, which will be different yet from a company focused on developer tooling.

Even for companies that fall within the same operating space, their reasons for building a community will vary. Some might be looking for a core group of customers to get periodic feedback from; others are hoping to set themselves up as thought leaders in a new space; still others want to follow trends within their niche and rely on their connections in the community to keep them apprised of these developments.

For companies that have both free and paid customers, the scenario for each of these customer groups is slightly different as well. Developer Relations is both the very top and very bottom of the funnel—responsible for brand awareness as well as making sure customers are taken care of. Free customers fall into the first category. They start out as the very top of the funnel and through relationship building, consistency, and trust can move into the "free customer" tier. One goal of the DevRel team could be to support these free customers and encourage their transition to a paid account, whether in their current company or in the next.

What's the core principle that brings all these scenarios together? Some may say the end goal of engaging with your customers is to generate more business. Although that's a great strategy and is often the end result of a strong community, it doesn't help define the goals of your DevRel team, as we'll talk about in the chapters to come.

Let's go back to our definition of community for a moment:

> *A group of people who not only share common principles, but also <u>develop and share practices that help individuals in the group thrive</u>*

The second part is what sets a community apart from a group of customers. You can have a group of people who share common principles (they want to send emails to their customers smoothly and seamlessly, or are using automation as a foundation for their high-velocity organization) without having them actively engage with each other, but it's difficult to have a true community without having folks who want to develop and share practices that help others thrive.

True communities have a desire to help each other, whether through contributing to open source SDKs, example code, and documentation or by mentoring other community members. Figuring out which of these accomplishments is the best fit for your product is an important step. What will help grow your customer base as well as create that "sticky" community that will ensure success for years to come?

Who Makes Up Your Community?

If someone tells you that their community is everyone and anyone, be careful. As I mentioned earlier, you want your community to be inclusive, but it's also important for there to be a sense of commitment and care for each other, even if that care is as broad as wanting each other to be successful in their programming ventures. This care leads to a desire to help each other—to mentor, encourage, and offer assistance wherever possible. This increases the "stickiness" of your community, ensuring that people who come are far more likely to stay. After all, why would someone want to leave a community that is both open and welcoming, and is also willing to help them out of a tough spot?

That being said, even the most inclusive of communities should have their limits. Saying your product is "for all developers" is awfully broad, and almost certainly not the case. Is your product truly easy enough to use that a brand-new developer can figure it out on their own? Is it oriented toward teams, or can a single engineer in a startup find value in it as well? Are you looking for the older, more experienced developer or sysadmin who knows the ropes and who can tell you stories about the old days when they had to do all this by hand? Or the fresh-faced, just-out-of-school developer, who's excited about the depth of your API and constantly looking for the next release? Are you willing to put up with the attitude of someone who has been everywhere and knows "everything"? Or are you only willing to accept those who are accepting of everyone around them, no matter their skill level? What about the expert who is capable of explaining complex topics but is also condescending to those who don't grasp the concept the first time around?

As you let yourself start to think about all of the possible character traits of your community members, you may start to reconsider your "everyone is welcome!" stance. Whether this means you establish community guidelines and a code of conduct prior to establishing an official community (hint: I highly recommend doing this and cover how to do so in Chapter 7), or perhaps look at redefining your overarching circle of inclusion, or both, it's safe to say that you'll find at least a handful of people who may not be the best fit for the community you're nurturing.

As you come across these people in your community, they'll either begin to weed themselves out as they figure out it's not the right fit or change their expectations (and behavior) to meet the expectations of those around them.

So, even if you say "our audience is developers," take a moment to figure out which developers you actually mean. It might actually be that your audience is just that broad—any and all developers, no matter the programming language or experience level—but chances are slim. At the very least, you should be able to narrow it down to your *primary* community: the one that will have the most impact on and benefit for the company, and your *secondary* community: those on the outskirts who dip their toes into the deeper community issues on occasion.

THE EXCLUSIVITY OF THE DEVREL COLLECTIVE SLACK TEAM

In my spare time, I help maintain a Slack Team for community builders and Developer Advocates.[5] The group started as a way for a handful of us in the Developer Relations industry to stay in touch online. We initially had a broad "invite who you know" mentality, and there weren't any rules about who was or wasn't welcome. Anyone who organized a meetup, helped out with a conference, spoke a lot, or even was vaguely interested in community building was welcome. As the group started growing, though, we realized that having the boundaries drawn that broadly was actually hurting the group rather than helping. Suddenly, the conversations, while still good, were revolving around "what's the hottest new conference?" rather than "how do we encourage our community?" and a few of us admins started wondering how to fix this problem.

These days, though conferences (which ones to sponsor as well as which ones to speak at) are still a popular topic of conversation, the process of joining the DevRel Collective community is a little more official. We now ask folks for information about who they are and how they're involved in community building on a day-to-day basis, as well as what their title is, before sending them an invitation to join the Slack team. Anyone who's casually involved in community building or who speaks at and organizes conferences on a regular basis is a great contact to have—but may not be a good fit for in-depth conversations around how to navigate CFPs when your title has "community" in it or what roadblocks we come across when trying to communicate effectively across various departments. And the folks who joined us early on who weren't the best fit? They were never officially asked to leave. They simply realized the group wasn't for them.

---

[5]If you're working in DevRel full-time, you can apply to join it here: http://devrelcollective.fun

In a world where everything is becoming more inclusive (which is a good thing!), it's a bit of an unexpected move to make your community more *exclusive*. However, sometimes it's not only necessary, but beneficial to do so.

Which Segment of The Community Do You Want to Focus on First?

If your company is relatively new, your primary audience is probably going to be anyone and everyone who's currently using your product. Set up a plan to connect with them on a regular basis, whether via email, video conference, or in person. Listen to their feedback, document the issues they're having (both with your product and in their general day-to-day work), and start making notes about how you can better serve them. What problems can you solve? What tools can you build? How can you make their experience better? Why is someone choosing to leave your tool and pursue another option? Even these "exit interviews" can be valuable learning experiences.

As your customer base grows, your primary audience will start to reveal itself. You'll learn to see patterns among the people who gravitate toward your product. Are they front-end developers? Project managers? Sysadmins? Experienced app builders? Open source developers? Whatever role these folks play, you'll want to make sure you're prioritizing their problems. As shown by the popularity of "+1" buttons on GitHub, JIRA, Google bug reports, and more, it's clear that for every person who takes the time to submit a user experience problem, bug, or feature request, there are 10 others wishing for it. Whether you're collecting this data via these "+1" feature requests, specific tags in support tickets, or in-person feedback received at a developer event, it's essential to listen and respond to each one, even with a simple thank you. What may seem like a simple response to you could be what makes someone decide to use your product instead of your competitor's.

Your secondary audience can be found in a number of different places depending on the sales structure of your company and the nature of your product. If your product is geared toward enterprise companies, it's likely that your secondary audience is made up of your primary audience's management. Although they may not be the end users of your product, they're the ones you'll have to convince to make the initial investment. And although it might make logical sense to make these decision makers your primary audience, you're actually setting yourself up for a difficult road if you do so. This audience is used to being sold to, and although building community involves nurturing a lot of relationships, sales should never be the primary goal for the Developer Relations team.

Your secondary audience might also be part of a different department entirely. Perhaps your primary audience is sysadmins who want to automate their services, but the web developers are the ones responsible for writing the automation scripts. You'll want to make sure your documentation is clear for both audiences and includes references that will help both the developers as well as the sysadmins as they navigate your product for the first time.

A successful product is one that can appeal to developers through its ease of use, attractiveness of the tool, and "stickiness" of the community—*and* simultaneously win over decision makers with pricing, business solutions, and practicality.

So, Do You Need a Developer Relations Team?

This is likely the most important question you'll ask yourself at this stage in the game. As I've already established, *community* is a buzzword these days, and hiring a community manager/technical evangelist/developer advocate is on every startup's checklist. But should it be? For companies that don't have any open source code, or whose users are self-sufficient once they get up and running, connecting via social media and conferences might be enough of a community presence. For others such as open source companies and collaborative projects, fostering that community is the difference between success and failure.

If you're thinking you might be one of the first types of company, don't close the book yet. Regardless of whether you're building an established community of customers or simply engaging a particular market segment, connecting with your customers on a regular basis to make sure you're on the right path is essential. Reaching out for feedback often, making sure that the decisions the company is making correlate with what your customers are looking for, and syncing up with the folks who leave as well as the ones who choose to stay can result in invaluable lessons and huge wins. Having a basic plan of how to interact with your customers (Chapter 7), understanding how to reach them where they are (Chapter 6), and how to find the events that your audience frequents (Chapter 8) are just as important as ever. At the other end of the spectrum, having a customer base with no plan for how to interact with them can result in causing your company far more harm than good, which I touch on in Chapter 2.

SINNERSCHRADER'S UNEXPECTED TRANSITION TO DEVELOPER RELATIONS

When Felicitas Kugland started developing in HTML, CSS, and JavaScript over a decade ago, she learned quickly just how helpful the greater developer community could be. These days, at digital agency SinnerSchrader, she's able to put her experience to use, helping the agency become a benchmark for technical companies in Germany and create attractive open source projects. But Developer Relations looks slightly different at an agency than it does at a SaaS or Open Source company. Felicitas explains:

"SinnerSchrader is an agency that builds digital transformational products, which means we're often helping companies reshape the usage of their products and transform their business reality. Developers aren't our audience, but Developer Relations is still incredibly important to us.

"By being involved in conferences, hosting meetups, and helping to organize various developer events all over Europe, we can show the community that we care about their interests. We of course want developers to know who SinnerSchrader is, understand what we do, and possibly even join our team. But we also want to show what we stand for. Our goal is to make SinnerSchrader a standard for what tech companies should be, so that other companies have an example of inclusion, diversity, and community service to follow. This means being involved in community work like organizing events, contributing to open source software, and offering open source tools, in addition to building a network and finding the right people to join our team.

"By enabling our developers to do all of these things, our company benefits from their increased knowledge, but more importantly, our developers are able to learn and grow from the community around them. These days, as principal product engineer working in Developer Relations, I'm also a crucial part of our technical hiring process, but even more importantly, I'm able to give back to this community which has helped me to grow and believe in myself throughout the years."

Likewise, if you're going to hire a Developer Relations professional, make sure you have a clear direction for them. Know what your purpose behind engaging the community is, and what your metrics around those goals are (more about this in Chapter 4). Again, the "need" for Developer Relations depends on the company-defined goals: maybe you're trying to break into a new geographic region or connect to your community beyond the confines of cubicles and desks, or perhaps your goal is simply to build brand awareness. Before committing to a Developer Relations team, make sure you have a clear understanding of the objective.

This goal setting also enables you to decide which role is the best way for you to start building your Developer Relations team. As Chapter 5 explains, there are a variety of roles that are good starting places. From a technical community manager who might not have a developer background but who can speak knowledgeably both on and offline about the product, to a Developer Advocate who can build out your documentation and sample applications, to someone who falls somewhere in the middle and who also excels at public speaking, your first hire is going to be determined by your goals.

This is why starting with *why* is so crucial to making any decisions.[6] Without having the foundation or touchstone you can come back to anytime there's a question about your roadmap, the DevRel team risks being pulled in too many incompatible directions, which dilutes your ability to prove business value. More importantly, without a *why* for hiring a Developer Relations professional (be they a community manager, Developer Advocate, or some role in between), you run the risk of trying to shove a square peg into a round hole because you don't have clear expectations for the individual.

At the end of the day, if you do decide to go the route of hiring a Developer Relations professional, make sure to give them leeway to make decisions as they see fit. Give them the tools they need to prioritize the needs of the many and set them up for success instead of leading them into a situation where they're simply a support system for marketing, support, product, and sales. I talk more about how to do this in Chapter 5.

Be Willing to Make Changes

In the beginning stages of community building, immediate wins are key to establishing your credibility and value to the company. At the same time, it's also one of the hardest times to guarantee wins, because you're just getting established in the community.

---

[6]Simon Sinek's TED talk "Start with Why" explains this concept in further depth: `https://www.ted.com/talks/simon_sinek_how_great_leaders_inspire_action`

This is where connecting with your core community members is crucial. The more you can optimize for what your primary audience is looking for, what motivates them, or what events they're attending (or organizing) that you might be able to sponsor, the better the chance your experiments have of succeeding.

There will still be hits and misses when it comes to what type of community engagement is right for your company. Maybe you thought a specific conference would be a perfect opportunity to connect with potential community members, but after attending you didn't see the desired result. Perhaps you tried to create a community of external advocates but couldn't find customers who were interested in the opportunity. By leaning on the support and insight of your primary audience, you can optimize for success and minimize failure.

We'll talk more about *quick wins* in Chapter 4, but in short, aiming for small successes that are sure wins in these early stages is a good way to set your team up for success. Save the big wins for later down the road when you have the backing of the community, a slightly higher budget, and the trust of your department. Aiming for the stars is great in concept, but in reality can lead to losses that can cost your team the small social capital you've been able to build up in the company.

Ask the opinions of other Developer Relations teams in your particular industry as well—though you obviously won't want to share your secret sauce, your fiercest competition might also be your closest allies. They may be willing to share insight into the best conferences and meetups, as well as the pitfalls they've experienced along the way.[7]

Overall, keep in mind that flexibility is always going to pay off. Be prepared to review and change strategy as your experience grows. For now, let's jump into the most difficult piece of community management: selling it to your company.

---

[7]https://twitter.com/mary_grace/status/923287669940948992

CHAPTER 2

Selling Community to Your Company

Convincing the stakeholders at your company that Developer Relations (DevRel) is not only valuable but worth investing in will simultaneously be your biggest struggle and most rewarding victory. It's not a "one and done" situation; you'll need to continue proving the value and impact of community building and Developer Relations.

Don't let that discourage you, however—just like the Sales department needs to prove its value by keeping the pipeline full, and Marketing is expected to provide relevant content to the proper audience(s), the Developer Relations team is expected to contribute value to the company.

The first step in this process is making sure that the objectives and goals of the team line up with the overall company goals. For instance, if the company has a generic goal of "selling to more companies," the Developer Relations team can help move the needle through brand awareness, relationship building, and representing the company as thought leaders in the industry.

Let's be clear about one thing, though: the primary goal of Developer Relations is not lead generation. Now before you close the book, be sure to hear what I'm saying. One of the many fantastic outputs of Developer Relations is an increase in the sales pipeline. But that should happen naturally as a result of relationship building and brand awareness. It's a fantastic way to make your product "sticky," which leads to customers becoming brand ambassadors on your behalf, spreading the word about your product to others in the industry. It's a wonderful side effect of your work and a great way to show the value of your unconventional efforts—but again, it should never be the primary goal. In short, the Developer Relations team should never carry a quota related to a particular number of leads or the amount of money they've contributed to the pipeline. The second that any developer community realizes your Developer Relations team simply wants them to sign on the dotted line, you've lost credibility with them.

© Mary Thengvall 2018
M. Thengvall, *The Business Value of Developer Relations*, https://doi.org/10.1007/978-1-4842-3748-9_2

Developer Relations is both the very top and very bottom of the funnel—responsible for brand awareness as well as for making sure customers are taken care of. These relationships start out at the very top of the funnel and through relationship building, consistency, and trust can move into the "free customer" tier, where they are then supported by the DevRel team as well as other departments throughout the company. This support can encourage a transition to a paid account, whether in their current company or in the next. With regard to both free and paying customers, DevRel supports the community's need for tooling, advocates for their needs on the product road map, and connects them to each other.

As community leader Eamon Leonard says,

DevRel is the people building the train tracks. Marketing builds the train station. Engineering builds the train. Sales drives the train home. It's essential to have each part or the train goes nowhere.

Before we get ahead of ourselves and decide which is the best way to show the value of Developer Relations (Chapter 4 talks more about metrics), let's take a step back: how do you convince your company that there's a need for Developer Relations in the first place?

Gathering of the Stakeholders

Perhaps one of the most important things you can do to further the case of spending company money on a relatively expensive department that only indirectly impacts the pipeline is consult the stakeholders. The *stakeholders* are, quite literally, those who have a stake in the business, though specifically who stakeholders are will differ from company to company. At an early-stage startup, the stakeholders might be the founder and the board. At bigger companies, they're likely the heads of the departments—the CTO and CMO, for instance. In short, these individuals have a significant interest in what overarching tasks Developer Relations will be responsible for, as well as what metrics will be tracked in order to prove value. They'll also be directly impacted by the actions of the Developer Relations team.

So, who are the particular stakeholders for Developer Relations within your company? You can usually narrow it down by asking these questions:

- Who outside of your immediate department is involved with the project?

- What team may be affected by the project's outcome?

- Who gains (or loses) from the success of the DevRel team?

- Can you clearly identify the benefit of this relationship for the DevRel team?

- If your relationship with this stakeholder improves, does it positively impact your team?

The *RACI matrix*[1]—figuring out who in your team or company is responsible, accountable, consulted, or informed—is an effective way of finding your particular stakeholders as well. By focusing on building these specific relationships, you set Developer Relations up for success with the individuals who will be making decisions for and about your team rather than trying to please everyone throughout the company.

Once you've established who they are, helping the stakeholders in your company understand the value of a Developer Relations team is key to securing the necessary funding. This will take some research on your part. You'll want a solid understanding of both what the company goals are and where they're coming from, as well as the areas where Developer Relations can offer assistance, expertise, or value within the company. Which departments could be doing more but never get the head count? Which processes could be streamlined if additional help were provided? What's out of the scope of your marketing team (for example, technical content), product team (for example, having one-on-one conversations with your community as someone who both understands your product and what the day-to-day developer life looks like), or engineering team (for example, being the public face of the company at various conferences)? DevRel is a beautiful Venn diagram of all of these things, and more.

---

[1]See www.projectsmart.co.uk/raci-matrix.php for more information.

COREOS DEVELOPER RELATIONS HELPS GREASE THE WHEELS

Paul Burt joined Red Hat as a technical liaison following the acquisition of CoreOS, where he served as a community manager and product marketing manager. CoreOS innovated container and distributed systems software, and Paul sees Developer Relations as the grease that keeps the machine running smoothly.

"If a business is a machine, DevRel is the grease that turns the wheels, making everything function more reliably. It almost always exists simply to make what's there more efficient. When I joined CoreOS, the wheel that I was greasing wasn't a completely new task. Rather, it allowed teams to direct their focus back to their specialties—PR, marketing, or engineering—and allowed me to focus on what I knew: gathering feedback from and connecting with the community.

"You can absolutely run a company without a community team! It just means that when passions ignite and the fire grows out of control, you may not have the right equipment to control the fire. It's likely you haven't yet built up the trust with the community that's required to put the fire out.

"It seems to be a common theme among a lot of DevRel teams, in addition to some sysadmin or QA roles—when things are going just fine, everyone wonders what your job is and what value you're providing. Yet when everything blows up, people are furious that you didn't do more to stop it, even though you weren't given the tools you needed to do your job successfully. With all of these roles, you're effectively combating risk, and it's incredibly difficult to put a number value on that, which makes it that much more challenging to ask for additional head count or resources.

"The key is realizing how much harder things would be without Developer Relations—what things would fall apart? Which relationships would you lose? How much more difficult would your processes be? What work would land on someone's plate who doesn't have the time or the expertise to deal with those issues? That's where DevRel fits in—they make sure things keep humming along so that everyone else can go about their work without worrying about the machinery breaking down, all while knowing that DevRel has a hand in the overall success of the business as a result."

Understanding these key points can lead to consensus around not only what the Developer Relations team is responsible for, but what the overall company goals are as well. As a consensus builder, you have to understand how each department relates to the overall goals. You also need to know how your work relates to the overall company goals while at the same time supporting other departments.

Let's start by asking a few key questions that will help you understand how Developer Relations can be helpful to your company. Understanding how the Developer Relations team fits within the overall company goals will help you figure out how to position your request to the stakeholders.

What Are You Trying to Accomplish?

This is the most important question to ask because the answer will drive goals and initiatives and ultimately be your true north as you navigate company politics and priorities. There are typically three options with Developer Relations, and which road you choose to take depends largely on your company and the product you're selling.

- *Are you looking to build a community of people who are drawn together solely because of your product?* This is common for companies whose products are predominantly open source as well as those that are focused on content sharing (for example, YouTube, Pinterest, and so on). For these companies, their product is completely dependent on people using, sharing, contributing, and being brand ambassadors for the company. The community is not a feature that's "nice to have"—it's an essential part of the company, and one quite literally cannot succeed without the other.

- *Are you looking to improve the Developer Experience?* For any technology company with a developer audience (for example, API-driven SaaS or PaaS companies), the *Developer Experience* (also known as DevEx or DX) is paramount. The initial experience that developers have when engaging with your product is a key determining factor of whether or not they will become a customer. From the ease of onboarding via your documentation to example code and SDKs, everything you can do to decrease their *time-to-value metric* (discussed in Chapter 4) significantly reduces both sales cycle time and the possibility of churn.

As we'll talk about more in Chapter 5, Developer Experience is often a subset of Developer Relations—they both require someone who understands the needs of your specific developer audience and who has the ability to translate that into clearly written technical content. This content could be anything from marketing and sales messaging and blog posts to documentation and sample applications.

- *Are you looking to help your company more clearly communicate with your developer audience?* Let's be honest: at most tech companies, very few people within the company don't have some sort of contact with the community—from sales calls and social media interactions to customer interviews and onboardings. So, what difference does the Developer Relations team make? In short, Developer Relations is the only team whose job revolves solely around the community.

  Although there isn't a "typical" day for a DevRel professional, their day always starts and ends with the customer—current, prospective, and potential. Whether it's helping Marketing with the most recent messaging, following up on mentorships within the developer community, working with a customer to solve a particularly difficult integration, or representing the company at a conference, the customer is front-of-mind at all times. This means they're the experts when it comes to how to communicate with the developer audience, from what language does—or doesn't—resonate to what types of content are valuable.

Your Version May Vary

Most companies are a hybrid of the scenarios we just worked through. The product might not be 100% open source, but with SDKs or various add-ons that have an open source presence, the community can see the value in contributing to these code bases. Using the open source community as a way to stay connected to the rest of the customer base can be helpful, as they may be inclined to quickly build out features they're waiting for rather than wait for the company to implement them.

Still other companies may only maintain a minimal amount of open source projects but might look to the Developer Relations team to help with messaging, brand awareness, and thought leadership, in addition to connecting one-on-one with developers in specific local regions. In other cases, DevRel winds up being a part of the retention plan for the platform—not from a sales acquisition standpoint, but because they can relate to the customers and help understand the pain points. This can lead to a decreased churn rate simply because of the increased trust and one-on-one connection with the community.

DEVREL AT RAPIDAPI MEANS HELPING THE CUSTOMER (AND THE CUSTOMER'S CUSTOMERS) SUCCEED

Like most companies, RapidAPI succeeds when its customers do, but in this case this premise is a little more explicit. RapidAPI is a platform where developers can find, test, and connect to APIs from one centralized location. That means its community is not only developers, but the API companies featured on its platform. Developer Advocate Alex Walling explains what this means for his job:

"My number one goal is to encourage the success of those API companies, because it pays off for us as well. Similar to most places, our community is made up of our customers, but in this case, we're not only supporting the various API companies, but their communities as well. So while we're engaging with companies like Imgur, FullContact, and Slack to make sure that they're having a good experience with our platform, we're also engaging with their customers to make sure that their experience is a smooth one too.

"My role is a mixture of selling, marketing, and getting people excited about the platform. I'm not the one signing contracts for new sign-ups, but I'm often the one talking to API companies about how we can help grow their community and work with them to increase the awareness of their APIs. Working with our partnerships team to figure out what might be an effective hook for these developer-focused companies is quickly becoming part of my job description, since I'm often the one on the front lines talking to our potential customers about our product. Given that I'm approaching that problem as a developer, I have a unique perspective. I can figure out what other developers might respond to well, and help arm my teammates with that information so that their future conversations are that much more successful.

"Working for a small company, my role isn't as straightforward as some other Developer Relations teams. Some days I'm working heavily with the Sales team, talking to them about what problems developers are hoping to solve with our platform. Other days I might be focused on marketing materials and case studies. Still other days I'll be working on support tickets, figuring out what the biggest problem areas are and then taking that data back to Engineering and Product to help with the road map.

"At the end of the day, I'm tasked with interfacing between the community of developers and my colleagues to make sure that both the API companies and their customers are having the best experience possible on our platform. It's a perfect combination of my technical knowledge and my interpersonal and relationship-building skills."

Setting Expectations

Once you've figured out what your Developer Relations team will accomplish and how they will contribute value to the company, it's time to bring the stakeholders to the table.

You'll of course want to present your plan, but you'll also want to find out what expectations the stakeholders have of the DevRel team. What are their underlying assumptions about the role that DevRel plays? What do they think are the most important things for DevRel to focus on? What projects do they intend to include the team on? How do they anticipate the DevRel team will help them?

Let me take a moment to make an important clarification: just because you're gathering information and gaining an understanding of how stakeholders throughout the company view a Developer Relations team doesn't mean you'll necessarily be delivering on all the items these stakeholders asking for. Although you will inevitably find yourself working with every department in the company, you'll want to make sure you check in with folks directly in proportion to how invested they are in what you're setting out to accomplish. If your Q3 goal is to improve documentation, for example, you'll want to connect often with the head of Customer Service, both to understand where the primary problems are as well as to make sure that your efforts are actively reducing the number of support tickets received.

Keeping your top goal for the quarter front of mind also helps you keep unnecessary work off of your plate. Given the variety of skills represented in the DevRel team, it's common to be pulled in different directions or looped into projects that could absolutely benefit from the DevRel viewpoint, but aren't critical to the DevRel's team goal. Be careful to avoid this type of interrupt-driven work. It's dangerous to your team's focus and also difficult to track the value of. When most of the work you're doing is attributed to another team, it's hard to turn in a successful end-of-quarter report that proves your work is valuable on its own. To use a sports analogy, you need to have more baskets than assists, even though assists are key to a team's success.

There's a fine line between being the advisors and experts regarding the community and being relied on or crucial to every project. This is where documentation is key. As you're gathering data (whether quantitative or qualitative), make sure it's being communicated back to the relevant stakeholders so they can make their own decisions regarding messaging, training, and positioning.

As mentioned earlier, the primary goal of community building is not lead generation. However, a good DevRel team will bring in new customers simply because of their connections and genuine excitement about the product. Building a relationship with your Sales team is crucial to a successful handoff in these places. You'll want to know the concerns and questions of each community member so you can pass them off to the right salesperson and have a smooth exit for the conversation—while still getting attribution for the "first touch."

As wild as it sounds, it's not uncommon for someone to begin using a product (or at least have a great impression of it) simply because they know someone who works there. Having a *Developer Advocate* embedded in the local community (even if the product isn't open source) can make a tremendous difference in everything from closing large deals to negotiating conference sponsorships to general brand awareness.

Having these conversations with your stakeholders early on can help you manage expectations as well as get a greater understanding of the company's needs. Although having a Developer Relations team can make a big difference for your company, it isn't a silver bullet. It can't fix your support team's attitude or solve the up-time problems you're having with your product. But it can direct your mission for the company as a whole and bring those disparate teams back together in a cohesive way.

This work will often be accomplished with the help of other teams. Whether you're looking to Marketing for help with SEO best practices or promotional materials, to Engineering for big-ticket technical items, or Customer Support for the bulk of the day-to-day support requests, this is a team effort. In order to make sure these interactions are smooth, it's important for the DevRel team to have a good working relationship with all the departments throughout the company.

My suggestion? Go in with a plan. Gather feedback. Get consensus among the teams. And then be prepared to adjust.

Your community team has the power to do a lot of good in your company if you let them, but that requires you to set them up for success and believe in them. We'll talk about this more when we delve into making your first hire in Chapter 5, but you need to be able to trust your DevRel team to truly be the experts when it comes to your community. They are the subject matter experts, after all—that's why you've hired them, right? Find someone who knows what they're talking about and then give them the tools, resources, support, and trust to do their job well.

Trouble in Paradise

Depending on the makeup and background of your stakeholders, getting them on board with your Developer Relations plan will either be a relatively simple process or an arduous experience. Chances are, if most of your stakeholders come from a developer background or have a general understanding of the developer audience, the idea of Developer Experience and time-to-value will be a fairly obvious sell.

But it won't all be smooth sailing. The key is to speak the language of each stakeholder group. For instance, Marketing will have very different questions than Product, and Engineering may have completely different concerns. It's important to address each of these conversations from their viewpoint. What are their reservations? What are their goals? What areas are they concerned about you "stepping on" as you offer feedback?

Be sure to engage as early as possible and define the project goals and scope clearly. Explaining what you can do to help and assuring that you won't be taking over is important. This is where your good working relationships come into play. The more your work can be represented as helpful and beneficial across the company, the more value other departments will attribute to your burgeoning team.

Lastly, you'll want to make sure to identify and manage any uncertainties. By knowing in advance what the possible risks are, you'll be able to clearly respond and dissuade any doubts. Additionally, acknowledging what the potential pitfalls are before anyone else brings them up makes it clear that you understand the full scope of your plan and have taken the time to explore any problem areas.

By listening and communicating with these stakeholders early and often, you're letting them know that their comments and suggestions are valued. Be sure to follow that up with feedback and regular status updates in order to keep them on board with your progress.

All Aboard

Once you've got the stakeholders on board, it's time to set the DevRel team up for success with the rest of the company. As I said, most people at a typical tech company interact with the community on at least an occasional basis. However, it's the job of the DevRel team to make sure that the customer is not only happy with the product, but with the website experience, the support team, the presence at events, the online resources, and the interactions they may have with other staff members. If that sounds like a lot for one person or team to handle, you're right! There's a very fine line here between being responsible for all the change within the company and being the *changemaker* who helps to drive that change.

There's a fantastic book called *Switch* by Chip Heath and Dan Heath (Random House, 2011) that walks through some of the challenges in influencing change in your company. One of my favorite quotes says the following:

> *When you're at the beginning, don't obsess about the middle, because the middle is going to look different once you get there. Just look for a strong beginning and a strong ending and get moving.*[2]

Let me offer a note of encouragement to the Developer Relations professionals who are reading this: in addition to building relationships with the community, it's our job to inspire, encourage, and excite the company about the community.

And as the subject matter experts on the community, it's our job to ensure that the company understands who makes up the community and why the company should care about these individuals.

It's a lot to take on, but the payoff is huge:

- A successful company

- A happy community

- A job that allows you to genuinely make people's lives easier

Getting the stakeholders on board with your plan is definitely the biggest struggle you'll face as a changemaker in your company, but it's the first of many steps to creating a healthy community, and as I mentioned at the beginning of the chapter, it's by far the most rewarding.

---

[2]Heath, Dan, and Chip Heath. "Chapter 4: Point to the Destination. p 93." Switch: How to Change Things When Change Is Hard, Random House US, 2010.

CHAPTER 3

Keeping a Pulse on the Community

I mentioned in the last chapter that it's not uncommon for developers to have a good impression of a particular product simply because they know and respect someone who works at the company. Likewise, if you've been in the technology sector for even a short time, you've likely seen how easily the tide can turn *against* a company if they take a wrong step or make a wrong choice in the public eye. In short, keeping a pulse on the public sentiment of your product is important.[1] It should be no surprise that this is one of the ways a Developer Relations (DevRel) team can add to the success of your brand.

It's a fine line for Developer Relations professionals to walk—they don't always see the email before it goes out, nor do they have control over the social media accounts, over the support or sales teams, or over what other employees say about the company during off-hours. But as the face of the company at events and online, they're usually the ones who receive the feedback and have to process the mixture of frustration, excitement, and criticism (good and bad) that the community communicates back to them.

In exchange, they're responsible for translating that feedback into business-speak: language that not only Engineering will understand but that can be seen as relevant and important by Sales, Marketing, and Product. They're also responsible for knowing who are the right people to relay that feedback to and, when necessary, for being the changemakers themselves.

---

[1]This is why the podcast that I cohost with Jason Hand and PJ Hagerty is called *Community Pulse*—as community professionals, we're responsible for keeping an eye on our respective communities and reporting back relevant information about the health of our community. Learn more at `communitypulse.io`

© Mary Thengvall 2018
M. Thengvall, *The Business Value of Developer Relations*, https://doi.org/10.1007/978-1-4842-3748-9_3

Ewan Dennis,[2] a member of the Developer Relations team at SparkPost[3] used to describe it like this:

To the community, I represent the company.

To the company, I represent the community.

I must have both of their interests in mind at all times.

In order to represent the community accurately, a Developer Relations team must be the internal experts on what products are hot, which languages are up-and-coming, and which topics are worth pursuing (or off limits) in the developer community.

During my years at O'Reilly Media, I saw a lot of "hot topics" come and go rather quickly. When I first took on the official role of community manager, it became my job to figure out which of these topics within the web performance and operations space was here to stay.

As a result of one-on-one meetings with community members, and by attending events all over the world, I began to get a feel for what was a new, "shiny" thing versus what was actually poised to make a difference in the tech scene. I brought this information back to the O'Reilly editors and conference chairs in the form of trip reports (see Appendix A for an example).

Each of these reports included information about where I had been[4] and what event I had attended, a general summary of the event and its value, a list of popular topics that had come up in various conversations, and a list of important contacts I had made while on the trip. This last piece often became a bullet-point list of its own, naming individuals that I'd met throughout the trip and listing the various people within the company I'd be connecting them to (editors, conference chairs, and so forth), as well as explaining why they were an important person to follow up with. These reasons ranged from "this person is the foremost expert on *X* topic" to "this individual runs an amazing meetup that we should sponsor in the future."

---

[2]Engineering manager, provider of scotch and also Scottish (aka Scotch Angel), @ewanovitch on Twitter.

[3]An email delivery API built for and by developers. I worked on building its community strategy for the better part of two years.

[4]Geographic regions are important to note, since generally speaking, from a technology adoption standpoint, the West Coast tends to be ahead of the East Coast, which is ahead of the Europe, which is slightly ahead of the Midwest, and so on.

Making these connections was one of my favorite things to do, partly because it engaged the "technical cruise director" side of me (hat tip to Amy Hermes[5] for that moniker) and partly because it was a really easy success metric—how many "handoffs" have I made for this particular event? for this trip as a whole? for this particular topic? I talk more about that in the next chapter, but in short, it was a great way to measure how successful each of these trips were.

It also made it really easy to take anecdotal evidence and turn it into metrics: "I've heard about this new topic from five of the thought leaders in our community in the past two weeks; we should explore that particular topic more." In-person conversations were preferable: not only were they an easy way to keep track of hot new topics and rising themes, they were a great way to connect with the community and build those relationships (or make already existing ones stronger).

However, for obvious reasons, in-person meetings weren't always possible. As much as I would have loved to visit New Zealand to connect with one of my core influencers in person, it simply wasn't practical. But thanks to the rise of social media (Twitter, Facebook, Google Plus) and the increased amount of personal blogs that focused on technical topics, I was able to connect with folks online as well and cultivate those personal relationships, even though we had never met in the same physical location.

Using tools like Google Alerts or Google Trends[6] is also an incredibly useful way to observe trends and keep track of what the community is saying about your company. One word of caution here: be sure to tailor your lists carefully. Use filtering systems heavily to make sure you aren't having to spend hours sifting through the end results. Otherwise, you'll find yourself deleting dozens of articles about a community college that has technical offerings when what you really want to see is news about local technical communities.

---

[5]Vice president and senior Mosaic specialist, KeyBanc Capital Markets; previously technical eminence program director at IBM; creator of #CloudMinds; also mentor, innovator, community cruise director, and all-around awesome individual; @amyhermes; I met her because of the *Geek Whisperers* podcast, Episode 93: http://geek-whisperers.com/2015/08/bringing-people-together-is-not-marketing-with-amy-hermes-ep-93/.

[6]Again, like most tools I'm mentioning throughout the book, there are two caveats: 1) There are likely others that are better suited for your use case, or at the very least, different from the ones I mention. 2) The tools I mention may not be the best fit for you. Take the outlined principles and apply them to your own goals, communities, and company to figure out what the right tool is for you.

The Role of Social Media in Community Building

I was in my sophomore year of college when Facebook became A Thing™ and was a senior when Twitter launched. When I joined O'Reilly Media as a full-time employee straight out of college, Facebook was the hippest place to "hang out" on the internet, and Twitter was the hottest way to share information (even if that was only what you were eating for lunch) with technology thought leaders. We quickly scaled up a Twitter account and a Facebook group, as did many other companies, and we learned by trial and error how to talk to our followers.

Over the years, I've learned two basic principles:

1. Developers hate being marketed to, and they have an incredibly sensitive awareness meter (or *BS meter*) for when they're being pandered to.

2. If a company is genuine in its outreach and actually cares about the community in obvious, quantifiable ways, it can build a large following on social media sites and use it as a valuable platform to promote their product.

Again, this is where the Developer Relations team comes in. Who better than your community experts to help shape the voice of the company in order to effectively reach the community?

In the process of keeping tabs on what's going on in the tech niche that your company falls into, chances are the team will also uncover interesting tidbits from the community, such as the following:

- Interesting news or ongoing studies

- Important developments in related areas

- Relevant events and/or calls for papers (also known as CFPs — the open calls that conference organizers put out to find speakers for events).

- Community members who have received accolades for their work

- Potential partnerships

- Problem areas that your company might be able to solve with a new feature (*quick wins*—more about these in Chapter 4)

- Ways to elevate the developer community that is active in or around the languages your product is built in, the technologies you use, or the topics your product falls into (for example, SaaS, PaaS, APIs, DevOps, and so on)

Whether or not the person who is actively in charge of maintaining your social media accounts is in your Developer Relations team or not, you'll want to make sure that you have a designated social media manager somewhere in the company. Leaving this up to the "whenever someone has time" column of your to-do list is a recipe for neglecting your social media accounts. Something that important to reaching your community deserves more attention. As we've already established, the Developer Relations team can (and should) help direct the voice of those accounts because of their experience and expertise. There are several ways to make this collaboration a smooth one.[7]

Establishing Voice

When I was at O'Reilly Media, we had what was called *The O'Reilly Voice*. It detailed everything from our policy on serial commas (we used them, which is the only proper way, in my opinion) to why we used contractions (it made the writing seem more friendly and conversational rather than formal and unapproachable). The document ended with a list of pet peeves from the O'Reilly writers. My favorite (which still influences my writing now) was this:

> *Pet peeve: Using the third person. How can we have a conversation with our readers if we're talking about them instead of to them? Example: "You'll get tips and tricks," NOT "The reader will get tips and tricks."*

As someone who maintained the O'Reilly Twitter and Facebook accounts for quite some time and who also contributed to the blog regularly, if I ever had a question about *how* to say something, I knew exactly where to find it. There was never any concern about things not sounding "O'Reilly-ish" because even though I could put my own personal spin on a topic, the company voice always shone through.

---

[7] I'm going to be using examples primarily from Twitter, partly because that's the current social media network of choice for most developers and partly because that's my largest area of expertise when it comes to social media networks.

Slack is another company that has been very clear about what is (and isn't) part of its company voice. Editorial director Anna Pickard has been interviewed many times[8] about how she crafted the voice of the company and how Slack's voice has evolved as more people have taken charge. Slack agrees that words are hard[9] and that once you scale past a certain size, it's necessary to have one voice but many hands.[10]

As both of these companies know, a style guide that defines voice is key when you have multiple people maintaining your social media accounts (note: it's helpful even if there's only one person running social media). It defines what you say in different situations and why. It helps others pick up tasks when someone gets too busy or goes suddenly be out of commission (see the Great Car Accident of 2012 that put me on medical leave for three months—and also, preventing burnout, which I talk more about in Chapter 9).

The simplest of rules, such as addressing the reader in second person rather than third, can make the difference between developers feeling that you value their opinions and developers clicking Unfollow.

Choosing Platforms

Over the last decade, I've seen most developers gravitate toward Twitter for interactions around technology—both to find resources as well as have an ongoing watercooler conversation about industry news. Among the top social media sites of today, Twitter seems to offer the best cross-section of both personal and professional communication, which provides a good way to connect with your community on many levels.[11]

Generally, Facebook is reserved for friends and family relationships and used as an escape from work, though Facebook Events can sometimes be appropriate for conferences and meetups. Tools like Google+ have largely faded away, though there are some open source communities that conduct most of their community interactions on Google+ pages or groups. LinkedIn, the other outlier, is chiefly used for industry announcements. It's a great place for thought leadership pieces about your industry or

---

[8]https://www.thememo.com/2016/08/11/slack-every-company-needs-a-voice-this-is-how-slack-found-theirs

[9]https://slackhq.com/words-are-hard-aabafc490d04

[10]https://slackhq.com/one-voice-many-hands-f8759968f9b8

[11]I talk more about this on Episode 15 of the *Teamwork* podcast from Dan Thomas: imdanthomas.com/15

"work in progress" posts about surveys your company is conducting or industry research you're involved in.

As with most things community related, where you choose to congregate is largely dependent on your community. As Chapter 7 discusses, finding where your community gathers is key to your success. This is not a "build it and they will come" scenario—you need to seek out your community and actively engage with them where they're already comfortable, whether that's on forums like Reddit, Hacker News, or Stack Overflow, social media sites like Twitter, Facebook, or LinkedIn, or community-run topical Slack teams.

One important note about forum sites like Reddit: corporate accounts don't tend to go over well on sites that prioritize individual feedback. However, members of your DevRel team (as well as engineers) can keep an eye on these forums to provide input, leave comments, and generally represent the brand, while still maintaining their personal integrity.

Working Together

Have your social media manager work closely with the Developer Relations team to make sure the company account is following the right people, talking about the important topics, and made aware of any outages (and how that will affect the scheduled posts). Personally, I've found Twitter Lists to be one of the best tools for keeping up with the constantly scrolling Twitter feed. Whether you make your list public or private is up to you and often depends on the situation, but keep in mind that a list could be a valuable resource to those outside your company. For example, you may have a list of upcoming conference speakers, or the top thought leaders in a particular market segment. No matter how you use them, as you're listening to your community and observing the trends, these lists are invaluable:

- *Looking for what topic is most important to your biggest customers?* Create a list for the developers at that company.

- *Interested in a big-picture look at the technology landscape?* Pop over to your list of technology thought leaders.

- *Want to know what your competitors are doing?* Take a look at that particular (likely private) list.

- *Hoping to find some retweetable content for a slow Twitter afternoon?* Have a list of your company's developers and another of your top community members on hand to see what's new and interesting to them.

You can also save Twitter searches using the Advanced Search tool. From searching for tweets that are particularly positive or negative in tone, to being specific about the term you're searching for (for example, if you're interested in tweets that reference "tea" but want to exclude anyone tweeting about the "tea party" political group), this can be a valuable tool.

As the Developer Relations team discovers new Twitter accounts that are engaging and potentially beneficial to the overall company strategy, make sure they pass those off to the social media manager—or better yet, give them the power to add those accounts to the various lists just mentioned.

The ongoing relationship that develops between your social media manager and your Developer Relations team will benefit the entire company. The social media manager will learn the best accounts to follow in order to gain insight into the community, which then benefits the Developer Relations team, who can use that information to strike up conversations with community members, who will feed more information and resources into the conversation, which can then be handed back over to your Product and Engineering teams, who will then take the information into account when determining priorities and core projects.

Making sure your social media manager is aware of any outages is incredibly important. While I was working at SparkPost in May 2016, our API suffered an outage. This was a very uncommon event for us, and one that created quite a bit of consternation among our users, for obvious reasons. In the midst of the outage, a scheduled tweet went out about what to do when your emails were delayed by various problems, including ISP and deliverability issues. This tweet pointed to one of our most popular pieces of content, which talked about how best to prevent deliverability issues. Although this would normally be a great resource to point to, in this particular case, *we* were the ones causing the issues for our customers as a result of our outage. Had we been better at communicating the outage internally, the social media team could have taken a quick pass at their tweets and deleted any scheduled tweets that might have caused further frustration for our customers.

Technically Speaking

If your primary audience is developers, make sure your social media manager can speak to a technical audience. This isn't to say that social media managers need to be developers themselves, but they should know that there's a difference between

Java and JavaScript (even if they don't fully understand what that difference is). This person should be able to connect the dots between popular technology topics and form cohesive tweets from the technical blog content that your developers are producing.

This will of course be a learning experience; one that will need to be guided and directed by the Developer Relations team, as well as the developers at your company. Don't discount the fact that you have your primary audience sitting in-house every day, eager to give you feedback on whether or not your marketing and sales efforts are on point or will fall flat.

If they seem hesitant to give feedback at first, be persistent (but kind). The stereotype that developers and marketing folks don't get along exists for a reason—there's a long history of disrespect and disregard for the other department's opinions. Don't contribute to this problem. Be open and willing to listen and change. If a good percentage of your developers say that something wouldn't work for them, don't take offense. Instead, ask for suggestions on how to change it and thank them for saving you from a failed campaign.

Focus on Developers

If you have multiple audiences (buyers versus users, or different levels of your product that apply to different job functions), consider creating a Twitter account that caters specifically to developers. Although this might seem counterintuitive at first because it splits your audience, consider that developers won't follow a Twitter account that isn't relevant to their needs. If your only audience is developers, this may not be as much of an issue. But it's rare that you won't be targeting other people as well.

As Chapter 1 talks about, even if your primary audience will always and only be developers, chances are, you'll be selling to one of the following groups:

- *Technical leadership (director or VP of engineering, CTO)*: The ones with the technical budget.

- *Project manager*: Looking to make a process quicker or easier.

- *Marketing/Sales/Support/Product*: The data the developers produce might be used by another team entirely.

That's not to say you should neglect your relationships with developers. More often than not, the developers will be the ones advocating for your product internally, so you'll still want to make sure you're building and maintaining those relationships. In short, these developer relationships are necessary but they're not sufficient to drive the company to buy. White papers and sales materials will often be owned by the demand generation arm of Marketing, but depending on who your buyer audience is (for example, lead developers, engineering management, and so forth), you may have a voice here as well.

How you decide to approach this audience split will determine whether you need separate content, messaging, and, in this case, Twitter accounts. In some cases, catering to developers and relying on that relationship to drive sales is the smartest way to go. In others, you'll want to target both the buyer and the user equally.

If the latter is the case, you'll want to split your messaging. After all, it won't do your buyers any good to see code snippets or retweets of technical content, and likewise, your end users won't want to see buzzwordy content pieces.

COMBINING THE @SPARKPOST AND @SPARKPOSTDEV TWITTER ACCOUNTS

When I first joined SparkPost, we had two separate Twitter accounts for our audiences. The one geared toward developers highlighted technical content, changes to our API, and tech events that we were sponsoring. The corporate account tweeted out information about the company culture as well as content pieces geared at the decision makers and the email marketing crowd.

At the time, separating these made sense, but as the company began to focus more on our end users, having the two different accounts didn't make as much business sense. In addition, as the Developer Relations team ramped up, we had less time to dedicate to the Twitter account, so it ran the risk of becoming idle. Rather than hire someone to focus on this account specifically, we decided to put more effort into ensuring that the voice of the corporate account was relevant and interesting to the developer audience.

Working closely with Marketing, we worked on a plan to engage with developers, increase internal sharing, and leverage conversations that were already happening in other places. We also found three categories of content that weren't already being tweeted about on the corporate Twitter account, which were not only relevant but important to developers. We worked together to come up with a plan for how to integrate those tweets on a regular basis.

Changelog

- Work with Product to craft tweets about changes that have occurred, which are posted in the weekly changelog.

- When patches are made, pull requests accepted, and new versions released to the client libraries, schedule three to five tweets about the changes.

Announcements and operations changes to the API

- When these occur, work with the person driving the overall communication to make sure the tweets are accurate and correctly represent the change.

- Schedule three to five tweets (depending on the timeline), increasingly in "pay attention!" mode, until the date when the change is made.

Events

- When our name goes up on an event site for a sponsorship, schedule around five tweets about the conference and our sponsorship between now and the date of the event.

- Find the Twitter account and hashtag for the event and follow it.

- Add the conference Twitter account to the private list of upcoming events so we can keep an eye on those tweets and reply to, quote, or retweet them when applicable.

We eventually transitioned the @SparkPostDev Twitter account into a status account that was automatically updated from our status page. That way, any developers who were currently following us would continue to get important alerts, but we also encouraged folks to follow our main corporate account, where they could find relevant, engaging information.

The other option is to engage your developer audience through developer-specific Twitter chats. This is particularly intriguing if you're building up your brand as the go-to place for particular types of content or are driving an industry change, such as PagerDuty's case study from Chapter 1. Keep in mind that for these types of online events to be successful, they need to be consistent. It's also helpful to start out with a handful of devoted community members whom you can rely on to show up and take part in the conversation.

Like many community initiatives, if you can get early feedback and input from key community members, you'll be able to build trust and, as a result, successfully engage the broader community as well. Even if you don't gain additional social media followers as a result, the engagement is a valuable metric (more about valuable metrics versus vanity metrics in Chapter 4).

Elevate and Amplify

Finally, and most importantly, make sure to use your company Twitter (Facebook, Instagram, <insert new social media platform here>) account to elevate and amplify the work the community is doing. No matter what you decide to use for social media, you want to make sure you're using your platform to highlight the work the community is doing, especially when it benefits you. This symbiotic relationship is one that you don't want to abuse, and showing the community that you appreciate them and are willing to shine the spotlight on them will go a long way.

In addition to the standard social media platforms, don't forget that your corporate blog is another valuable way to reach developers. Most companies tend to treat their blogs as soapboxes to promote "exciting" news about the company (which tends to only be exciting to those at the company). Although there is a time and place for this, companies often fail to realize that if they were talking more about the technical problems they're solving while building their product, they'd have far more traffic on the site from interested developers.

Though it takes some effort to build up a group of internal developers who are interested in writing, it's relatively easy to build up a mentorship program around blog posts:

- Set out a basic template with writing prompts. For example: What's the problem you're trying to solve? How did you discover the problem? Why is this interesting to other people? How did you solve the problem? How can other people relate to it?

- Don't worry about the tone and grammar. First focus on telling a story.

- Remember, done is better than perfect. There's always room for edits and rewrites down the road, but getting a first draft down so that you have something to work with is essential.

Automate this process as much as possible—your developers are busy. Don't wait for a project to be completed before approaching a developer or project manager to see if they'd be willing to write a blog post for you. Work with your Engineering managers to build a blog post into the official project epic so that it's accounted for time-wise and is required to be completed before the epic can be closed out.

Why is this important? If the developer community sees you publishing good, interesting content that solves common (or not-so-common) issues, they'll begin to see your engineers as knowledgeable, which then attributes value to your product indirectly:

"$COMPANY has interesting and smart engineers. They must be building an interesting and well-written product."

This observation will hopefully lead them to come back to you in the future to help solve a problem that they're facing.

One final note with regard to content: in a day and age of information overload when content is everywhere, syndication is key. Relying on developers to either seek out your specific content or stumble upon it is ideal—but not particularly realistic, especially as you're just starting to build out your brand. Dev.to[12] is a perfect example of a syndication site that benefits the community as well as the company. With its ability to use canonical links to attribute any traffic back to the original website, you can benefit from the page views and resulting Google-fu while also taking advantage of the fantastic community of curious and engaged developers.

Personal Brand vs. Company Brand

This brings us to the question of how social media fits in the day-to-day for the Developer Relations team. Chapter 10 talks about this more indepth, but as a company, you'll want your Developer Relations team to continue to foster their own community. After all, their network is a large part of the reason why you hired them—when you hire them, you automatically acquire their following. However, if they begin to neglect that following, you lose some of the value they can provide for your company.

---

[12]Founded by Ben Halpern, Jess Lee, and Peter Frank, dev.to is one of the most welcoming and inclusive environments for sharing content that I've ever come across in all my time working with developer communities. @thepracticaldev on Twitter.

Relying on your Developer Relations folks to retweet relevant content from the corporate blog—or even better, quote the tweets and give them their own spin—is a great way to leverage their network. They're not only helping to promote your site content, they're also pointing people back to your corporate Twitter account.

There are times when it makes far more sense for something to come from a personal voice that has a face and a name attached. This is when your team can step up to wish community members a happy birthday, commiserate over poorly written code, or post group selfies from a local event. Then, quoting the birthday message on the corporate account or highlighting a recent contribution that particular community member made can be seen as a genuine way to elevate and recognize the community member.

You'll want to find the balance between your Developer Relations team's Twitter activity and that of the company. Most importantly, make sure that communication channel referenced earlier stays open. Creating a private Twitter List specifically for your Developer Relations team members can be valuable—it gives you an opportunity to see who they're talking to most often and the conversations that they find valuable. At some point, it's likely that they will move on to another company, and you'll want to make sure you haven't lost their entire network at the same time. If you've successfully followed and interacted with this community in the past, keeping up with them will be a far smoother transition than if you're scrambling to find them once your only connection is gone.

CHAPTER 4

Measuring Your Success

One of the most difficult things to do in Developer Relations (DevRel) is prove that the investment is worthwhile. (If it were easy, this book wouldn't exist!) It's a pain point that the DevRel teams feel as well—one that's been mentioned over and over in various interviews and articles as the "hardest part of the job." After all, DevRel can easily become one of the most expensive departments, with sponsoring events and various community-driven projects, paying for travel to speaking engagements and sending out custom swag to community members. Any board worth its salt is going to want to know where the value is in all this money being spent, and any executive worth their salt will need to have an answer for them.

Without the ability to account for the value the DevRel team is contributing toward the overall company goals, you'll be hard-pressed to keep the team together. In addition, you'll have a hard time keeping your team motivated. As Rob Spectre says in his "Measuring Developer Relations" talk,[1] the primary reason why you track metrics in DevRel is so that "everyone on your team knows—not thinks, but knows—the difference they are making with their work."

So, how do you show the incredible potential and value that can come from a DevRel team? The answer may not come in traditional form. You're not necessarily going to be looking for number of leads created, traffic to the site, or any of the other ROIs that usually come from Marketing or Sales. You also can't judge success based simply on whether or not the job gets done, as is typical with Engineering. You can draw a few pointers from the Product team, which typically gathers metrics on general customer satisfaction and feedback, as well as the number of support tickets or bugs. At the end of the day, DevRel is a grab bag of these goals, plus a few that are unique to them. There's no doubt that the returns are there, but you'll find them in unconventional places.

---

[1]https://GitHub.com/RobSpectre/Talks/tree/master/Measuring%20Developer%20Evangelism

M. Thengvall, *The Business Value of Developer Relations*, https://doi.org/10.1007/978-1-4842-3748-9_4

DEVELOPER AVOCADOS: THE GOOD KIND OF FAT

When I joined SparkPost in November 2015, I saw quite a few references to avocados within the Developer Relations team and on various channels that we maintained.[2] Although I'm all about the avocados (and avocado puns),[3] I couldn't make heads or tails of the reference and finally asked about it one day. It turns out that one of our project managers had a hard time saying *Developer Advocate* when she was talking quickly. Instead, it often came out as "Developer Avocado." Given how much my coworker Aydrian Howard[4] loves avocados, he took on the mantle of Developer Avocado without much prompting. This grew into a brilliant analogy for Developer Relations, which he and I have used countless times since then:[5]

- As we all know, avocados are a good kind of fat. Used at the right times, in the right ways, with the right combinations of items, they can be amazingly beneficial.

- Avocados are also expensive, to a point where some food establishments in Los Angeles list avocado toast at "market price" on their menus.[6] Similarly, as mentioned earlier, Developer Relations teams tend to be one of the more expensive departments, but the goal is to create a good, healthy, inviting environment for our community.

- Avocados tend to take on the flavor of things around them. Likewise, Developer Relations teams tend to be fluid regarding goals, which department they're in, and what the group looks like, depending on the needs and goals of the company.

---

[2]https://twitter.com/SparkPostOps/status/667420447345102848

[3]https://www.sparkpost.com/blog/building-internal-community/

[4]A great guy that I had the privilege of working with for 2 years at SparkPost; passionate about making things easier for developers; @ahoward on Twitter

[5]This is also the reason why my consulting firm is called Persea Consulting. *Persea* is the scientific genus for the family that avocados falls into, and also lends to thinking about *persons*, which nicely translates to community and developer relations. https://www.marythengvall.com/blog/2018/1/31/developer-avocados-the-good-kind-of-fat

[6]https://twitter.com/sherlyholmes/status/938934404251971584

- Avocados work well with many different types of dishes. From Mexican dishes to omelets and scrambles to the classic BLT, you find avocados in all sorts of cuisines. This couples nicely with the previous point that Developer Relations teams are fluid. Not only can their goals and departments be different depending on the company, but the tactics that they use to build a community change depending on the circumstances and the type of product. There's rarely a set way to engage with the community—you experiment and figure out what works best for your community by pulling a variety of levers and observing the outcomes (more on this in a bit).

- Avocados take a long time to ripen, and it's an even longer process if you take into account that it takes five years for an avocado tree to be fruitful. But once the fruit is ripe, it's not only delicious—it yields a good profit for the farmers. Developer Relations is also a long game and it's not something that often has an immediate impact on sales. However, with a good up-front investment and careful nurturing, the final harvest is rewarding.

The more you look into the research and data on avocados, the more you realize just how good they are for you. Likewise, with more research and data around Developer Relations, you'll realize that it's not only good for your business, but in many cases, it's essential to maintaining a healthy product. And no one can deny that a happy community and a healthy product are good for the heart of every company, just like avocados.

As a starting point, it's good to have a handful of day-over-day, month-over-month numbers that are clear-cut and straightforward. This data can help you make decisions about the following:

- What's going well?

- What's going poorly?

- What should you be doing differently?

Those three questions are part of any standard retrospective and are a good place to begin when you're looking for ways to measure the value that you're contributing to your company as well as the community.[7]

---

[7]This is a good exercise to do on a monthly or quarterly basis with your team as well. It helps you keep ahead of any problems and issues that may be cropping up before they become too large to handle.

Some of the answers to these questions will be quantitative (for example, we're posting technical content on the company blog twice per month and getting a good amount of traffic to the site as a result). Others will be driven by observations and qualitative trends (for example, the last three conferences we've sponsored have had a track on this new technology, but people are shifting toward this other topic instead—we should consider producing content on that new topic or bring it up to product as a feature request).

Sensu VP of Community Matt Broberg[8] refers to this as the difference between measuring things with your brain and with your gut. Those who measure things with their brain are looking for the raw data: the number of pull requests on your GitHub repos, the number of engagements on Twitter. This is a quantifiable way to point to the health of the community and, therefore, the value that your team is contributing. Those who measure with their gut have an overall impression of the community's needs and the right (or wrong) thing to do based on time spent talking with them day in and day out. It's not a quantifiable thing per se, but it's no less valid of a measurement and should be taken with the same consideration, particularly if it's a shared sentiment.

Storytelling Is Part of the Job Description

To understand why I feel so strongly about this, you need to understand a little about how I got into Developer Relations and Community Management in the first place. I've been a writer since I was young—my 3rd grade teacher left a note in my yearbook telling me to send her an autographed copy of my first book.[9] I realized in high school that I needed to have a slightly more practical dream than "be an author," and pivoted to feature-writing and journalism as an outlet.

But by the time I was halfway through college, newspapers across the country were laying off reporters due to the drop in subscriptions and the rise of online blogs. I pivoted yet again, this time to public relations, and took an internship at O'Reilly Media, which turned into a full-time job out of college. Although I was still writing regularly, both personally and professionally, I missed the "feature story" aspect of journalism. I was writing clean-cut press releases and researching the latest trends in programming

---

[8]A good friend of mine; He's a passionate community builder who has tremendous insight into and passion for the open source community; @mbbroberg on Twitter.

[9]https://www.marythengvall.com/blog/almostanauthor

languages—not talking to the people who were creating those languages or building the next great technological innovation.

After asking questions for a few years about how we knew that these were the right topics to pursue in our conferences, books, and webcast offerings, I made the jump into community management thanks to O'Reilly's President Laura Baldwin. She gave me the freedom to not only figure out what this brand new role meant, but to find out what kind of information I would need to bring back to prove that the work I was doing was valuable.

In Chapter 3, I mentioned the trip reports I used to circulate after meeting up with community members. Those allowed me to tap into my storytelling side and gave me the motivation and drive to find out how I could best help these customers and community members. However, I also had to show my effectiveness through the number of new conference speakers or authors I attracted, as well as engagement around upcoming events. If I couldn't prove that it was worthwhile for me to be traveling around the country speaking at events and meeting up with thought leaders, there was little chance that it would continue, and rightfully so.

Ultimately, we're storytellers—communicating feedback to the Product and Engineering teams and helping Marketing and Sales craft the stories the audience will listen to. The storytelling piece comes directly from our "gut," but having analytics to back it up gives our story the validity to be respected up and down the org chart.

There's no doubt our gut knows exactly what to do, and we should continue to do that. But unless you sprinkle the metrics and analytics in there as well (salt to taste), you won't be able to prove your business value, which is necessary in order to protect the DevRel organization for the long run. We're always telling stories—even with numerical data—but the narrative becomes more convincing to the business when you invest in the quantitative to complement the qualitative.

At the end of the day, someone has to account for the cost associated with your department. Community doesn't fit too nicely into the traditional org charts that we're used to seeing (more on that in Chapter 5), and until it does, it will continue to be difficult to measure. So many of us have experienced the heartache of being re-org'd (or our team dissolved) simply because we haven't effectively measured our value. And with that re-org, we often also lose our community.

Checks and Balances

It's my firm belief that you need both qualitative and quantitative measurements when you're trying to show the value of DevRel. Why?

Trust Your Gut, But . . .

While at SparkPost, I built an event scoreboard (see Appendix B) to measure the success of each event we sponsored. We had a Good Experience column for our gut impression of the event, but there were also columns for number of partnerships formed, whether or not an employee spoke at the event, how the foot traffic was at the booth, how much feedback we got (both about our competition and about SparkPost), and more. These quantifiable data points helped us balance the "Did this event go well? Y/N" question that was traditionally asked at the end of every event. The data points also ensured that the number of sales opportunities wasn't the only number used to judge the success of an event, since not all the events we sponsored as a DevRel team were prone to lead generation (nor should they be—more on that in Chapter 8).

There were a number of times when I felt like an event had gone extraordinarily well, but when we ran the numbers, it turned out to be only mediocre. Alternately, there were a few volunteer-run events that were incredibly difficult to handle from a logistics standpoint, but wound up being really valuable from both a lead-generation and relationship-building standpoint. In both cases, running the numbers allowed us to take a step back from our emotions and evaluate the conference from an objective standpoint.

It's Not All About the Data

If you invest too heavily in the "brain" side of metrics and spend all your time gathering data points like number of Twitter followers, GitHub stars, or people in a Slack forum (what I like to call "vanity metrics"), you'll lose touch with the people of your community—a sacrifice that comes with dangerous consequences.

A large part of the reason why DevRel teams are created is because we have a unique set of skills that allow us to communicate with Marketing, Product, Engineering, and Sales, as well as our community of developers. This liaison role requires spending time with each of these groups and then funneling feedback to the right people, making the right introductions, and keeping tabs on our customers. But arguably, the most important part of our work is continuing to build relationships within the larger developer community.

If we're suddenly tasked with defining and creating metrics, we run the risk of losing touch with the most important people in this equation: our community. Without them, we quite literally can't do our jobs. So although it's important to keep running tabs on metrics that prove our value, we have to automate that process in order to allow us to continue to do the most time consuming—but most important—part of our jobs.

As Matt Broberg said in his talk "Community Metrics Are a Trojan Horse for Real Relationships" at the 2017 Community Leadership Summit,[10]

> *"When you start mistaking pageviews for community health … you'll spend so much time measuring things that you forget to be a member of the community. No one wants a tribal leader that's not part of the tribe. That's called a dictator, and it [will prevent you from growing] something meaningful in the long run."*

ROI Is a Difficult Metric for DevRel

If we don't figure out a way to quantify the things our gut tells us, we'll be left with ROIs (returns on investment), which are difficult to measure for a community team. ROI is typically measured in profits. You calculate it by dividing the return by the total cost of the investment, and the result is expressed as a ratio or percentage. This ratio is used to evaluate whether an investment was worthwhile, or whether a future investment is worth considering. In the marketing world, a "good" ROI is 5:1. This typically means you've gained $5 in sales for every $1 spent in the marketing budget. ROIs are usually applied to things like pay-per-click ads, paid media, and content production costs.

This ratio is meant to give marketing campaigns a simple "pass/fail" test, and when applied to straightforward ad campaigns it's a relatively good measurement. Either people have clicked the ad and purchased a product or they haven't. There's a spectrum here as well. Perhaps someone clicked the ad and perused the website for a while but didn't actually become a customer. If your Marketing team is running any sort of multitouch attribution software, they can see what site the person came from, how long they spent on the website, whether they went to another website on your domain, and (bonus!) whether or not that same person came back at a future date. This often allows the Marketing team to connect *early engagement* (the first time someone visited the website) to a final sale. The content that originally drew that person in can then be attributed as a *first touch* in the sales journey, which increases the recognized value of that specific piece of content.

---

[10]http://cls.mediaspace.kaltura.com/media/CLS+2017+-+Matthew+%28Brender%29+Broberg+%E2%80%93+Community+Metrics+are+a+Trojan+Horse+for+Real+Relationships/0_ro0yrlfk

ALGOLIA TRACKS DEVELOPER AWARENESS

Tracking metrics for brand awareness is particularly difficult. Algolia, a platform that helps developers build fast, relevant search features for their websites and applications, looked at developer awareness trends to figure this out. Developer Relations Lead Josh Dzielak describes developer awareness in this way:

"It was the number of hands raised in a room when you ask how many people have heard of Algolia, and the increased traffic to web content that developers might find interesting— basically as high or early on in the traditional marketing funnel as you could get. There was an organizational belief that ramping up developer awareness led to results and business value down the road. There was also an acknowledgement that it's a very nonlinear process between when a developer finds out about a tool versus when they learn more about it, integrate with it, or choose to pay for it. The awareness that ultimately leads to acquisition and revenue can happen months or years beforehand, which as we all know, presents challenges to analytics models that track traditional, linear steps through a funnel.

"We tried to track this awareness as much as possible through traffic to the site: organic search versus referrals versus direct traffic. However, since there are hundreds of open source projects and developer portals using our DocSearch product, a lot of that traffic was coming through as direct referrals straight from their sites.

"This is where better multitouch attribution tools would have come in handy, as we could have seen more clearly where the customer's journey had started. As a result, one area that we struggled with was tracking those initial click-throughs all the way through to acquisition. There was no doubt that it happened—like I mentioned earlier, we knew that ramping up developer awareness led to business value based on the many anecdotes we heard from developers about how they first discovered and then tried Algolia, but mapping the initial awareness to particular links was difficult.

"For example, we'd have hundreds of people coming to our website every day from Bootstrap (the biggest site that uses DocSearch), and yet less than half of one percent of those people signed up at that moment in time. Basically, that means there might be thousands of people who became aware of Algolia and eventually became customers as a direct result of the link to algolia.com in the Bootstrap documentation, but we only have a few dozen where awareness and acquisition happened simultaneously, which means we couldn't see the impact using traditional, funnel-oriented marketing tools.

"The better thing to look at is when people sign up, what percentage of them have looked at developer content in the past? How many of them clicked through to the site based on a talk that we gave at a conference? How many of them had attended one of our Search Parties? If you're only tracking results through the traditional, linear marketing funnel, you might be wrong about the reasons why developers ultimately sign up. Sign-ups seem to be the one thing that people can agree on when it comes to metrics, which is hard, because DevRel is about building relationships first and foremost. Those relationships would often lead to sign-ups down the road, but since there isn't a direct way to track those face-to-face interactions, it's difficult to quantity the impact of building relationships, and easy to underestimate the role that plays in the full customer journey."

As you may have already guessed, ROI, the (mostly) simple and straightforward way of approaching marketing campaigns, doesn't translate well to the complex and chaotic nature of relationship building. One of my favorite articles on community management and metrics[11] says it this way:

> *"The inherent challenge is that when you're measuring community building efforts, you're trying to measure things that are mostly intangible. Community building is fundamentally about relationships. How do you conduct a cost-benefit analysis on a relationship? We don't go up to a friend and say, 'Well, it took me a cumulative sixty-eight hours of conversation, sixteen cups of coffee, and a birthday cake to go from being an acquaintance to a close friend (as defined by the discovery of common ground and the mutual exchange of confidences). However, I have derived 1.21 gigawatts of emotional satisfaction, three new friends, eight book recommendations, and three homemade dinners in return. Also, if I hadn't been at your house eating one of those dinners, I would instead have been on the freeway during the thirteen car pile-up last month.'*

> *"It just doesn't work like that."*

---

[11]https://genuinely.co/2013/08/measuring-community-kpis-social-metrics-community-building/

Qualitative + Quantitative = Sweet Success

I've talked about what we can't or shouldn't track (number of leads, done/not done goals), as well as why it's important to track both qualitative and quantitative measures (to balance our gut and our brain), but where does that leave us?

Online Engagement

Online engagement is the easiest thing to track—track *everything* that you can possibly track here (but make the initial investment to automate it).

From GitHub pull requests and forks to Twitter engagement and comments on content, online engagement is the easiest way to show growth and give numerical metrics to the higher-ups. I mention these metrics in particular because they're not just vanity metrics, like how many followers you have on Twitter or how many people have starred a GitHub repository. Those things are often nice big numbers to throw around, but they don't give any indication of whether people are actually seeing your content or not, and more importantly, they aren't proof of community engagement.

Although collecting this information involves a lot of data gathering, there are a handful of tools[12] (many of which have useful APIs) you can use to pull together a nice set of graphs automatically. Although this often requires an initial investment of both time and money, the time you'll save from not curating it all on a daily/weekly/monthly basis is worth the overhead. I've listed a handful of tools in the footnote and could probably list more, but by the time this book is in your hands, there will likely be five more. In short, the tools change by the day. The key is to prioritize the metrics that need to be automated, find a tool that works for you, and make it happen.

---

[12]Bitergia is a fantastic resource if you have a large stake in the Open Source world. Their dashboards help you see who your biggest GitHub contributors are, in addition to stats around mailing lists, forums, bugs, and more. Netflix's OSSTracker is another (`https://GitHub.com/Netflix/osstracker`) as is MeasureOSS (`https://GitHub.com/MeasureOSS/Measure`). Pulling Twitter Analytics and other API metrics into something like Keen or Datadog can be useful from a visibility standpoint. Without being able to see the trends from the past month, how can you make well-informed decisions on what to do next?

In addition to proving value, these analytics can be used to show trends within your community. For example, if your main product is an API, you can run a simple query using GitHub's Search API[13] and JQ[14] to track how many people are creating GitHub repositories that have your product name in either the title or description of the repository. This shows you at a glance how many people are not only engaging with but actively building tools using your API, and at what rate that engagement has been growing. You can sort by number of "watchers" to gauge the popularity of each repository, or add "language" as an additional qualifier to see what the popular programming languages are and whether an additional SDK might be useful to your community.

When this search is run in conjunction with a user agent string, you can track how many customers are using particular SDKs or tools. If hooked up to your customer database, you may even be able to see exactly which customers are using which tools, which leads to visibility into revenue streams, allowing you to put a dollar value behind each tool. And everyone knows a high dollar value is what leads to more resources.

Multichannel Endeavors

Multichannel endeavors are trickier, but are still worth trying to track if possible.

Multichannel marketing works because you're meeting your community members where they already are, not where you want them to be. This theme comes up a lot in Developer Relations—we'll talk about it more in Chapter 7 with regard to how to find your community. In this case it means reaching your customers on multiple levels such as social media, email, in-person events, and even billboards.

Chances are, most of these channels are going to fall to your Marketing team to track, but when it comes to speaking at events (whether online webinars or in-person conferences), you'll want to make sure your time has been well invested.

When speaking at an event, the best way to track engagement is online. Most tech conferences have hashtags that people use throughout the event. Even if they don't mention the name of the speaker, by going through the hashtag soon after your talk, you can often see which tweets are a direct result of your talk. Collecting these tweets into a Twitter Moment offers you an easy way to reference them down the road, as well as publicly showcase your involvement in a particular event, which can be a nice bump for your personal brand.

---

[13]https://developer.GitHub.com/v3/search/
[14]https://stedolan.GitHub.io/jq/

Additionally, you can track on-site metrics, such as number of hands raised when you ask how many people are familiar with your product, as well as the number of questions received after the talk or how many people came up to engage with you. If it's a multitrack conference, taking a quick count or estimate of the number of people in the room is helpful as well. However, when reporting these numbers, be sure to use percentages rather than direct numbers, because the total number of attendees will change per event.

Promo codes can come in handy at in-person events as well. Whether these are cards handed out at the sponsor booth or easy-to-remember codes that you put in your slides, promo codes make it easy to track sign-ups precisely. These can either be codes specific to each event, or a generic "DEVREL" promo code that works across the board. Either way, it's an easy way to attribute value to your team.

Tracking a geographic location for sign-ups can be useful if you're frequenting meetups or region-specific conferences. If you track historical data as well, you can start to see how big of an impact your speaking at or sponsoring events in a particular region can have. When this data is compared to the dates of events, direct correlations can be made. This, like most aspects of Developer Relations, is a long-tail goal, and you shouldn't expect immediate results. But with an investment of time and energy in a particular region, you should be able to see sign-ups and community engagement. Be careful to not use this as a metric for large events, though, as they tend to pull attendees from around the world, which will skew your data.

In-Person Connections

Solely in-person connections are nearly impossible to track quantitatively, which is where the qualitative analysis and storytelling skills come in.

As I say in Chapter 3, in-person interactions and building relationships through listening to community members are among the most important parts of Developer Relations. They're also among the most difficult to track in a quantifiable way. This is where the trip reports I mention earlier come into play.

Similar to the event scorecard mentioned earlier, these trip reports can serve as a gut check and a way to analyze how the trip was as a whole instead of just an overall "yes, it was effective" or "no, it was a waste of time." The exact questions that you ask will depend on the goals of your company, but here are a few items that should translate well across all industries (see Appendix A for a sample trip report):

- Types of people in attendance

    - Geographic demographics

    - Types of developers (front end or back end, specific language preferences, and so on)

    - Job titles (managers, individual contributors, or C-suite or VPs)

- Sponsor interactions (did people spend a good amount of time in the expo hall?)

- Caliber of talks (sessions as well as keynotes)

- Overarching themes from the sessions or hallway track

- General impression of the conference

These reports encompass both qualitative analysis of a (sometimes significant) investment as well as what I call *warm handoffs*. These handoffs aren't limited to sales—they could be handoffs to a variety of groups:

- *Business Development/Partnerships*: A potential company to integrate with or list as mutual partners

- *Marketing*: A customer to feature in a case study or a community member who's willing to write a blog post about an interesting way that they've used your product to solve a problem

- *Product*: A customer who's willing to give extensive feedback about a new feature or who's interested in beta testing features before they're released

- *Engineering*: Someone who's stumbled on a particularly hard-to-solve bug and is willing to help Engineering get to the bottom of it

Of course, Sales should be included in these handoffs as well. Depending on the person you've met in the community, you will determine who exactly in Sales you pass them off to—whether you start with the Solutions Architect (the technical side of sales) or go straight to the Enterprise Sales team will depend on the need and (usually) the community member's title. Sometimes, the handoff won't be with the community member you've engaged with but with their manager or the lead of the team that they report to.

These warm handoffs are incredibly important to keep track of for a number of reasons—the most obvious being, of course, that it's a definitive way to attribute value to the activities that the Developer Relations team is involved in. Additionally, in aggregate, it's a valuable way to see which activities overall are more effective than others in the long run, as well as to track themes throughout the industry.

Whether you choose to keep these contacts separate from the company CRM until you make the warm handoff is up to you. However, if you do put all the names in one pot, there should be a clear distinction made between Developer Relations contacts and Sales contacts. This decision will depend on whether your CRM can reliably handle the distinction as well as whether you have a good relationship with your Sales team. You'll need to be able to trust your Sales team to not reach out to developers too early in the process, even if they work for a target account. As we've already established, developers typically don't want to be sold to, and putting them in a position where they'll be added to a drip campaign, signed up for the company newsletter without their permission, or even worse, cold-called, isn't just bad practice,[15] it can serve as a big turn-off to the developer audience. Remember, word spreads quickly, and you don't want the tide to turn against your product simply because you've failed to segment your sales prospects from your community members.

Anecdotes vs. Facts

Before we move onto the next area of metrics, we need to address the difference between anecdotes and facts. These trip reports you bring back from events, as well as the feedback you collect from community members on a regular basis, are all easily seen as *anecdotes*—one-off stories or situations about a particular person who's having a particular experience, which is specific to them and not indicative of your entire community.

---

[15]https://www.ftc.gov/tips-advice/business-center/guidance/can-spam-act-compliance-guide-business

This can in fact be true at times, and I'm not suggesting that we start acting on all pieces of feedback. We shouldn't confuse anecdotes for facts. However, enough anecdotal evidence can reveal patterns that disclose data that should be acted upon. As mentioned in Chapter 1, chances are, for every one user experience problem, bug, or feature request you hear about, there are ten other people thinking the same thing who simply haven't spoken up.

In a fantastic article entitled "Anecdote as Epithet",[16] Michael Quinn Patton makes this case:

> *"An anecdote is nothing more than a short story about something. But anecdote has become an epithet. "That's just anecdotal" is a common way of dismissing qualitative data. . . . It's just an anecdote when told in isolation and heard by amateurs. But I'm a professional anecdote collector. If you know how to listen, systematically collect, and rigorously analyze anecdotes, the patterns revealed are windows into what's going on in the world. It's true that to the untrained ear, an anecdote is just a casual story, perhaps amusing, perhaps not. But to the professionally trained and attuned ear, an anecdote is scientific data—a note in a symphony of human experience. Of course, you have to know how to listen."*

We not only need to be good storytellers, but excellent listeners as well. It's our responsibility to represent the information we're being given by our community, sift through it to find the things that are not only anecdotes but evidence of a problem or opportunity, and then effectively communicate that back to the company stakeholders so that something can be done.

SENSU'S PHILOSOPHY IS TO KEEP PULLING LEVERS AND TELLING STORIES

The storytelling we've been talking about throughout this chapter also plays into how we report on our metrics. Matt Broberg is the VP of Community and DevRel at Sensu, which provides a framework for monitoring infrastructure, service, and application health, as well as business KPIs. Over the years, he has figured out how to combine pulling the right levers with telling the right stories when reporting on metrics for his DevRel team.

---

[16]https://www.betterevaluation.org/en/blog/anecdote_as_epithet

"At the end of the day, the overarching priorities established for a DevRel team need to be broad enough to set us up for success, even if the ways that we report on the success of those priorities change as we pull various levers. It's essential that these priorities are stack-ranked so that we understand which ones to tackle first, second, third, and on down the line. Without this ranking, DevRel is left feeling unsuccessful because despite the sheer quantity of valuable work that they provide, they often aren't able to check high-priority items off of their list. Ranking these items means there is no question what the agreed business value of the team is and therefore what your overall focus should be. This is where we get to shine—by choosing to frame our metrics of success with stories of the community member's journey. If you can agree on your business value, the deliverables you provide alongside your metrics will paint a clear path to follow.

"The importance of finding business alignment shines through when we think of the lead time required for most DevRel deliverables. We need to communicate that each deliverable—whether it's conference talks given, merged pull requests, or the level of conversation in our community forum—takes hours and sometimes days of preparation in order to succeed. If we're constantly being told to pursue new metrics or too many "key" performance indicators, we're being set up for failure by people who don't understand the ramp-up time of our craft. Think about the first step of presenting a talk at a conference: we have to submit a CFP, which means tracking the event, knowing the audience, reaching out to the organizers, designing a great story, prepping the abstract, and so on. DevRel needs business alignment to have the ramp-up time to succeed on these longer commitment timelines, which building a community frequently requires.

"There's also a conversation of moving from raw metrics to aggregate views of metrics. In doing so, we reveal the stories that communicate the significant impact of our actions as DevRel. The raw metrics never speak to us as effectively as the aggregate—it requires framing and storytelling to establish ourselves as truly valuable. That can come in the form of competitive share of voice, customer acquisition, or even top of funnel marketing. DevRel is also a force multiplier elsewhere in the business in the forms of product and user experience feedback, case deflection, or even recruiting. However, all these benefits can come at the cost of a simple narrative of business value, which is what keeps DevRel consistently funded. This means DevRel teams have all the more reason to stay focused and show aggregate success metrics that are supported, but not driven, by the nice-to-have additional benefits.

"In the end, DevRel can (and often is) offering all of this value and more, but it's crucial to not feel obligated to measure it all. The key is figuring out the best story for that particular metric, which aligns it to our business core values and goals, showing that what we're doing is not only interesting, but an effective tool, and a valuable asset for the business. These are the levers you have pull to figure out your unique story.

"If you're able to pay attention to metrics that align both to your company goals and your DevRel goals, then you're setting yourself up for success. And success has bigger budgets, fewer reorgs, and a better life for your team. No one will be able to deny the business value of what you're doing, and you'll be able to continue pulling various levers to make a difference both in your community as well as your company."

Time-to-value

Time-to-value is one of the most important metrics, albeit one of the most difficult to coordinate.

Time-to-send. Time-to-launch. Time-to-deploy. Whatever your goal is for your customers, how long it takes them to reach that point is an important metric to track. The shorter the time, the easier the route, and the less likely they are to leave before they actually give the product a fair shake.

Once you've convinced developers to sign up for an account, you have a limited amount of time to show them the value of your product. No one wants to spend a lot of time or effort setting up and learning a product that might not even do what it claims.

This means your documentation and user experience for new customers needs to be top notch, and you need to make it clear from the get-go that you value your customers. This is one place where the teamwork around documentation, sample applications, and Developer Experience I referenced in Chapter 2 really comes into play. You'll of course get some of the user experience feedback from conference attendees as they're navigating your website, API, or demos at the booth, but more often than not, your Customer Support team will be on the front lines for this fight.

Depending on the tool your company uses to track and triage support tickets, the support team should be able to tag items, create standard response macros, and have a general idea of the common issues that come up on a regular basis. This is another place where automation is key. In addition to replying with a standard macro when they hear the same question about how to navigate a particular part of your API for the 105th time, there should be a report compiling in the background that tells how many tickets tagged with that same problem came through in the past month.

This is where the Developer Relations team can step in—either a Developer Advocate or a developer experience manager (more about these roles in Chapter 5)—and comb through the report to figure out what's actionable. Sometimes this will mean rewriting documentation. Other times the best solution will be coming up with clearer explanations for complicated code segments, or figuring out a better way entirely to walk developers of a varied skill level through a concept, whether that's through a sample application or a video.

This type of work is what I call a quick win—it's a relatively easy fix that can have a great impact across the organization. Suddenly, your Customer Support team has fewer tickets to deal with, your Marketing team has fewer complaints to answer on social media, and your customers are having an easier time figuring out the product. In addition, your community has seen that you have their best interests at heart and that you not only listen to their concerns, but act on them—and that's quite possibly the success metric that will have the biggest impact in turning your customers into advocates for your company.

Quick Wins and Weekly Reports

These quick wins don't just apply to your customer support queue. They also come into play with situations like submitting a PR to list your API on a GitHub gist of cool APIs to build tools around, or getting your logo up on a site that features developer tools. These quick wins directly correlate to brand awareness and additional places for your audience to find out about your product. Ideally, these are one-person projects that take less than a day but have a positive impact for the brand and a lot of potential for growth.

These quick wins are an easy way to show immediate impact in an industry that depends on long-tail success and relationship building, which can sometimes take years to come to fruition. Reporting these in a weekly email that goes to your boss, or even better, to the leadership team at your company, is a good way to stay front-of-mind and show that even if you're not able to show direct sales as a result of your work, you're accomplishing things on a regular basis that contribute to the overall goals of the company and keep pushing the needle forward.

Finding Your Specific Metrics: Libby Boxes

For the most part, I'm not suggesting exact metrics to track because these will depend on your company's goals and the direction that your specific DevRel team is taking. But Libby Boxes (Figure 4-1), a predictive framework popularized by Cornell Accounting Professor Robert Libby, are a great way to figure out what these general practices look like for your team.

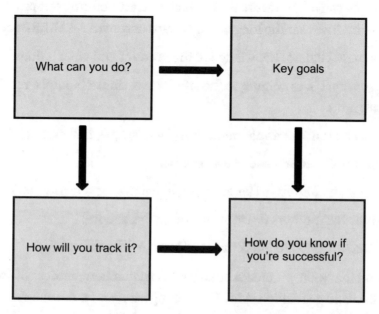

Figure 4-1. *This framework is used to illustrate the relationship between the strategic objectives you're trying to achieve and the initiatives (or levers) you use to reach those goals*

This framework is used to illustrate the relationship between the strategic objectives you're trying to achieve and the initiatives (or levers) you use to reach those goals. In short, they're a way to trace your everyday actions and deliverables back to the overarching company goals that you're trying to push forward. This direct line makes it easier to prove that your efforts, though unconventional, are making a difference for the company.

Pirate Metrics

Each of your *conceptual outcomes* (the overarching outcomes or goals you're striving to meet) will relate back to one or more pirate metrics[17] or AAARRRP, the updated version specific to DevRel from Phil Leggetter.[18] These metrics are a good foundation for creating goals, as they represent the behaviors of our customers and directly correlate to the outcomes you'll be looking for. Although tracking all of these metrics at once isn't reasonable, it gives you a framework from which to start building out priorities.

Here are the metrics that the long and awkward acronym AAARRRP stands for:

- *Awareness*: General knowledge of the product and what it does
- *Acquisition*: Users coming to the site from various channels, resulting in a sign-up
- *Activation*: Product implementation (for example, makes first API call)
- *Retention*: Continual use of the product
- *Revenue*: Pay for usage (for example, subscribe or buy product)
- *Referral*: Refer others (become brand ambassadors)
- *Product*: Provide feedback or contribute to the product

Keep in mind that what your team uses to track acquisition metrics will be very different than what the demand generation side of Marketing uses, and there should be very few (if any) ways that DevRel is responsible for items that track back to the revenue metric.

Leggetter has created an AAARRRP mapping template[19] for DevRel teams to chart out which metrics each task falls under. It should be noted that although this list covers a large spectrum of tasks, not all of them will (or should) be covered by any one DevRel team, especially if you have a small team that's just ramping up. These are often tasks that will be shared among teams, and some may not apply to your company at all (for example, if you have technical account managers or a Sales Engineering team, DevRel won't be involved with pre-sales discussions and integrations). However, this framework allows you to put in your own DevRel team deliverables and figure out which metrics those deliverables relate back to.

---

[17]http://startitup.co/guides/374/aarrr-startup-metrics
[18]https://devrel.net/strategy-and-metrics/introducing-aaarrrp-devrel-strategy
[19]http://bit.ly/aaarrrp-template

Setting Objectives

To set your *deliverables*, or objectives, this section asks four questions.

What Outcome Are We Striving for and Which Pirate Metrics Are Impacted?

This upper-right quadrant back in Figure 4-1 represents your key goals, which are usually determined by overarching company goals. Let's say at Avocado Industries, the company goal for the coming year is to grow the customer base, resulting in higher revenue. DevRel isn't responsible for sales, but their work can still impact this goal through awareness, acquisition, activation, retention, and referral, as you can see in Figure 4-2. The key is to make sure that these are goals you can actually impact. Focus on the umbrella of adoption (awareness and acquisition), retention (largely impacted by Developer Experience, content, and community building), and satisfaction (referral), and be sure to make the warm handoff to Sales when it reaches the revenue metric.

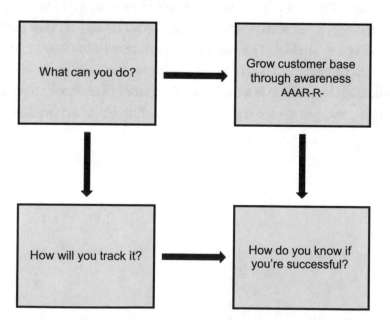

Figure 4-2. *The upper-right quadrant represents your key goals—in this case, growing the customer base. The pirate metrics this refers to are awareness, acquisition, activation, retention, and referral.*

What Will Help Us Achieve That Outcome?

The upper-left quadrant is the first *input* metric you'll run into—what could you implement that might influence your outcome? Keep in mind that input metrics in one context can be outcome metrics in another context. For example, we could say that customer engagement (input metric) drives adoption (outcome metric). Customer engagement may be your final outcome metric, but it may be an input metric for another part of the business. For example, the executive team could posit that adoption drives revenue—which, while very important, is outside the scope of your team.

By taking a look at our pirate metrics, we can see that awareness is going to be key to grow the customer base. If we can increase awareness, we'll likely drive acquisition and activation. By using content as a key awareness input, we also impact retention— creating quality content and a better Developer Experience for our customers who are already on board. All of these things lead to a happy customer base, which results in referrals.

As you can see in Figure 4-3, choosing to focus on one key pivot point (growing the customer base *through awareness*) allows you to impact many different parts of the business. Choosing the handful of key inputs to implement allows you to spend less time switching between projects and more time focusing on the few that will make the biggest impact. The question to ask here is what general inputs will likely drive your chosen output? Keep this conceptual—we'll start to break it down into actionable items in the next step.

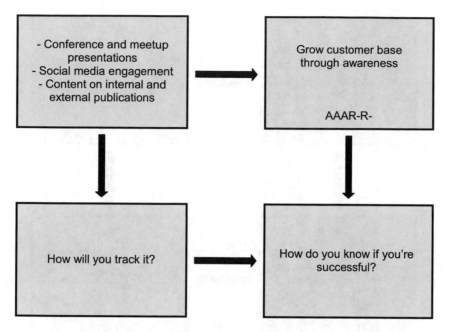

Figure 4-3. *Conceptual inputs drive the overall outcome*

How Can We Measure Our Progress Toward That Outcome?

The lower-left quadrant starts to delve into the actual measures you'll look to in order to implement the concepts. These initiatives begin to make the conceptual inputs more concrete and give your team a general direction in which to head. Again, the way you choose to pursue this narrative will depend on the specific talents of your team (remember the specialization discussed in Chapter 4), but the conceptual inputs from the upper-right quadrant give you a starting point.

Let's say your team is made up of a strong speaker and a strong writer, both of whom have a solid presence on Twitter. By playing to their strengths, you can leverage their skills to move the needle forward on awareness (Figure 4-4). Given that you have a small team, it may be worthwhile to build an internal speaker's bureau to amplify the voices of developers who might be interested in speaking at conferences but who need help when it comes to CFP topics or presentation skills.

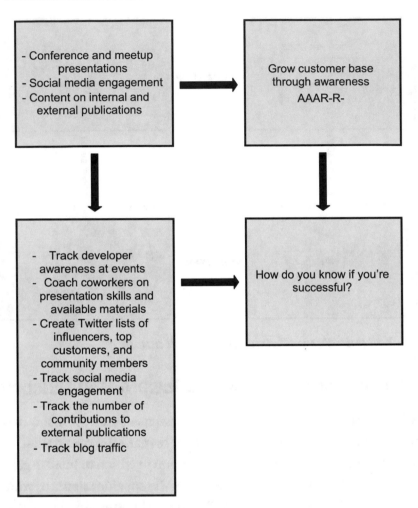

Figure 4-4. *The lower-left quadrant starts to delve into the actual measures you'll look to in order to implement the concepts*

What Objective Measures Can We Put in Place?

This last box is where you can put the deliverables, or objective measures, for your team (Figure 4-5). What are you expected to have accomplished by the end of the quarter? How many conference talks is it reasonable to give in one quarter (keeping in mind, of course, that these conference talks require accepted CFPs or invitations to speak)? How do you know whether you've succeeded in pushing the needle forward on the overarching company goal?

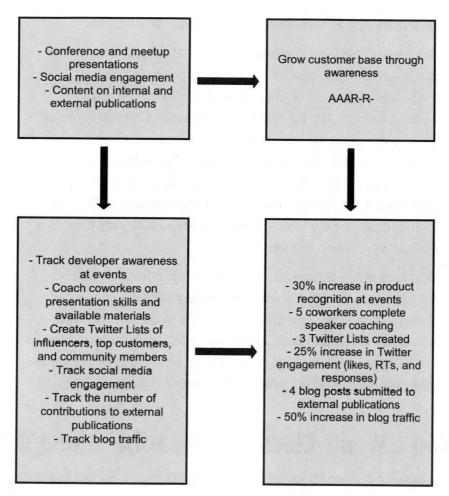

Figure 4-5. *The last box is where you can put the deliverables, or objective measures, for your team*

Setting these objective measurements allows the DevRel team to know exactly what it is they're responsible for (and therefore, what they're not responsible for). It becomes an easy way for them to push back against work from other departments, or at the very least, gives them (and their management) a clear understanding of which of their objective measures won't be met as a result of a different project that popped up. In addition, because these metrics can be traced back to the overarching company goals, you can draw direct business value from your work. There's no longer any question of how the work the DevRel team is doing will drive more people to adoption and revenue.

Two words of caution as you set these objective measurements:

1. Starting with production metrics (such as the number of events you sponsored, spoke at, or organized) tends to increase awareness of the cost of your program instead of the results. Instead, focus on the outcome of those events. Can you increase the awareness of your platform? Will you receive valuable feedback about the Developer Experience? How many warm handoffs can you make to Marketing and Sales? By focusing on these metrics rather than "speak at five conferences," you're highlighting the value that you provide to the company instead of the money you've cost them.

2. Don't conflate a statement of work done with the goal you're trying to achieve. A flat number of things you're doing or have done (for example, "submitted three CFPs in Q3") is an output measured, not a net effect. The important thing to pay attention to is whether all your team goals and measurements (work done) are contributing toward the overarching company goals.

Building a World-Class Developer Relations Team

The last measure of success I'll present is one that I'd wager most folks would see as a goal and not as a metric. Although I think building up a world-class Developer Relations team should be a top priority, I also think the success of this goal can be a metric of the overall success of the community you're attempting to build.

Making sure that your Developer Relations team is getting the training, support, and assistance they need in order to become the best possible community builders will not only make them successful, it will drive the company forward. Any investment you make in your team's happiness will free up their energy to invest in the community, which will continue to motivate them to move forward and spread the word about the work that you're doing as a company.

It's possible that this metric is one of the hardest to measure. It's a people metric, which automatically means it's squishy and messy and hard to get your hands around unless you're actively listening and responding to what's being said, just as your team is expected to do with the community.

Remember the three questions I listed at the beginning of this chapter for a quarterly retrospective about how things are going with your community?

- What's going well?

- What could we be doing better?

- What should we do differently going forward?

Asking those questions (and actively listening to the answers) will get you a long way down the road toward creating a world-class Developer Relations team. We'll talk about this in Chapter 5 as we explore how to hire a DevRel team, but the more your team knows you have their back no matter the circumstances, and the more you understand the value they bring to the table, the more willing they're going to be to pull levers, take risks, and try new things that might wind up being the key to the entire company's success.

These things are important not only for the success of your team inside your company, but because as your company succeeds in effectively fostering a strong Developer Relations program, you'll start to see a direct impact in the awareness of your brand in the developer community as a whole. As mentioned in Chapter 2, sometimes all it takes for a community member to be drawn to your product is a simple awareness of someone on your Developer Relations team.[20] These days, it's not uncommon for someone to ask, "What companies have the strongest Developer Relations (or community) teams?" Developers know that if the community team is strong, their feedback will be heard.

TWILIO'S WORLD-CLASS DEVREL TEAM

Twilio has long been regarded as the prime example of a "world-class DevRel team." Twilio is a cloud communications platform that gives developers the building blocks to add messaging, voice, and video in their web and mobile applications, and it's no surprise that they've had a strong Developer Relations team from the start, given that developers have been their first and only focus. Developer Evangelist Phil Nash has been with the company since 2014 and has seen this consistent attention from the beginning.

---

[20]https://twitter.com/mary_grace/status/843975759890800640

"We've been fortunate to earn that reputation because of how the company started. The three co-founders of Twilio are all developers and it's always been a developer product—we've been 'API-first' from the very start. As a developer-first company, we've been lucky enough that the business doesn't only value developers, but *demands* that we put them first in everything.

"Because of this, there is a strong belief that Evangelism and Developer Relations works, so we've had to do less outright proving of that value. This has freed us up to build relationships and give back to our respective communities without worrying that we have to have metrics to back up all of our work. We of course have goals and expectations like every other team, but we don't feel the need to defend our work as often as it seems like other Developer Relations teams do.

"Our Developer Evangelism team has a mission to inspire and equip developers to change communications. Those two points—inspire and equip—dictate all of the work that we do. We keep these two main focuses because if you aren't able to inspire or excite someone about a project, they're not going to pay attention, and once you've got them inspired, if you don't follow up with equipping them to actually go and do that thing themselves, then you've also failed. This applies to all of our content, events, talks, and projects.

"In order to fulfill this mission, our team tends to hire for technical credibility first. We do this for two reasons: first because we need people who can talk credibly about code with their communities, but also because these folks tend to be the ones who are already embedded in these communities. We're more than willing to mentor someone in public speaking or writing blog posts if they don't have as much experience in those areas or want to grow more. What matters the most to us is their willingness to help the community and their technical ability to do that within their specific stack.

"Lastly, given that we're a distributed team, we have a quarterly in-person summit for our Developer Evangelism team. We spend two intense days talking about what we do and evaluating our work—holding retrospectives for various initiatives and planning out the next major projects. We're a team that values psychological safety, and we have from the beginning. These meetings are very open, vulnerable, and authentic. Because we're able to trust each other, we're able to be our true selves, which makes the team stronger as a whole.

"This combination of these things results in a strong team that trusts each other to do their best work and a company who believes in the work that we're doing. This empowers us to do our jobs well as we continue to grow and learn along the way."

What does it look like when a company has a high bar for Developer Relations? Among other things, you can expect them to have a smooth developer experience end-to-end (or at least be actively working on improving it). They are likely looking for feedback in an open and transparent way, whether through a bug bounty program, a beta tester program, or actively talking to their customers both online and in person. Lastly, their passion for the developer community is built into the very foundation of the business, not added on as a checklist item or shunted off into a singular team who is only consulted when there's a crisis.

Like many of the things we talked about in this chapter, this "world class DevRel team" status isn't a tangible, measurable concept. However, the distinction that your company has one of the best Developer Relations teams, above all of the other metrics, can make a significant impact on the livelihood of your company. Ultimately, as the article I quoted earlier from Genuinely says, not all metrics are tangible, but we instinctively assume that they are.

"Tangible makes us feel better. Tangible helps us predict a good ROI, but brand loyalty, relationships, and other key foundations of community are inherently intangible but almost incalculably invaluable. We can conduct surveys and look at indicators like all of those we've just listed, but as it stands, there is no perfect measure."[21]

---

[21]https://genuinely.co/2013/08/measuring-community-kpis-social-metrics-community-building/

CHAPTER 5

Building a Developer Relations Team

Now that we've covered how to define your company goals around community and how to build a business case for including Developer Relations (DevRel) in your success strategy, it's time to figure out who's going to help fill those roles.

In this chapter, we'll talk about benchmarks for growth (drawing a mall map), titles (what's in a name?), what your first hire should be and what that job description should look like, where this person (or team) should live within your company, and how to help your newfound hire(s) succeed.

Draw Your Mall Map

Although building out a plan based on your current situation is of course necessary, if you're only planning for the current situation, you're being short-sighted. We'll talk more about this in Chapter 7, but you always want to be thinking ahead to the next steps. What are the resources you need for the current scenario, and then what will you need once you've surpassed your goals? If you desperately need a technical community builder or Developer Advocate now, great! Once they're onboarded and successful in meeting their goals, who will you need next?

I've always loved the analogy of drawing a *mall map* for your DevRel team. In San Francisco, we have a mall that is 9 floors tall and over 1.5 million square feet. With 180+ stores, a map of where all of them are located is essential. Similarly, with as many directions as a DevRel team can head in, a map that identifies where you are now, where you'd like to go, and what you might see along the way so you know whether you're heading in the right direction is integral to the success of your team.

© Mary Thengvall 2018
M. Thengvall, *The Business Value of Developer Relations*, https://doi.org/10.1007/978-1-4842-3748-9_5

Focusing on the basic hygiene of your Developer Experience first is important: what are the biggest issues that need to be addressed? Going back to the pirate metrics from Chapter 4 can be helpful to find the basic categories you're looking to address. Do you need to work on general awareness or is activation the main problem? Do you need external help with referrals or more feedback from your active users? Figuring out the category you need to focus on can help you figure out what your starting point is, both in terms of hiring a new employee and what their initial goals will be.

From there, you can visualize a company in which that category is no longer the biggest issue. What would you focus on next if the activation issue were taken care of? What circumstances might occur if you're suddenly retaining customers? By stepping through these scenarios one by one, you can start to build out your mall map with your "anchor stores" (the bigger department stores sprinkled throughout a typical mall), helping you to identify the major places where another hire will be necessary. The mall map can also show you what to avoid, similar to the makeup vendors or people who have "just a quick question" for you as you search for your next location. These distractions are important to identify as early as possible so that they can be avoided when your team comes across them. Lastly, the mall map analogy allows you to acknowledge that you might accomplish your main goal (finding the perfect suit coat for example) at a different store than you originally anticipated. As mentioned earlier, this flexibility is key in ensuring that your team meets their main goals as quickly and easily as possible.

Having a long-term strategy built out (even if that "long-term" timeline is only 18 months) can be key in showing the stakeholders at your company that this Developer Relations team isn't just a passing fad. By sketching out what each hire will be capable of and the goals they will hit along the way, you can show the potential value that Developer Relations will bring to the company. This map also allows you to outline the initial goals that the team will be responsible for, setting them up for success to build a strong foundation for the industry's next world-class DevRel team.

What's in a Name?

This topic is no stranger to the DevRel community. Case in point: there are *community manager*, *developer relations*, *community leadership*, and *Developer Experience* events— all geared toward the same (or similar) audience. It's a popular question in various community forums as well.[1] If you go looking for the appropriate title in various salary surveys, you're going to have a hard time narrowing it down.[2] Mobilize even started keeping a Google Spreadsheet with various alternatives to the *community manager* title.[3]

From *community architect* to *chief engagement officer* to *developer evangelist*, there are more titles than I can possibly cover in this chapter, but I think you'll notice one key theme for all of them: at a glance, none of them does a particularly good job of describing exactly what the role involves.

The title *community manager* has risen drastically in popularity since I first started saying, "I want to talk *to* our customers instead of *at* our customers," from within the Public Relations department at O'Reilly Media. I'm grateful for the heightened awareness of the job role, but like all popularity, it comes with downsides. From the folks who assume that I "handle the social media stuff" to conference attendees who want to talk to someone "who actually knows what they're talking about," it's a tough battle to convince people that I, in fact, can hold a technical conversation with them about various products.

In many previous jobs, I didn't disclose my title until someone pushed for it or I handed them my business card. It was my hope that by that time, we'd talked about what our product can do for them, I'd exhibited my in-depth knowledge of the code base, and I'd pointed them in the right direction to find more information. We'll talk more in a bit about why it's so important for every community manager (whether technical or not) to be able to do those three things, but as you can see, there is a wide range of assumptions made about the title *community manager*, which often doesn't accurately represent our day-to-day job. Part of this struggle is that there *isn't* a typical day-to-day job that applies to us, but nailing down a job title that best encapsulates the expected day-to-day for the role that you're hiring for is key.

At the end of the day, I've figured out a set of titles that work well for a predominantly proprietary (with some open source tooling or SDKs) tech company with a developer audience. The first three titles I list (*DevRel Manager*, *Developer Advocate*, and *Technical Community Builder*) are ones that I feel strongly should be a part of every Developer Relations team. The last five (*Developer Experience Manager*, *Technical Ambassador*, *Technical Engagement Manager*, *DevRel Project Manager*, and *Full-time Engineer*) are

---

[1]https://www.communityleadershipforum.com/t/alternative-title-to-community-manager/923
https://www.quora.com/What-are-some-good-alternative-titles-to-Community-Manager
[2]https://experts.feverbee.com/t/alternative-title-to-community-manager/5159/8
[3]https://docs.google.com/spreadsheets/d/164ZkdeyJ5wzOmsvvisBpS1ygFAh3ZPNfUAipCp-OMdU/edit

relevant for some teams but not others. As usual, your needs and business cases may vary for each of these examples—for example, you may have an awesome social media manager who can keep up with the technical lingo, or a great marketing colleague who heads up an influencer program.

Team Title: Developer Relations

This title addresses who the team is working with (end users versus buyers), which is an important distinction when you're lining up your team goals and trying to prevent work from creeping onto your plate from other departments. It also establishes that the DevRel team members are the subject matter experts on that community.

The responsibilities of the team are determined by the specific goals of the company, which will also determine which department the team falls under—we'll talk more about this later in the chapter. However, in general, it's the overarching responsibility of the Developer Relations team to ensure the success of the developer audience and communicate their needs back to the rest of the company. As I've established previously (and will touch on again at other points throughout the book), almost every department interacts with the customer community on some level, but it is only the Developer Relations team whose sole focus is the community's well-being.

When starting with a small team, focus on the basic hygiene necessary to keep things up and running: good documentation, excellent support, and free developer accounts. Once those things are up and running smoothly with only occasional maintenance, you can start looking at a forum or another place for the community to congregate, sample applications, SDKs, "superuser" or champions groups, sponsoring open source and community projects, general brand awareness, speaking engagements, and more. But unless you have the basic foundation that every developer is looking for, in a reliable and trustworthy product, no one wants to see the bells and whistles. If the first experience a developer has when they visit your site is poor, what's the motivation for them to ever come back, or for that matter, to send anyone else your way?

Strategic Lead: Developer Relations Manager

Although this title isn't all that out of the ordinary, finding someone perfect for this role can be a little like finding a unicorn. It's incredibly important that this person have experience in Developer Relations and isn't just the VP or C-suite person that all the individual contributors on the DevRel team report up to. This person serves as both the umbrella and conduit for the rest of the team. They protect the team from outside requests, bouncing unrelated work back to the departments it came from. They also provide a way for the feedback that the team is receiving on a regular basis to get funneled up to the right places and people.

So what are the responsibilities of a developer relations manager? This isn't just a typical people-manager role. This person not only handles the day-to-day aspects of what the team needs but sets the strategy of where the team (and therefore, the community) is going next. You're looking for someone who may or may not have a technical background but who can speak the lingo and keep up with the conversation. They know the right questions to ask and have experience with technical products. They don't necessarily have day-in-and-day-out coding experience, but they know the basics and can follow along with simple instructions enough to know whether your *Getting Started* guide is clear and easy to follow. They're also able to take a "forest" view of the situation rather than getting stuck in the weeds of sample apps, bug fixes, and community forum wrangling.

This individual will be heading up the conversations with the other teams in the organization; having regular check-ins with Marketing, Product, Support, Sales, and Engineering. They'll be involved in the planning discussions and present for all the product launch calls, offering feedback and insight into what the community is looking for and why. This requires them to be in constant communication with their team, sifting through the community needs and triaging the feedback the team is receiving on a regular basis. They'll then coordinate with the other teams to find out not only how to handle the requests, but who will be responsible for seeing it through.

Technical Contributor: Developer Advocate

The title *Developer Advocate* covers two of the biggest questions in the community space:

- What are your qualifications?

- What do you do?

This title helps establish the fact that these employees are first developers, and second that their primary objective is to be the voice of the community at the company, which sets them up to be the spokespeople for and experts about the community.

Remember what I mentioned in Chapter 3 about representing the company to the community, and vice versa—representing the community to the company? This is the role that owns most of that responsibility. They're the ones who get the most face time with the developer audience due to speaking at conferences, working the booth, and interacting with developers online via forums, Slack teams, various websites, and social media channels. Some of these platforms will be maintained by the company, but more often than not, Developer Advocates will spend their time in community-run channels rather than the company-maintained ones.

#EMAILGEEKS: THE SLACK COMMUNITY WHERE EMAIL MARKETERS, DESIGNERS, AND DEVELOPERS MEET TO TALK SHOP

Although building out a community Slack team or Discourse channel for your customers may be a good place for people to collaborate, hanging out in discussion channels created by the community is often a better way to keep up with the latest trends. These places are also a great way to get to know folks who are part of your core community but who may not use your product. Lead Developer Advocate Avi Goldman learned this secret while working for SparkPost, an email delivery API built for and by developers.

"Shortly before I joined the Developer Relations team at SparkPost, I was starting to create small projects that illustrated email in a fun, engaging way. As I dug into these projects and did research on various blogs, I started making a list of some of the bigger names in the front-end email community. I followed them on Twitter so I could keep track of what they were talking about and noticed that many of them were tweeting with the hashtag #emailgeeks. As I started to engage with them more often, I heard about a Slack team for these "email geeks" to hang out in as well.

"While this community-run Slack team has obviously been beneficial to SparkPost (more on that in a moment), it honestly started out as a great resource for me. It helped me learn more about this topic that people were looking to me to be an expert on. It also allowed me to engage with people in the industry who hadn't been our primary customer audience at SparkPost. While email is a fairly big piece of most businesses, it's not something that developers usually spend a lot of time on. This Slack team allowed me to find a segment of developers whose primary focus was email and who were really passionate about pushing the email industry forward.

"As I became more active in the community, I really wanted to find people in my geographic area who were interested in similar topics. I started talking to Justin Khoo and Sue Cho in the SF area who were fairly well known in the email community and also excited about this idea.

As a result of our combined connections, it was surprisingly easy to spin up the #emailgeeksSF meetup. Because we started with people who were already influencers in the community and cared deeply about the topic, we were able to draw others into the group simply because of their network effect. The community already existed—it was just a matter of pulling them together in an in-person forum.

"This in-person meetup allowed SparkPost to get in front of developers who were thinking about email at bigger companies, which historically had been incredibly difficult. There was immediate value to show because I could very easily say, 'We spoke to these people who work on $COMPANY'S email system full time—they've been to two out of the three recent meetups and are interested in learning more about what we're working on.'

"The meetup also sets SparkPost up as an industry leader in the community—we're giving influencers a platform to speak from, which not only helps with brand awareness but tells the community that we care about their needs and want to support their projects. As a result, the success of this meetup has paved the way for other community events and sponsorships that previously might have been difficult to make a business case for."

As the team starts to grow, you can begin to segment these advocates into specialities—technical as well as interpersonal—and even geographic locations. You'll find that some excel at speaking, whereas others thrive in one-on-one conversations at events. Others will become known for their writing skills and ability to create content that resonates with the developer audience. Still others will be able to break down the details of your product step-by-step into clear, easy-to-follow documentation, or will have an innate ability to find the community where they are, digging into the particular niche of your industry, as discussed in the "#Emailgeeks" case study.

One note of caution when hiring for this role: although it's tempting to require that this individual produce several pieces of technical content per month, as well as speak at conferences regularly, as well as keep up with all the latest and greatest code developments, as well as take a deep dive into the product code base and create sample applications and SDKs, you need to be conscious of the fact that there are easily three full-time jobs within that job description. Pick and choose the skills you're looking for and the corresponding responsibilities based on your mall map and then, as your team grows, begin to find your holes and hire to fill those spots. Whether it's language-specific needs or particular skills, you can flesh out your team until you've got everyone focusing on their specialties. This allows each individual to carve out a spot for themselves that best suits their talents, permitting them to not only bring the most value to the table, but also to pursue particular areas in which they want to grow and learn.

Remember how we talked about building a world-class Developer Relations team as a metric in the last chapter? This is where that starts to take shape and be noticeable to others outside of your company.

Cruise Director: Technical Community Builder

This is the role traditionally referred to as *community manager*, but I've very specifically chosen to name this role *community builder* instead. My reasoning here is dual purpose: it escapes the problems addressed earlier regarding the title becoming muddied, and it very clearly denotes what this role is intended for: building a technical community around the product at hand. Although this title does have *technical* in the title, it's similar to the developer relations manager in that the individual doesn't have a developer background. The important distinction is that this role needs to be filled by someone who's willing and able to learn the basics of the technology.

One of their most valuable skills is being the "cruise director" mentioned in Chapter 3—knowing the right people to connect with in the community as well as whom to point community members to when they have questions or concerns. This person is the primary owner of the processes, systems, and constructs built up around the external community you're fostering. Whether this is a public forum or Slack team, an invite-only group of top customers or your most prolific contributors (content, GitHub PRs, and so forth), the community builder is the one behind the scenes. They're the person making sure everything's working as it should, enforcing the Code of Conduct (more about the importance of this document in Chapter 7), looking out for potential connections to be made between community members and others within your company (think about the warm handoffs metric discussed in Chapter 4), and more.

This role is also key in collecting anecdotal data. Together with Developer Advocates, they gather information about the problems they're hearing about from the community, as well as potential content and collaboration opportunities.

Developer Experience Manager

Developer Experience is something that plays heavily into the success of your product. If you think back to Chapter 2, it's one of the three questions we asked to first categorize your goals around Developer Relations. I put this role immediately after the three essential DevRel roles because I believe strongly that once your team starts to grow and your community starts to scale, you need someone who can take over the Developer

Experience pieces. As mentioned earlier, Developer Experience is the cornerstone of your product, but once your team starts to grow and specialize in different things, you won't want them context-switching back to the basics often. This person now owns that Developer Experience, from start to finish. They may not manage a team of people (though if your team grows large enough and you have the need, that's a possibility), but they'll be overseeing the cross-team task forces across the company who are working on everything from the UX and design of the site to the documentation and SDKs.

This person won't necessarily be responsible for all the actual implementation, but they'll be in charge of making sure that work in this area gets done in a fluid and timely manner. From keeping an eye on the documentation and organizing it in a way that will make sense to your customers,[4] to overseeing the *Getting Started* pages and the general user experience, this person plays a key role in the time-to-value metric mentioned in Chapter 4. You'll be looking for someone who can both delegate and step in to do the job when necessary. This is another job where a developer background isn't necessary, but in this case, if they weren't a developer in a past life, they need to at least hold their own in technical writing skills.

Technical Ambassador

I very specifically call these folks *ambassadors*, not *evangelists*. The word *evangelist* implies a religious affiliation, which has a negative connotation in many countries and can make it difficult to even get in the door at some businesses, let alone build credibility. Guy Kawasaki popularized the term *evangelist* as well as the concepts of *evangelism marketing* and *technology evangelism* in the mid-to-late 1980s while marketing the early Macintosh computer. Though the term made sense at the time—he was, after all, an evangelist of sorts, focused on spreading the good news about the Mac—it has since lost its favor in a lot of circles. In addition to the problems just listed, evangelists are now often viewed as extensions of the sales team, which makes it even more difficult for them to make headway in developer communities. The term *Technical Ambassador*, on the other hand, distinguishes this role from Developer Advocate and establishes this individual as an ambassador of goodwill on behalf of the company.

---

[4]I'm a fan of this documentation matrix from Daniele Procida: https://www.divio.com/en/blog/documentation/

Though this might at first glance seem very similar to the Developer Advocate role, this role has more of a sales focus than a community focus. These are the folks who excel at speaking on large stages and selling not just the product, but the *importance* of the product to the larger technical community. Your Developer Advocates are the folks who will connect easily with the developer community, selling them on the what and why and life-changing ease of your product, but the Evangelists will sell the leadership (VPs and C-suites) on the importance of your product for the longevity of their business.

These folks don't have as much of a community bent. Although they should understand the importance of community, they aren't going to be on the front lines at meetups and developer conferences. They will, however, be speaking at the business and tech leadership conferences, keynoting on various stages about why this particular technology is important at this particular time in the industry. This role fits best in new industries within the tech realm (for example, SendGrid's revolutionary email servers as a service, or the DevOps cultural revolution), where it's not only necessary to educate the community on what the company brand is, but what need they're filling.

Technical Engagement Manager

This title is convoluted, and may not suit every business. However, having someone who—similar to the technical community builder and developer relations manager—has enough of a technical understanding to contribute to the social media channels and engage the developer audience online is a huge win. However, making sure that this title isn't simply a version of *Social Media Manager* is important—you don't want this individual to wind up being solely responsible for spreadsheets of tweets and Facebook posts, running online ads in their spare time.

This person is the last pair of eyes on any content intended for the developer audience. You'll notice I didn't say they're responsible for *writing* all the content. Rather, their responsibility is to make sure the content aligns with the company voice and also caters to the developer audience without being too "markety" or sales focused. This could include all tweets and social posts intended for the developer audience. It could also mean that they do the day-to-day writing for these developer-specific accounts as well. Again, the exact who and what is going to depend on your company and the resources you already have. If you already have a Social Media Manager who's capable of engaging the developer audience and is doing a great job of bringing them into the conversations, you may only need help from the Developer Advocates to point out who the relevant community members are, or who's contributing on a regular basis (look back at Chapter 3 if you need a refresher on this).

DevRel Project Manager

Given that a catch-all role in a DevRel team can be pulled in so many different directions, I very specifically put this role in the project management world. Wikipedia has a very clear definition behind *project management*: "The discipline of initiating, planning, executing, controlling, and closing the work of a team to achieve specific goals and meet specific success criteria at the specified time."[5] This distinction keeps the individual protected from being pulled in every direction, which can easily result in them doing the work for others rather than simply delegating the work.

Depending on the size of your team, this role can manifest in a few different ways:

- This could be the person who handles all your events logistics, making sure everyone submits CFPs in time, that all the boxes are checked for various sponsorships, and that the swag inventory is kept up-to-date.

- They could also handle all the overarching project details for a larger DevRel team. Considering how much DevRel tends to cross over into other departments (Marketing, Engineering, Product, and so on), having one point person who knows where all the moving pieces are is invaluable. This person can then be the point person at the regular status meetings for other departments, freeing up the rest of the team to get other work done instead.

Full-Time Engineer

This title is fairly straightforward—this is a full-time engineer or developer. The only difference between them and their counterparts at the company is that they're dedicated to the Developer Relations team.

I've found this role to be incredibly helpful to teams that are either relatively small (say, one Developer Advocate and one community manager) or relatively large (with ten or more individuals on the team). In either case, having a full-time engineer on the team means that the one-off bugs or smaller tickets that community members have reported but that aren't urgent enough for the Engineering and Product teams to address won't fall through the cracks. This also means that if you need a particular application built for an event or a tool to automate some of the DevRel processes, you don't have to make a case for Engineering time. Many larger companies are pivoting to this process—Google,

---

[5]https://en.wikipedia.org/wiki/Project_management

and Twitter both have partner and on-call engineers, as do Oculus and RiotGames. This position allows for greater focus among the team in general—each person can focus on their speciality rather than needing to focus on content and strategy as well as tooling and community applications.

Who's First?

The titles I've highlighted are all ideal, but having this full team structure is rarely seen outside of large companies. Your first hire is going to be responsible for bits and pieces from all of these roles. Keep in mind that although every hire is an investment, hiring your first Developer Relations employee is especially crucial. This person brings with them not only their experience, but their network, and if you can find someone who enjoys the community and is also valued by the company, this person could be instrumental in setting the tone for your entire relationship with developers down the road. As you can imagine, choosing both the role you'll be hiring for and the person to fill that role is extremely important.

Know Your Strengths and Weaknesses

Do you need someone to come in and lay down structure and a vision for where you'll be taking the Developer Relations team? You'll be looking for a more senior hire in this case—someone who has experience at a previous technical company doing Developer Relations work. This person will have seen the pros and cons of how to interact with and build out a technical community in the past and, with the support and direction of the stakeholders addressed in Chapter 2, will be able to create a successful strategy for a fledgling team.

On the other hand, if you have an executive who's handling most of the initial strategy and direction for the Developer Relations team, you don't necessarily need someone to handle that role right now. You can instead focus on hiring someone to take care of the execution side of things, such as a Technical Community Manager or Developer Advocate, who can come in and start to build out the community but who won't necessarily be as involved in the overarching strategy and planning of where to take the team. This person could be experienced or relatively junior. You won't be looking to them for as much of the strategy and planning, though you will want to listen closely to their feedback, because they're the ones in the trenches day in and day out, talking to the developers who are using your product. With mentorship, this person may be able to take over the team in a few years, guiding and directing the strategy and next steps of where to take the team. Or you may use this person to shore up the gaps until you can make the investment to find a team lead who can take the reins and start building out the team on their own. Either way, keep in mind that you're hiring for a career, not just for the moment.

This is a good place to stop and talk to current Community Managers or hopeful Developer Relations team members—just because you're the initial hire at a company doesn't mean you're alone. When taking on the myriad responsibilities covered in the first half of this chapter seems overwhelming, don't forget that there's no expectation for you to take on all of those roles at once. It's your job to see where the needs are and fill the gaps for now, while identifying which role needs to be filled next based on the goals or initiatives of the company.

You can also rely on people in other departments:

- *The social media manager who has a good eye for interesting developer content*: Rely on them to curate a good stream of information from which you can gather data. Work with them to amplify the voice of your current community members while also finding other potential community leaders from the popular developer content that they're surfacing.

- *The sales engineer who's really good at explaining things in a clear, step-by-step fashion to their new prospect*: Ask them to help you fix the documentation or give feedback on the first draft of the *Getting Started* guide you've created.

- *The engineer who helps run the local programming meetup*: Help them realize their hidden speaking talents and work with them to craft CFPs for local conferences.

You can even rely on your community members for content creation and brand awareness. Know of a few community members who are excellent writers or speakers? Work with them to build content for the Engineering blog as a guest blogger, or offer to help them draft a CFP (and pay them a stipend for their travel expenses) for a conference talk about how your product helped them accomplish a long-term goal at their company. Or scope out which community members live in an area where you're going to be sponsoring a conference. Offer to pay for their conference ticket if they're willing to help staff the booth for a few hours and answer questions about your product.

The lesson is: don't try to go it alone in these first few months (or years). Keep an eye on yourself and make sure you're taking care of yourself as well as your community. After all, if you get burned out from working too many hours trying to do all the things, who will take on the reins of community building? More on this in Chapter 9.

As Bear Douglas,[6] developer advocacy lead at Slack, said, "It's okay to let balls drop as long as you tell people to move their feet out of the way. If you're just one person, it's okay to cut scope! It's okay to say, 'Sorry, we're not going to be able to do these 15 events, because I'm just one person, and that's not where the highest impact is right now. I'm going to focus on these priorities because those most closely match the goals and mission of the team at this time.'"[7]

Make the Investment

This first hire is an investment. You're bringing on someone who will be shaping your reputation and relationship with the developer community, and you'll want to make sure they're a good fit for your needs. This goes back to building the foundation that we talked about in Chapter 1—knowing the *why* behind a community, as well as what you hope to accomplish. Without these important questions being answered, your hire won't have a good foundation to build on, and your plans will be shifting more quickly than the community can keep up. Conversely, being clear on both what your current needs are and what you're able to support right now will set you (and your initial hire) up for success.

Finding this first hire can be a difficult task sometimes. It's an investment to find someone who's qualified to not only take on the mantle of Developer Relations but to also plan out the strategy for your company's future community endeavors. Although this might seem like a daunting task, this section talks about a few places to start looking.

Look Inward

Look at the folks who are already working for your company—who already know the product and already have a slightly (or more than slightly) technical bent. Chances are, they're familiar with not only the ins and outs of how your product works, but also the pitfalls. They also know the advantages and how your product is different than your

---

[6]Bear is an awesomely strong DevRel professional with a lot of experience building communities at large companies. She is @beardigsit on Twitter.

[7]https://www.heavybit.com/library/blog/building-developer-relations-teams/

competition's. You might find this person in the technical side of your Sales or Support departments, or in Engineering itself. Find someone who is not only familiar with the product but is excited about it and excited about making it better for the community.

Look to Your Community

Who are your top customers? Who is passionate about the product and excited to help others in the community? Who are the folks who are constantly suggesting features or pointing out bugs—or even better, who take the initiative to build out open source tools for the rest of the community? These folks are already your biggest cheerleaders, and it often won't take too much coaxing to get them to join the company, since they know that in doing so, they'll be able to continue to help others around them.

Your customer support and marketing teams can be good resources to find these folks. They should be aware of who's active on Twitter or good at organizing the local events, and you may find that the person organizing the local meetup that you've been sponsoring for some time now is actually a great fit for your company.

Look Outside of Your Community

If you're not looking for a senior strategist, stop to look at code schools and college graduates. Who is actively contributing to open source code or plugged into local meetups? Who is actively looking for mentorship and seems to be self-driven? If they're drawn to the developer community already instead of just dragging themselves to events for the job opportunities, they may be just enough of an extrovert to thrive in an environment of mentorship and community building.

One note of caution if you're hiring a more junior individual or someone who hasn't done Developer Relations work previously: make sure you have someone internally who can mentor them in the world of DevRel. If you don't have an individual with DevRel experience internally, make an effort to set them up with an external mentor. At the very least, encourage them to find a mentor and receive mentorship on company time. This investment will not only benefit them, but will benefit your community, and therefore your company in the long run.

Look for Common Characteristics

Wherever you go looking for your first hire, there are a few characteristics that you'll want to keep an eye out for.

Self-driven

Given how independent of a department Developer Relations tends to be, you'll be looking for folks who are self-driven and highly motivated. They will often be working on their own, finding and building relationships, sourcing opportunities, and moving quickly from one project to the next. You'll want to find people who can work well in a team setting, but who are also able to take on a project and see it through from beginning to end, largely on their own, motivated by the fact that they're making their community's lives easier.

The traits of responsibility and accountability go along with this self-directed nature. However, this also means that the manager overseeing the team needs to trust that their employees are following through with the work. In short, putting a micromanager over a Developer Relations team will end poorly for everyone involved, because not only will it frustrate the self-directed employees, the micromanager will never get the instant data they're looking for, as established in Chapter 4.

Flexible

As mentioned in Chapter 1, Developer Relations teams need to be flexible. The boundaries of your community are flexible. The plans are flexible. The roles are flexible. How you approach each unique situation your community faces will depend on your company's goals and needs. In other words, your approach will be need to be flexible. This requires a high threshold for handling change and unexpected circumstances with grace and patience.

Good Communication Skills

Speaking at a conference or two does not a good communicator make. However, someone who has experience in a TA or mentoring/tutoring role has not only learned how to communicate in a way that makes sense to a variety of skill levels, but has also received feedback from students and knows how to apply it to their future communications. This will also come into play when communicating successes to the higher-ups. Being able to parse the communication styles of engineers as well as non-technical managers is a skill set in and of itself—one that can be improved upon, but not necessarily taught. Good communication skills also includes being able to listen and observe. Knowing the right questions to ask to get more information about a situation is key, as is being able (and willing) to sit back and watch as patterns form.

Full Understanding of the Role

This doubles as a willingness to be a Jill or Jack of all trades. Someone who expects that being in Developer Relations means simply traveling to events and mentoring at hackathons might have a unique skill set for that particular area, but won't be interested in writing documentation, working with partners, helping to build scalable content, or doing the dirty work of researching local meetups and figuring out which ones are most effective (sometimes all in the same day).

Setting expectations early—before you bring someone new onto the team—is key. Make sure the individual understands the full scope of the job and everything that's involved, and that they're truly excited about the variety and context switching. Although Developer Relations can seem like a glamorous lifestyle from afar, in reality it often means doing whatever it takes for the good of the community, which may or may not involve someone's dream of becoming a household name at technical conferences.

Willingness and Desire to Learn

Most importantly, look for a willingness and desire to learn—a curiosity about the developer world around them. At the end of the day, it doesn't matter what they currently know. It matters whether they can see patterns, keep an eye on the overarching industry, and make decisions about what to pursue next as a result. If they're willing to learn new things, they'll never get bored, but they'll also be able to increase their breadth of knowledge, allowing them to interact with additional developer communities.

The All-Important Question of Where

The placement of your Developer Relations team is largely determined by their core goals. During my time in the community realm, I've seen Developer Relations teams shift between Marketing, Engineering, Customer Success, and Product. All of these departments are viable options, but the structure of and metrics for the team will of course change based on the internal priorities of that department.

Marketing

Many companies place Developer Relations within Marketing, since that department tends to have the most budget for things like events, swag, travel, and brand awareness. Whether DevRel will fit nicely within Marketing boils down to whether or not the leadership understands that there are two equally important goals for Marketing: MQLs (*marketing qualified leads*, usually handled by the demand generation team) and community. Brand awareness, content, and event sponsorships all overlap in this Venn diagram, so it makes sense that the efforts would fall together under the same umbrella.

The key to making this relationship work is ensuring that there are different goals and priorities for both teams that come directly from the CMO, and that each is equally represented under the Marketing umbrella as a whole.

If there aren't separate goals and priorities set up for DevRel, it can easily lead to minefields with regard to goals, combined CRMs (which can lead to Sales reaching out to developer contacts), the expectation of defining the value of your work via ROIs (go back to Chapter 4 for a refresher on why this is a bad idea), and tracking everything you do through the microscopic view of "did it lead to a MQL?"

If these are the metrics your Developer Relations team is held to, you run the risk of setting them up for failure and restricting them to the traditional marketing funnel, which drastically limits their ability to be spontaneous and creative in solving community needs. This will eventually lead to relationships breaking down and your team burning out from trying to prove their value instead of simply being able to do things that will bring the company value by default.

Engineering

This is another common place for Developer Relations to sit. After all, a majority of the team is technical. But most engineering teams are set up with a pass/fail system of goals—either they accomplished the project within the designated timeframe or they didn't. This makes things awkward when it comes to metrics for Developer Relations, as checking the box that you successfully sponsored a major conference isn't quite enough to call the event a success.

Budget is another constraint within Engineering. Their budget is usually limited to tooling and infrastructure for the product, which doesn't leave much room for sponsoring events, traveling to speaking engagements, or buying swag for your community members. Although you can absolutely can make the argument to move that budget over to Engineering, it's difficult to segment off what are considered to be "Marketing events" (usually sales- and MQL-based shows that cater to the buyers rather than the day-to-day consumers) from the smaller developer-focused shows.

One of the biggest benefits to being based in Engineering, however, is your direct access to the engineers. This is a key point. Remember the Engineering versus Marketing wall mentioned in Chapter 3? Being in Engineering allows you to start that bridge-building. You're "one of them," which makes it easier to mentor the engineers with regard to writing blogs, submitting CFPs, and helping out at local events. In addition, you're often a part of the daily standups or at least the weekly reviews, which allows you to keep an eye on projects and step in to suggest non-code-based tickets as I suggested in Chapter 3 in the discussion about the corporate blog.

FINDING THE RIGHT HOME FOR DEVREL WITHIN GE DIGITAL

GE Digital is the leading software company for the industrial Internet, reimagining the industry's infrastructure by connecting software, apps, and analytics to industrial businesses. Given how much innovation and change there is within this new industry, it's no surprise that there's been change within the Developer Relations team as well. Developer Evangelist Leah Cole explains:

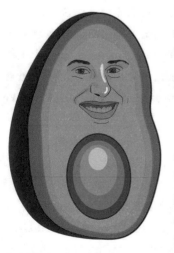

"Like most companies, GE Digital has experimented with where to place the Developer Relations team within our company structure. We've been part of the Marketing team in the past, but have found the right place now—we report directly to Engineering, but have a dotted line to Marketing.

"In day-to-day work, this relationship with Marketing is less of a dotted line with regard to metrics and responsibilities, and more of an open line of communication. Being able to have continual conversations with Marketing means that we can approach our developer audience with confidence about what they're seeing and hearing from the company, but also support it with the work that we know our engineering team is doing.

"As we hear what's coming down from the Marketing side, we're able to work with them to finesse that message to fit the needs that we're hearing about from our community, but also understand what the Marketing priorities are. In addition, we understand what's being committed under the hood, so we're in the perfect position to both meet the needs of our community as well as strategically feature items on the Engineering roadmap.

"It really feels like we're in the right place: under Engineering leadership, working under people who value our work output, and talking regularly with people who value our expertise."

The key to being in Engineering is keeping an open line of conversation with the VP of Engineering and CTO in order to make sure that they continue to understand the direct value of Developer Relations as it relates to Engineering. From feedback on the main product to users willing to beta-test the new features before they're released to not only supporting but amplifying the work of the engineers, there's a lot that you have to offer from within Engineering.

Customer Success

I touched briefly on how the Developer Relations team can work closely with Customer Support to triage tickets and decrease the overall number that are coming in. But whether or not the DevRel team belongs directly within the Customer Support (or Success) team is another issue. This is a tempting choice for a lot of companies, as the broader scope of Customer Support is typically termed *Customer Success*, and Developer Relations is largely focused on the success of their customers. However, the danger of DevRel actively being managed within this team is that they can easily drop into the role of technical support, never to be seen again.

Developer Relations often ends up being the default technical support team regardless of where they live in the company. From answering questions on the forum to maintaining a community Slack team to helping customers find the bug in their code, it's an easy trap to fall into, but a dangerous one as well. Although helping the community be successful is an important part of Developer Relations, the fulfilment of this need should be geared more toward the general community than one specific community member. The team can help build out documentation and resources that take care of recurring support questions, but you don't want to pigeonhole them.

On the other hand, similar to Marketing, if the head of Customer Success understands that there are two goals within the greater Support team: *customer support* and *community success*, this is a marriage that could work. Suddenly, you've got direct access to the support queue and visibility into the most commonly asked questions, putting you in a position to facilitate content creation, relevant speaking topics, a redesign of the documentation, and the biggest problem areas that you'll likely need to address at an event as well.

The key to making this work is separating the goals and metrics of the support team from that of the DevRel team, ensuring that your team's time is protected. Though you can be a resource, your primary role is to teach people how to fish, not fish for them.

Product

Similar to Engineering, Product teams are often set up with a pass/fail system for metrics: were you able to push out the features in the timeline that was set forward or not? You'll also run into similar issues when it comes to budget—Product isn't typically the department that's being borrowed from when someone comes up short at the end of the year.

However, given that a large piece of the Developer Relations goals is to parse relevant feedback from the community and distribute it internally at the company, being based within Product is often a strong move. For Kara Sowles,[8] Manager of Community and Evangelism at Puppet, moving into the Product department, which in her case includes UX, Engineering, and Documentation, felt like "finally coming home."

Product is one of the few departments that often has a good relationship with every other department—they work closely with Marketing to create plans around launching features and often facilitate monthly product newsletters to customers. They work with Sales to help the team understand the benefits (and pitfalls) of the latest release, with Business Development to ensure that the latest partners are happy and that any future work is prioritized, and with Engineering to triage upcoming tickets and jointly set goals for the next sprint.

Having the ear of the Product team means having input regarding the next items that Engineering will be working on. This gives you an opportunity to advocate for the small fixes that can result in quick wins for your community, such as tickets and bugs that your

---

[8]A fantastic women and amazing community builder, Kara and I connected over the DevOps community while working at competing companies (she at Puppet and I at Chef) and became fast friends. She is @FeyNudibranch on Twitter.

community members have filed, which keeps these issues from being lost in the backlog. Be careful with this power, though. It's easy to turn every anecdote into data. Gather enough data to make sure you truly understand the top priorities and problems that are plaguing your community and then present those at the appropriate time.

Training or Content Division

There are a handful of companies I have observed that have a Training or Content division. These divisions seems to be few and far between these days, but they can be a great fit for Developer Relations as well.

As with Product, this placement allows the team work very closely with different departments on strategy, positioning, and the general ecosystem of the industry. Because this team is often focused on partner enablement or Developer Experience, the department isn't expected to directly drive revenue, which allows the DevRel team to do what they do best: interact with the community, pass along feedback, and do what they can to make the product the best it can be for the community.

Internal Consulting Firm

I once saw a unique situation where the DevRel team lived outside of any department, but instead of being their own team entirely, they served each of the departments in turn. One quarter they would work with Product, offering feedback from the community and helping to build out the product road map. Another quarter they would work with Marketing, perfecting the company voice and community messaging and helping build out a content plan, and so on. The team was essentially an internal consulting firm, offering advice and structure to each department who interacted with the community.

Though I love the idea of this setup, I struggle with understanding where the direct value message comes into play. If you're so often switching gears to work with a new team, when do you get the opportunity to show the value that you're contributing in your own right? Your relationships get built up within each department, which is arguably incredibly valuable, but unless those departments are willing to give you partial credit for the work that is ultimately on their plate to finish, it's a hard sell to keep the department around for the long run. Like any other consultancy, once their job is done and each of the departments has been trained in its particular speciality, what's to keep the company from dissolving the DevRel team?

Community Department

I believe things will eventually head in the direction of Community and Developer Relations being its own department. As a department that so closely works with the entire rest of the company, we can't easily fit into only one department and still expect to be as cross-functional as we're expected to be. Being segmented into one department or another forces us to take on the mantle of whatever department we're currently in, no matter how well intentioned the separate goals and initiatives are.

At the same time, once moved into our own department, we're placed under even more scrutiny, because suddenly we don't have the security of being part of a larger team. We're now solely responsible for our own metrics, our own value, and our own bootstraps to pull us up and sustain the long-tail relationships during the dry spells.

Then again, aren't we already in that position? Most of us have been through so many reorgs that we've lost track, or have been let go from a company when our entire team has been dissolved, when they simply can't find the right place for us to fit, or when no one wants to take responsibility for us anymore. At least being in our own department puts us in a position of authority—which is what we really are. We are the authority on our community and the experts giving advice to the rest of the company regarding how to approach the customers that can make or break our success story.

Geographic Location

The second question of "Where" relates to the best geographic location for the DevRel team. As usual, this decision varies from company to company. In some teams it makes the most sense for the DevRel team to be in the office (for example, if they're working primarily on content, social media, or documentation and training). But there seems to be a disconnect when companies requires "butts in seats" even for the DevRel team, yet simultaneously wants them to be interacting with community members in person.

Much of this decision goes back to your overarching goals. If you're looking to make a splash in a particular geographic location, it makes far more sense for your Developer Relations team (or at least one individual) to be based in that location. If your headquarters happen to be elsewhere, quarterly in-person check-ins can assuage any concerns about a lack of face-to-face interaction.

Many companies, as they begin to expand the DevRel team, find themselves spread between the East Coat (primarily New York City or Boston) and the West Coast (San Francisco, Portland, and Seattle are all popular choices), possibly with an advocate or two in between (perhaps Austin or Chicago), as well as a presence in Europe (London, Amsterdam, Berlin, and Paris are fairly common locations).

Again, where you choose to locate your team should depend on your customer data. Where is your biggest concentration of active customers? Where is the biggest concentration of community advocates? What city is ideal for getting to know peripheral communities that might need a little more encouragement? Ideally, this will be a location that is close to community members, allows for frequent attendance at meetups and local events, and has a good proximity to an international airport.

If you do choose to go with a fully (or even mostly) remote DevRel team, commit to having all your team members on-site at least once per quarter. This face-to-face interaction, teamwork, and brainstorming can make a significant difference in the effectiveness of the team.

In between these onsites, weekly team meetings and biweekly one-on-ones can break down some of the invisible barriers caused by computer screens. Holding the team meetings on Mondays allows you to start off the week with status updates and weekly goals and then bookend the week with an asynchronous team check-in where members can report their quick wins as well as progress on larger projects. Biweekly one-on-ones round out the communication, allowing for time to talk about productivity during the week, any concerns that need to be addressed, or career goals.

Where Does That Leave Us?

Unfortunately, unless your company has fully invested in Developer Relations, you still have to figure out which department is the best "bucket" for you to fall into at this point. There are two different ways to figure this out.

The first option is figuring out which department you'll often be blocked by. For instance, if you're going to be asking Engineering for their help most often, being based within Engineering is likely your best bet. You'll already be a part of the team and working with them on a daily basis, often involved with their processes and schedules, which gives you insider access.

Likewise, if your goals are largely around brand awareness and building up the recognition of your product via time spent at developer events, you'll be spending a lot of time working with Marketing and spending their budget. It makes more sense to make that argument from within Marketing, where you already have an allocated piece of the budget, rather than asking Marketing to give up their budget, which typically comes with directed ROI requirements and metrics that are expected to fall within that realm.

Considering goals and function is the second way to figure out where the best location is:

- Are you building tools for your customers? Product might be a good fit.

- Are you assisting with brand awareness through conferences and sponsorships? Marketing.

- Are you helping to triage issues that your customers are running into and solve the overarching problems that are causing the support queues to fill up? That usually falls under Customer Success.

- Are you working on a content strategy that highlights the work that your Engineering team is doing in a way that will both attract developers to your product and build up the personal brands of your engineers? This could fall under either Engineering or Marketing, depending on whose time you're most dependent on.

- Are you trying to integrate with as many APIs as possible to get your product up on various websites throughout the industry? Partner or Business Development may be your best bet here.

Ultimately, as I said in Chapter 2, everyone within the organization should be touching the community in some way, whether they're in Business Development, Customer Success, Marketing, or Sales. But it's up to the Developer Relations team to not only have the community as their foremost focus at all times, but to infuse other departments with that mindset as well. Finding the right place to put the team is less about which department is best suited to handle Developer Relations and far more about which department can best help Developer Relations be successful.

At the end of the day, wherever you decide to put your Developer Relations team, do whatever you can to sustain their existence in that department. I heard horror story after horror story while doing research for the book—some people had been in as many as six different teams in less than two years. Such departmental reorgs not only destroy the confidence of the team and instill a fear of being let go with the next reorg, but also delays their ability to fulfill their goals as they adjust to their new management structure, which further weakens their place in the company. One individual put it this way:

> *"Every time we switched departments, we had to shift the way we were communicating the story of our success so that yet another executive would understand where we were coming from. We weren't able to simply continue our projects—we had to take the time to make sure our new management was on board with what we were doing so that we wouldn't lose our jobs. You can't expect us to be educating our new department as well as shifting priorities, and at the same time hold us to consistently meeting the metrics that are often outside of our control."*

Another interviewee noted that they had found a bittersweet benefit to being shuffled from department to department:

> *"We've now convinced most of the senior leadership in the company that DevRel is an important and valuable team, which is great! But at what cost? Our productivity has suffered drastically in the meantime."*

It's clear that DevRel can work well within a lot of different departments, but there are two threads that run throughout every successful team:

- The head of the department understands the value of Developer Relations and is willing to fight for them.

- The team is made up of an awesome group of people who work well together and is able to seamlessly move between teams and roles.

Wherever the DevRel team lands at your company, provide them with the tools to succeed, put them in an environment with management who understands their value and trusts them, and then leave them there to do their best work.

Set Them Up for Success

No matter where you put them, what their individual roles look like, or how much budget they're given, setting up your new team for success is the best thing you can possibly do for them. What does this look like?

- *Be their cheerleader*. Call out successes that you see from them to the rest of the company: ways that you have seen them contribute, quick (or not so quick) wins that others may miss, or quotes from the community that illustrate the relationship building and supporting qualities of the team that make your product "sticky."

- *Be their advocate*. Keep an eye out for areas in which they may need support: verbal affirmation to other departments, keeping extraneous or inappropriate work off of their plates, or getting support from other departments to build out necessary tooling.

- *Be their mentor*. I say this assuming that you, the internal advocate for Developer Relations, has experience and expertise in Developer Relations yourself. But if you don't, pull on the resources around you. Find the meetups, figure out the right conferences, and introduce your teammates to other community members. At the very least, give them permission to do these things themselves. Give them a budget to spend on personal development and training. After all, if they're the ones driving your community efforts, which is in turn driving your product forward, keeping them up-to-date on the latest and greatest things in the Developer Relations industry is in your best interest.

- *Be their enabler*. Put them in a position where they're empowered to make decisions, and then have their back. Of course there will be times when the plan needs to be reworked or reconsidered, but in general, trust them to be the experts they are when it comes to the community. Don't second-guess their suggestions. If the initial idea doesn't make sense, ask for clarification and help them to rework the arguments, but then allow them to make the case for what they need.

As I said in Chapter 2, your DevRel team has the power to do a lot of good in and for your company if you let them, but that requires you to set them up for success and believe in them. A report from CMX says a lack of internal support is the most cited reason for community failure.[9] At the end of the day, if you've decided to build a Developer Relations team in order to create a community that will strengthen your product, be sure to give them the leeway to make the right decisions and follow the right metrics, pulling levers and making changes as the community leads and directs them down the proper path.

In short, bring in the best and brightest. Give them stretch goals and a general direction to go in, as well as the tools they need to achieve those goals. Trust them to do their jobs well, and then step back and watch the magic happen.

PART II

Building and Engaging with the Community

CHAPTER 6

Finding Your Community

Figuring out exactly which segment of the community is *yours* is one of my favorite parts of community strategy. It's like the logic puzzles where you're presented with five elementary school children who all have a different sandwich and juice in their superhero lunchboxes. You have to figure out which child has the peanut butter and jelly with the apple juice in the Wonder Woman lunchbox, and, just like that, everything else falls into place.

It isn't quite that simple, of course—those logic puzzles never are. But once you have your niche of the market carved out, figuring out who your primary and secondary audiences are and where to find them is an easier task.

Chapter 1 touched briefly on primary and secondary audiences. When a company is starting out, your community is fairly defined for you: it's the people using your product. You don't want to differentiate between programming languages, job titles, or industries at this point. You want to keep yourself open to whomever is interested in the problem you're solving.

However, as you begin to talk to your customers, you'll likely start to see patterns in job titles, industry issues, and problems that they're trying to solve with your product. You'll also start to see patterns from inside your company: what languages are we using to build this platform/product? Are we an API that expects our customers to use the same programming language, or can anyone implement this product without caring about what language the code is written in? This is important data that will lay the groundwork for sales materials, marketing content, and product enhancement.

You may not be the only one in on these conversations, or even the person leading them. Often, it's the product managers or the technical account managers who are gathering this information from the customers. But the data that's collected from those calls should be shared back with all relevant parties, including you. This data will help your company figure out exactly what segment of the market your product belongs in. Are you targeting B2C or B2B companies? Does the size of a company make a difference

M. Thengvall, *The Business Value of Developer Relations*, https://doi.org/10.1007/978-1-4842-3748-9_6

in whether or not it could benefit from your product? Who else is in that same market and where are the gaps? How could you differentiate yourself?

Once you've figured out which segment of the market you belong in, you can start to learn about the people who work at the companies in that segment. What are the technical problems they're facing? What blockers are keeping them from being efficient and effective? What's the market segment for their product, and what problems are they trying to solve for their customers? With each question you answer, you begin to gather more information about which needs you can meet. Additionally, you're making progress toward figuring out where your primary audience lives, works, and finds their information, which gets you closer to finding other community members like them.

If your founder or product manager has already done this legwork for you, count your blessings. Now you get to take this one step deeper by exploring where your primary audience hangs out. Which communities are they involved in? Take a deep dive into those communities. Who are the thought leaders? What are the popular in-person events? Where is the best content?

Relationships 101

As with starting off any new relationship, your focus needs to be on what your community wants and the things they're interested in. Who are their favorite people to hang out with (virtually as well as in-person)? What books, articles, magazines, and Twitter feeds are they reading? Whom do they look up to? What are their favorite topics? What do they love and hate about their job? What's the one thing that would make their professional life easier? What are their priorities?

As you can see, it really is like cultivating any new friendship. Digging deep into the personal aspects of your customers—getting to know them on an individual level rather than just as employees of a company that pays you money—is an investment, but it's one that can provide you with valuable information about your community and also lead you to future customers. These initial community members are also the ones who will help you shape where your business is going and may very well open a completely different market segment to you—one you might not have ever considered. It may be that one of the market segments they reveal to you is your true primary audience. Think of concentric circles—you start in the center, with your initial, core community members. The next layer may be an area that all of these community members fit into, or it may be a Venn diagram of sorts. The next layer likely overlaps slightly but leads in a slightly different direction, and so on.

EXPLORING THE SPARKPOST MARKET SEGMENTS

When I first started working at SparkPost in 2015, we had a few different audiences. SparkPost is an email API for developers, so the DevRel team was focused on developers, but the Marketing and Sales teams were primarily focused on email marketers and C-suite folks. Though it wasn't outside the realm of possibility that these audiences would be interested in our transactional email offerings, it was splitting the company's attention and causing issues when we tried to redesign the website. With so many different audiences, how were we supposed to appeal to all of them with just one landing page?

We pivoted in early 2016, deciding to cede the email marketer audience to MailChimp and other companies that had slick UIs for non-technical audiences and focus on the things we specialized in. We took on the developer audience with a new fervor, with our CEO harkening back to Steve Ballmer's famous "Developers, Developers, Developers!" speech. For the Developer Relations (DevRel) team, this was a turning point for us. We suddenly had all of Marketing, Sales, and Product looking to us for our expertise on our primary audience.

But we made the classic mistake of pursuing "all developers, everywhere!" mentioned in Chapter 1. Without the narrow pursuit of our primary audience, we spent far too much time trying to build content that would be suitable for any and all developers rather than figuring out which developers would truly care about implementing an email service that would make their lives easier.

After a few conversations with my better half[1] it became clear that in pursuing a broad swath of developers, we were missing an entire segment of the technical audience. Though our API appealed to the developer audience, the sheer fact that we were handling email servers as a service, which had historically been the job of Ops folks, was still revolutionary to many people, despite SendGrid having paved the way for that conversation several years before.

---

[1]Jeremy Price, @jermops on Twitter. I'm lucky to have him by my side!

This opened up a completely different market segment to us—one that quite honestly we hadn't thought of before, because we were so focused on our API users. It also forced us to reevaluate our "all developers, all the time" philosophy, because adding a segment wasn't a scalable option for us at that point in time. Bit by bit, we started scaling back on "all developers" and started figuring out which developers were most likely to use us and that we could support.

We had a fantastic hold in the JavaScript community, thanks to Developer Advocate Aydrian Howard's work in NYC, and our PHP audience was strong, thanks to the widespread use of PHP frameworks and the recent refactoring of our PHP library. Deciding to focus on these two segments as well as explore more generic developer conferences for the time being allowed us to expand into the DevOps market (albeit slowly) and approach our core audience from both sides of the technical spectrum: those who would be installing the software and making the changes (Ops) as well as those who would be maintaining the code moving forward (Devs).

A lot of this is simple market research and business strategy—work that will hopefully have been done before you joined the company (though if it hasn't been, that's the place for you to start). It's about first defining (through segmentation) and then understanding (through targeting) your primary audience: what makes them tick and what are their struggles? This information informs the messaging they'll respond to (positioning). From there, you can figure out the next audience you should focus on.

This next audience could either be a slightly different market segment or it could focus on the buyer persona. As I've said, it's fairly rare that the end users of your product are also the buyers. Both of those audiences will usually recognize the need for the product, but the buyers are the ones with the ability to pull the trigger and make the decision to purchase or use the product. Your Sales team will usually be the ones targeting the buyers, assisted by the Marketing team with classic drip campaigns and gated content. Your involvement in this audience will likely be minimal. Your role here will be making the right connections (again, with the cruise director analogy and the warm handoffs metric) and continuing to provide content for the end users. Though they might not be the ones making the ultimate decision about whether to use your product at their company, they do have a fair amount of influence over the code base, and by providing relevant content specific to their needs, your company will continue to bubble to the top of the list when a need arises.

Additionally, the work you do regarding which developer segments are most likely to use your product will direct the specific content that the secondary buyer audience is looking for as well. This is one reason why working closely with your colleagues in Marketing, Sales, and Product is key, no matter which department you report into—the information that each department finds will help add details to the persona of your ideal customer. It might seem counterintuitive to narrow your scope, but having a specific set of criteria helps to bring in the people who are looking for your exact product. Once you've built up a following of loyal customers, you can start to expand into more segments of the developer audience, slowly scaling outward in concentric circles.

Don't Start from Scratch

No matter what else you learn from this chapter, please take my word on this one salient point:

Don't try to start your community from scratch.

You'll wind up spending too many resources and you won't see the return that you're hoping for. This is no "If you build it, they will come" situation. This is where you need to roll up your sleeves, get your hands dirty, and dig into the depths of Meetup, Twitter, GitHub, and conference-land to figure out where your community is and what they're interested in. (See Chapter 3 for how to connect with your community online and Chapter 8 for information on in-person events.)

This takes time and energy and effort and is probably the longest of all long-tails you will encounter in community building.[2] But if you don't do this research at the beginning, you'll wind up spending money to sponsor conferences that aren't a good fit or pursuing relationships with segments of the community that won't be a suitable investment in the long run.

---

[2]This is why it's important to get the automated data-gathering I talked about in Chapter 4 in place to begin with. That way when you need to take the time to do the research, you aren't having to backtrack to prove the value of what you're doing. Libby Boxes come in handy here as well, so that even when you don't have dollar values to put with your metrics, you can at least show how you're making an impact with the metrics you've defined.

As I've mentioned a few times, the best place to start finding these answers is with your current customers. Work with Product to gather a short list of your most active customers, both in terms of usage as well as feedback.[3] Schedule 15 minutes to talk to them on the phone or put together a short survey for them to answer. If these are folks you've spent a fair amount of time getting to know already, there may be no need to offer anything for their time. In fact, as we'll talk more about in Chapter 7, offering monetary compensation might actually be a turn-off to the loyal audience who simply wants to help. However, an unexpected thank-you note or small token of appreciation that shows up a few days after the conversation will never go unnoticed. If you're sending the survey out to more than your trusted inner circle, offering a prize to a random participant is an option as well.

However you choose to gather this information, it's important to get answers from a good variety of your customers. You don't want to skew your results by basing decisions on a limited number of responses from one particular group or another. This will also come into play as you establish an inner circle of community members as well (addressed in Chapter 7). You don't want to only talk to folks who are using your free developer tier, or vice versa, only chat with enterprise users. You want to speak to some in each of these levels and everywhere in between to make sure you're getting the full spectrum of your community's needs.

This spectrum will also protect your team from the classic assumption that your community is only made up of free customers. Making it clear that you have the same amount of respect and appreciation for the paying customers as you do those who use the free developer accounts helps maintain your credibility. This also adds weight to the requests you're making on behalf of your community. If you're working with developers at Fortune 500 companies who are having similar issues as lower-paying customers, you're able to pin direct value to the feedback that you're receiving, which also makes it harder for people to dismiss it as "anecdotal."

---

[3]If you're working for a large company, you might need to check with Sales and Support to make sure there aren't any customers you should avoid talking to (as in, customers that are considering another option or who have been having difficult experiences lately).

Once you've gained a little more insight into your customers[4]—which programming languages they use,[5] where they find information on new and interesting technologies, what meetups and conferences they frequent, what sites they visit when they're having trouble deploying something new, and what the makeup of their team is, for instance—it's time to find other people who fall into these similar categories. This information will help define your geographic area of focus (this is more necessary when you're a small startup with limited people and budget) as well as your focus for content and potential SDKs or tools.

This information is all useful because of what I said at the beginning of this section: *don't try to build your community from scratch*. Figure out where your customers already hang out and meet them at their level rather than force them to find you in an obscure Google search or your latest press release. Whether it's the local JavaScript meetup or a syndicated blog platform, position your content and spend your time connecting with the people who are most likely to share the same qualities as your current customers.

One thing that's important to remember is that regardless of what types of companies (startups, mid-market, or enterprise) your company is trying to target, developers hang out with other developers and get their information from the same places. Although some may be looking for information on how to scale particular products, and others are focused on implementation, they're all developers, looking for successful tools and resources.

As Keen CEO Kyle Wild said in a presentation at Nylas's Empower conference in 2017,[6] smart companies focus on *developer* retention, not just *organization* retention:

> *"Orgs will either grow, get acquired, or shut down. If you retain the loyalty of the developer, all of these scenarios are wins for you."*

---

[4]You'll notice I'm referring to these folks as your customers and not your community. There's a reason for this. In general, as established in Chapter 1, the *community* can be anyone who is currently using your product, is considering using your product, or could benefit from your product. But in this circumstance, you're using the information about your current *customers* (paid or free) to gain insight into your larger community, of which the customers are a subset.

[5]Remember that if you're an API company and you offer SDKs, you can find out this information by implementing user agent strings in your SDKs. See Chapter 4 for more information.

[6]https://www.youtube.com/watch?v=0q6tsM57JZ0

That, in a nutshell, is the core of Developer Relations. Build relationships with developers across the industry and show them that your company is not only willing but *excited* to meet their needs, and they'll take you (and your product) to the next five companies they start working at.

Open Source Communities

I've mentioned open source communities as outliers a few times throughout the book, and though the differences between open source and proprietary communities are numerous, at the end of the day you've still got a developer community full of people looking to connect with other developers facing similar issues. Setting aside the monetary value for a moment, let's establish what the primary differences are between open source and proprietary communities.

Read vs. Write Communities

Open source communities tend to have a far easier entry into the world of community building, simply because if it's a project that's been happening for any amount of time, it's already got a group of people interested in it (whether simply using or actively contributing). It also has a set of expectations and its own system of checks and balances. Although there's often one person making most of the final decisions at the beginning of the project, there's a group that's relying on each other for the success of a greater whole.

Communities like these—ones that rely on others to help—are called *write* communities,[7] a concept (along with *read* comminities) introduced by Jono Bacon in *The Art of Community* (O'Reilly, 2012). Although they may have a fan base of sorts as well (the people only using the product, but not contributing), the people who are its biggest fans are also the ones contributing to the project and actively working to make it better. They aren't simply using the project on a day-to-day basis at work—they're heavily invested in making sure the project continues because they believe in its success.

Alternatively, a company with a sales model of "install our software with this one easy command and you never have to think about it again!" likely isn't going to be building an active write community. Though they may have a group of top users that they rely on for feedback and active input into the product road map, trying to build a

---

[7]Jono Bacon first introduced this concept of Read vs. Write Communities in *The Art of Community*, Chapter 2.

community of users that will be returning to the site would undercut their entire sales pitch. That's not to say that this company couldn't have a successful user conference, but it will often be structured as a customer networking day that they invite prospects to, rather than a conference where people come together to learn and share ideas and make strides on bringing the product further along (such as OpenStack Summit). This community is called a *read* community—one that has an active user base who are fans of the product but not actively contributing to an open source product.

As I've said before, this doesn't necessarily mean you shouldn't have a community-minded person at the company. If you have a "superusers" community, you'll need someone to manage them. Or you may need someone to be the liaison between departments, making sure there is a constant flow of communication between Marketing and Product, Sales and Engineering, and ensuring that the customers are put first in all decisions and outward-facing materials. But don't expect to have a community that is excited about giving back to your open source SDKs, client libraries, or tools. This is a community that's happy to pay for your services and let you do the heavy lifting.

The "Stickiness" of Open Source Communities

Open source projects tend to naturally bring together what I defined as *community*:

> *A group of people who not only share common principles, but also develop and share practices that help individuals in the group thrive.*

Given that the very nature of open source projects lends itself to building tools that help other people while allowing for collaboration and a "do-ocracy"[8] of sorts, it makes sense that a strong community forms around many of these projects.

THE KUBERNETES COMMUNITY CHOPS WOOD AND CARRIES WATER

While the phrase "chop wood and carry water" from a Zen proverb was originally picked up by the DevOps community, it's quickly become one of the calls to action for Kubernetes—an open source system for automating deployment, scaling, and management of containerized applications. Sarah Novotny leads the Kubernetes Community Program for Google and sees that the mentality of "chop wood and carry water" isn't just a nice thought, but a core tenet of what makes the community work.

---

[8]https://www.noisebridge.net/wiki/Do-ocracy

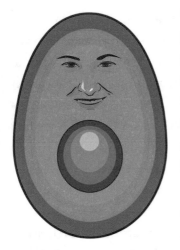

"In order to avoid some of the bad behavior we've seen in other communities, we wanted to make sure that when companies were coming into the project, they came in humbly and with the intent to help the project, as well as helping themselves. One of our core values is 'community before company,' which means people are here to contribute to a good project first and foremost, and *then* have their company benefit from the work, rather than the other way around.

"We've spent a lot of time and effort rewarding people for the things that are unglamorous, thanking individuals for a variety of contributions instead of only when they include code, and making sure that we talk about members entering the community humbly and with a heart for the whole community rather than just building out the extension that they need for their own benefit. At its most basic, it's teaching people to prove the value of what they're doing before asking for reward.

"We still have situations where people show up and drop a 10,000-line pull request without getting to know anyone involved in the project, but we calmly walk them through why that's not something that we allow, using Aja Hammerly's 'We Don't Do That Here' example as a model.[9] It's taken a lot of coaching and laying out our expectations with our Coding Guidelines,[10] along with value- and culture-setting. Since Kubernetes is a distributed orchestration system, we've tried to build a distributed governance system. We teach people through influence and servant leadership that they have the power to respectfully curb and correct new people in the community and guide them in order to set expectations.

"Our belief is that, like Peter Drucker said, 'Culture eats strategy for breakfast.' If you build a thoughtful, resilient, respectful community that listens to many perspectives and makes good decisions, then you are going to have a good product. It may always not win or be the best in its league, but it will have a very strong perspective and well-thought-through use case. You will have engaged with potential users. You will have a more diverse and inclusive community. Ultimately, you will have a group of people who are in it for the sake of the community and you will solve more problems as a result. That's what we're aiming for with Kubernetes."

---

[9]http://thagomizer.com/blog/2017/09/29/we-don-t-do-that-here.html
[10]https://kubernetes.io/docs/imported/community/guide/

What is considered "sticky" by proprietary products—their shared knowledge and inside jokes, choice of tooling, or knowing the right people to approach about the right topics—pales in comparison to being a core contributor, or even an episodic (occasional) contributor, to an open source project. But even with core contributors, the questions around community remain the same: the project might bring people together, but what keeps bringing them back?

The Person in Charge of the Community

This may seem like an odd place to start, considering that you need to have a community in order for the person who's leading the community to make an impact. But when you stop to think about the organizations you're part of or the things you do in your free time, it's often because the person bringing everyone together has a special talent for making people feel welcome, or establishing a rapport, or, if they're more behind the scenes, introducing the right people in order to make everyone feel special and included. This is akin to the *benevolent dictator* concept popularized by Eric S. Raymond's essay "Homesteading the Noosphere," which delves into the social workings of open source software development.[11]

Remember the cruise director analogy from my friend Amy Hermes? This is exactly where that persona comes into play. Even if your fledgling community is only five customers who have volunteered a little of their time to talk to you about how your product is working for them, those are five people who have something in common: they're all interested in making your product better for the greater good of their company and the sake of the community.

When one of them mentions that they're struggling with a particular piece of the integration or looking for another tool to use in addition to your product, find the other community member who mentioned that same issue in a recent call and make an introduction. If there isn't another community member to introduce them to, find an engineer who's interested in bouncing some ideas around and brainstorming a solution for them. You're not volunteering that engineer to do the work, but you're making an introduction for a relationship to build and grow and then taking your exit when the job has been done.

---

[11]https://www.catb.org/~esr/writings/homesteading/homesteading/

At the end of the day, you're the person bringing them all together. Although they still might be willing to give feedback if you weren't there, they likely wouldn't reach out to figure out who that person is at your company if you weren't there to nurture the relationship and get the conversations started.

The People Around Them

Different communities are known for different things. For instance, the DevOps community is known for #HugOps—empathy sent via virtual hugs on Twitter when a particular service goes down and the community knows that the Ops team is having a rough day as a result.

The Go programming language is known for its mascot, the Gopher.[12] You've likely seen variations of this Gopher around, represented in various costumes or combined with other tech logos.[13] Similarly, the GitHub octocat[14] is easy to recognize, and the various stickers have become collectable items at conferences and events around the world.

The Extreme Programming project (XP—one of the agile processes introduced in the mid-90s) is famous for its emphasis on pair programming[15] as a way to increase the quality of work produced by engineers. Pivotal Software practices this religiously to this day.

These outward symbols and practices identify people as part of the same community and spark instant conversations, allowing people to connect over the similarities that are apparent from their laptop stickers, Twitter hashtags, or programming habits.

---

[12]Originally created by Renee French (reneefrench.blogspot.com), the Gopher has taken on a life of its own, namely under the direction of Ashley McNamara. An amazing artist, she's also an incredible DevRel professional herself and a wonderful person to boot; she is @ashleymcnamara on Twitter. Erick Zelaya is another Gopher artist who is also responsible for the amazing cartoon avocado versions of my case study individuals; he is @erickzelaya on Twitter.

[13]If you want a cartoon gopher version of yourself, point your browser at https://gopherize.me.

[14]Originally created by Simon Oxley and expanded by Cameron McEfee. Full story at http://cameronmcefee.com/work/the-octocat/.

[15]http://www.extremeprogramming.org/rules/pair.html

Feeling Like They Belong

Making your open source community open and welcoming is one of the most important things you can do. Create a Code of Conduct so that people know what to expect and what is expected of them (more about this in Chapter 7). Make it clear that you're looking for people of all skill levels and strategies. Set your project up with a clear *README* and *Getting Started* guide, as well as a *Contributions* section to make it clear that contributions are not only welcome, but encouraged.

When new folks join your community, whether via an online forum or initial contribution, be sure to welcome them and acknowledge their presence. Even a simple "Thank You" or "Welcome" tag on GitHub can make all the difference with someone coming back again, looking for another way to contribute and get more involved. SendGrid tweets out a thank-you message every time a community member submits a pull request to one of their SDKs. This small token shows appreciation for the time and dedication of the community and amplifies those who are willing to take the extra time to make the community their own.

Open Source Is an Investment

Like all other things community, open source software is an investment. It's not the answer to your community problems. It's not a one-stop shop for finding free labor. And it's definitely not a simple way to attract people to your product. It takes work and effort to balance an open source product alongside your proprietary moneymaker. And if you're a solely open source shop, you know that maintaining a happy community who is also willing to contribute is a difficult task.

FOSTERING CHEF'S OPEN SOURCE COMMUNITY

The world of open source software is full of dedicated people who are passionate about creating and contributing to software that they use. The Chef framework is used to automate building, deploying, managing, and securing all manner of IT systems. Much of Chef's software is released as open source projects that a large community of people help to maintain. Nathen Harvey, VP of community development at Chef, explains how fostering this segment of the community can be beneficial to the entire company.

"Not every product or company is built on top of an open source foundation, yet every company has the opportunity to foster a community of open source contributors around their products and services. Chef's core projects are open source, which means it is possible for people to inspect the code, contribute new functionality, and fix bugs. Chef's architecture includes open APIs that provide access to the automation capabilities of the platform. Developers have built entire tools around these APIs that have gone on to become the de facto standard set of tools a Chef developer uses when interacting with the platform. Tools built around the Chef framework are mainly aimed at streamlining and enhancing developers' interactions with the framework.

Some examples include Berkshelf, a tool that helps manage dependencies; knife, which helps users interact with and manipulate data stored in the Chef server; and foodcritic, which inspects Chef recipes to ensure they are following best practices. Additionally, contributors across the community can share and contribute to one another's infrastructure policies (cookbooks), compliance and security definitions, and application packages. Potential contributors have a number of ways to participate in the open source ecosystem, contributing directly to Chef's projects or working with one another on projects in the ecosystem.

"Making a project open source requires more than simply clicking the 'Make public' button on a GitHub-based repository. Understanding your audience or customers has always been paramount, and the same is true when deciding to make a project available as open source software. It is also important to be clear about the reasons for making software open source. Knowing for whom and why will inform the decision about which open source license to use for the project. The next step is to make it clear to developers how they can contribute and provide clear expectations about how their contributions should be proposed.

"The 'real work' begins when contributions start flowing into the project. Activity on a project typically begets more activity, which means it is important that new contributions are acknowledged and new contributors feel welcome. However, not every contribution to the project will be a welcome change, which means you will need to consider how to handle these contributions early on.

"You will always want to keep these principles in mind:

- Consider which parts of the product can be open sourced.

- Provide guidance on how to contribute.

- Acknowledge contributions and welcome new contributors.

- Celebrate contributions and amplify their impacts on the community.

"Fostering this constituency of your community requires dedication, patience, and hard work, but there are few things more rewarding than seeing a passionate individual make something you have built even more awesome."

If you've got products that are proprietary as well as open source, it's important for you (and your stakeholders) to remember that your open source customers who typically aren't paying for your product are just as valuable as your paying customers. Their feedback, contributions, and support are integral to your success. Because of this, you need to protect the open source offerings that your company has. Don't make the open source products subpar to your paid products. Offer support to them just like you would to your paying customers. And treat your open source community just like you would your paying customers—with respect and appreciation.

If done right, an open source community can be a great advantage and can lead to some of the best community relationships, turning your customers into true advocates. Just make sure you have the time, energy, and ability to scale the program. Developers can smell a half-baked idea a mile away, and if they think your sole reason to create an open source piece of software is to attract a new community that you don't plan to maintain, you won't gain any traction to start with.

Giving Back to the Community

Often, building a new community starts with giving back to the ones that already exist—allowing your engineers time to invest in community-driven open source projects, for example, or monetarily supporting the core maintainer of a particular open source project that's integral to your tech stack. Even just calling out which open source projects you use and giving credit back to the creators can do a lot to garner goodwill. By taking these steps, you're showing that you care not only about the code, but about the people responsible for the code—the movers and shakers who are actively trying to make the industry a better place for everyone.

As I'll discuss more in Chapter 8, sponsoring a local meetup where your community might be gathering—either monetarily or providing a space to meet—and then spending the time to network before and after go a long way toward building brand awareness and exchanging ideas about how your product can be even more useful to the community. Paying meetup fees for meetups that cater to your specific audience is another way to help volunteers in your community.

Sponsoring podcasts and events geared toward new developers can be beneficial as well. If nothing else, the relationships you'll build with the organizers can pay off tenfold in additional connections. These connections can result in engineering hires, partnerships with local code schools, or external recognition from the organizer as a company willing to go out of its way to help out a good cause. CodeNewbies is a perfect example of this. Founded by Saron Yitbarek, CodeNewbies is a community for new programmers that offers a podcast, a weekly Twitter chat, and a conference. Though being actively involved in this community may not directly contribute to the bottom line, it demonstrates that your company values up-and-coming developers as much as they do senior developers.

Sometimes these simple acts of giving back is all it takes for people to give you a second look and realize that maybe your product really is the way to go. Because if the company is willing to make an investment in a community without getting much, if anything, in exchange, perhaps they're willing to make an investment in the people in that community as well.

USING DOCKER WORKSHOPS TO GIVE BACK TO THE COMMUNITY

Jérôme Petazzoni is the Tinkerer Extraordinaire at Docker—a platform to build, ship, and run any app, anywhere. Although he's now known for his excellent workshops and tutorials on Docker and orchestration, he learned early on that there was a way to use these tutorials to further his personal goals.

"Delivering the first few workshops turned out to be a huge investment. However, in the long run, it paid off, since updating and refining the content required significantly less work. Over time, these workshops became a well-oiled machine, and it resulted in a high satisfaction rate. I realized that good workshops were in high demand and they gave me access to conferences that I couldn't have attended (let alone spoken at) otherwise.

"Soon after, I recognized that this was also a really easy way for me to give back to the community, especially to underprivileged people. Docker training has a fairly high price point due to its popularity, but I could spend a single Saturday or an evening or two and give these trainings for free with the help of organizations such as Girl Develop It or GoBridge.

"There were also direct returns for the company as well; at almost every workshop, someone from the class would approach me, asking us to come to their company to train their team. I've also had people tell me over the years that they either brought Docker into their company or pursued a job at Docker as a direct result of one of my workshops.

"As the popularity of these workshops grew, I started reaching out to our partners to see if they wanted to help facilitate them. I created a rider with my list of requirements, but left most of the details in their hands. They were responsible to find the venue, which meant the size of the workshop and all of the publicity was up to them, and in return, they were able to charge admission if they wished. My one request was that they reserved a certain percentage of tickets for me to distribute. I'd reach out to local chapters of GoBridge or other organizations and offer tickets for free to those members, allowing me to continue to give back to the community while at the same time bringing direct value back to Docker."

Although you may not be able to convince your stakeholders that you should sponsor these events or projects out of the goodness of your hearts, keep in mind that the organizers of these events or creators of these code bases often have a fairly large following. They may be working with the next generation of developers, but they're the thought leaders and pioneers, and having the support and appreciation of these core individuals can sometimes be a pivotal moment for your product.

CHAPTER 7

Building a Healthy Community

Making a name for yourself in the developer community isn't as easy as making a splash at a major industry conference or getting to the front page of Hacker News. Sure, that's good publicity, but not all publicity is good publicity when it comes to the tech world. You'll want to be sure that both your company's name and your personal brand are associated with concepts like inclusivity and diversity, as well as being welcoming and receptive to feedback. In general, you want to be empathetic to developers' needs while also curating a community that is kind, helpful, and includes individuals who are committed to maintaining a welcoming and helpful environment. After all, who wants to be a part of a community that's antagonistic and full of vitriol?

There are a few communities that survive despite the negativity, solely out of necessity. The Linux Kernel Mailing List (LKML) comes to mind. A simple Twitter search often reveals a number of people asking why members of the mailing list are so mean to each other.[1] As with many things, the solution lies with the people at the top:[2] if the individuals leading the charge don't care to create an open and welcoming environment, others are hard-pressed to enforce any type of goodwill among the other members of the list. Although Linux continues to be successful, this isn't an example you want to follow. It's a success borne of demand, but it's a toxic community environment and one that people try to avoid more often than not.

If you're like most community builders, you know you don't want your community to be one that's talked about in hushed tones and accented by eyerolls because of the drama. But how do you ensure that your community is not only beneficial for your company image but genuinely helpful to those that are a part of it?

---

[1] https://twitter.com/mattklein123/status/949387830588948480
[2] https://twitter.com/DrPizza/status/955552718126551041

© Mary Thengvall 2018

M. Thengvall, *The Business Value of Developer Relations*, https://doi.org/10.1007/978-1-4842-3748-9_7

Finding Your North Star: Community Mission and Vision

This is where your goals we established in Chapter 2 come into play: those goals should be built around an overall vision and mission for your community team—the *why* factor that drives the cultivation of a developer community. Without a clear vision, you don't know what you're aiming for, which makes it difficult to define goals that will help you reach what you're envisioning.

This vision should be forward-thinking and progressive, pointing to where you want the community to be in five or ten years. It should challenge and inspire your team to continue moving forward and innovating on what you've built, until you've achieved all your strategic goals. This vision statement will be an umbrella for your mission, values, and goals—shaping where and how you grow over the next few years.

Your mission statement, on the other hand, should be a clear and straightforward statement that reflects your purpose as a team. This statement should also make it clear that you value trust, empathy, and a caring community. As simple as it sounds, being explicit about this in the mission statement makes it clear to everyone when they join that there's no room for negativity or abuse in this group.

For example: Keen's community team mission—listed publicly on their Keen Community Team repo[3]—clearly states that they want to help their community be successful in every way possible. They emphasize support and a care for the health and well-being of everyone involved in Keen:

> *We use our super powers to help Keen IO grow into a sustainable business, by supporting other teams within the organization (our internal community) in accomplishing their missions and helping our customers, partners, investors, advisors, fans, friends & family, etc. (our external community) be everything they dream to be.*

Likewise, Twilio's Developer Evangelist team is very straightforward in their mission: inspire and equip developers. They are committed to developing tools and training to help their community be the best that they can possibly be:

---

[3]https://github.com/keen/community-team

Our job is to inspire and equip developers to build the next generation of amazing applications. This means understanding what they are trying to do, pointing the1m to tools and training and generally helping them be successful.[4]

Having your mission statement clearly defined gives your team a way to explain your goals in a clear and concise manner and also proves to be an instant litmus test for your projects and priorities. Does that most recent idea align with what you need to do for your community right now? If not, put it in the backlog and move on to the higher-priority items. Is your current project taking a turn that means it won't be as effective for or encouraging to your community? Take another look at the *mall map* from Chapter 5 to see if there's a way to change it and reincorporate the community initiatives.

CMX HUB'S EXPECTATIONS AND GUIDELINES

CMX is the premier community for community professionals, and they offer education and training opportunities for these folks. In their Facebook Group, CMX makes both the mission statement and reason for the group clear from the start:

Our mission at CMX is to help professional community builders thrive, and this group is the temple where we gather.

A pinned post in the group details why the group exists, how they define *professional community builder*, what they expect of group members, and what they provide in exchange. There's no confusion around who is welcome, what is (and isn't) tolerated, and the value you'll get out of the group.

This makes things clear and straightforward not only for the CMX group members, but also for the organizers. They know their mission, have their goals in place, and know exactly what falls outside of those goals and what their focus should (and shouldn't) be as a result.

---

[4]http://ahoy.twilio.com/heroes

Erica McGillivray, Director of Product Strategy and Community Experience at CMX, explains:

"Any community space you have is like your living room—you wouldn't let someone in your house without giving them some basic guidelines. Likewise, you need to lay out boundaries for your community. Saying that you expect people to 'Be excellent to each other!' is a great starting point, but that's just the beginning. When you're addressing people's behavior, you need to be explicit about what you expect, as well as what you won't tolerate. The more specific you can be both with regard to general behavior (for example, we won't tolerate you being racist, homophobic, or transphobic, and here are the consequences) as well as behaviors specific to your community (such as don't use affiliate links), the healthier your community will be.

"Once you've covered the bad behavior, the next step is to think about how you want people to behave, and how to express that within your guidelines. Does your company have values that you can translate into rules or examples? Keep in mind that setting these expectations is the easy part—making sure that you're emulating it yourself gets a little more complicated. For example, one of the rules in the CMX Facebook Group is 'no promotional materials.' But that means we have to follow that behavior ourselves, or risk getting called out as hypocrites. If we're modeling this behavior, how do we go about promoting our own events or courses? We typically wait until the 'Share your promos' post every other week, just as we expect everyone else to do.

"The last piece that you need to be conscious of is that your expectations of the community are understood throughout your company. As a public face of the company, you need to know that your colleagues have your back. They need to support your decisions even if an irate customer turns up, complaining that you aren't allowing them to participate in the community when you're simply doing your job in a sensible and reasonable manner.

"Being up front and honest about these expectations (as well as keeping them front-and-center for people) allows your community to be open and vulnerable about the topics that they need and want to talk about, without fear of being shut down or treated poorly. At the end of the day, the expectations for our community need to line up with the company values. If the values make sense for who we are as a team, a company, and an industry, they will trickle down into the community, making for a healthy, strong, and encouraging place for our community members to gather."

Setting Expectations: Code of Conduct

Despite our best efforts, there will always be a bad apple in the group who insists on pushing the boundaries—or perhaps someone who has the best intentions but simply doesn't realize the power that their words have. This is where a Code of Conduct comes in handy. This document clearly states what the company expects of these community members and what the consequences are for breaking this contract. Having a check box where the community member has to actively acknowledge the Code of Conduct upon joining a group is essential, because then there's no questioning their awareness of it when a situation arises.

Although there are a variety of open source Codes of Conduct around these days, the Geek Feminism Wiki has an excellent anti-harassment policy that has been largely accepted at most tech-related conferences in the last few years.[5] A Code of Conduct that begins with positive expectations of a community gets things started on the right foot. Rather than assume the worst of your community, you assume that their intentions are good and that they mean to treat the rest of the community with respect and consideration. Starting with "TL;DR: be excellent to each other" instead of "We won't stand for *X*" sets the tone for the rest of the Code of Conduct and establishes what type of community you are running.

Your job isn't over once the Code of Conduct document is put together. It's now your responsibility to make sure everyone on the DevRel team (as well as others throughout the company who are interacting with the community on a regular basis) knows how to respond to Code of Conduct violations.

The article from Aja Hammerly[6] that Sarah Novotny mentioned in her Kubernetes case study from Chapter 6 can be helpful. Enforcing a set of standards like this can be difficult, especially in an online community where it's hard to understand intentions and tone. By using phrases like "We don't do that here," you establish an expectation without casting blame. This also empowers the rest of the community to handle potential Code of Conduct violations by giving them an easy way to explain to a new member that their words or actions aren't acceptable in this particular community.

---

[5]http://geekfeminism.wikia.com/wiki/Conference_anti-harassment/Policy
[6]http://thagomizer.com/blog/2017/09/29/we-don-t-do-that-here.html

It's important to remember that regardless of your geographical focus, you likely have an international community. Keep this in mind both while writing your Code of Conduct—is the wording clear and straightforward? can you get it translated into other languages for non-English speakers?—as well as when enforcing it, because cultural misunderstandings can be common, particularly in online communities.

In most cases, "We don't do that here" will be a sufficient reprimand, but there are times when situations can spin out of control swiftly, and you'll need to call in reinforcements. Make sure you have a policy for how to handle any and all types of Code of Conduct violations, both online and at in-person events. Some violations will require a one-on-one conversation to explain why there was an issue and the impact the violator's words or actions had. Other violations will require an immediate expulsion from the online or in-person community (or both, depending on the circumstances of your community). By establishing these practices openly from the start and being transparent not only about the expectations but the consequences of violations, you make it clear to your community that you care about their safety and well-being and won't tolerate abusive behavior of any kind.

Keeping Topics on Track: Community Guidelines

Community Guidelines help keep the conversation on track and edifying to the community as well. Looking back to our CMX Hub example, there's nothing inherently wrong with posting about an exciting project that you're working on, but establishing a particular day and time where that is appropriate keeps the group from being overrun with information that may or may not be relevant to a majority of the group.

This brings us back to your mission and values statements—these documents should help shape the topics of conversation that will be most prevalent in your community. What topics drive the community toward the overarching goal? Looking back to our definition of community from Chapter 1, if the purpose of the group is to "develop and share practices that help individuals in the group thrive," then the conversations should be actively working toward that end.

Providing Stability: Community Rituals

Rituals, or traditions, provide a good source of the community "stickyness" I've referred to previously. People come to expect that a changelog or release notes[7] will be released every Friday, that the community meets every Wednesday at 8 a.m., or that tacos will be served at the community meetup on Tuesday nights. This can generate traffic to your site, increase community connections, provide motivation to show up to a free event, and even lead to community members becoming external advocates if done right. Similar to the traditional content calendar that establishes what categories will be covered every week or month, or the newsletter that goes out every third Wednesday, these items provide structure both in the community as well as in the DevRel team. It gives your community a shared sense of belonging and identity—something that, despite whatever other differences exist, brings them together and gives them something in common.

A Gathering Place

If you're working on building an actual community of individuals, whether they're contributors to a particular open source project, content creators, or "email geeks," you'll need a place for them to gather. Again, going back to your mission and vision statements will help you evaluate what the best solution might be. First things first: make sure you have a quorum of customers who are actually interested in this type of a forum or gathering place.

Again, as I mentioned in Chapter 3, you'll want to rely on your community to tell you where they're already present. Be careful setting up a Facebook Group unless you know that's where your community congregates. Be cautious moving everything over to Google+ unless you know it's readily accepted among your primary community of potential customers. And think hard about whether you want to create your own, or simply join in where the community already resides, whether or not it's maintained by you (for example, StackOverflow, Reddit, topic-related Slack teams, or IRC).

---

[7]*A changelog* (or *release notes*) is a record of all noteworthy changes made to a project (most notably an application), including bug fixes, new features, and so on. One example of a company that does great app release notes is Slack. I consistently read the app updates, which is not my normal practice. See `https://slack.com/apps/mac/release-notes`

- *Are you looking for a place for people to share what tools or projects they're building using your service?* Having a place on your website where you can highlight these projects is key. The Chef Supermarket is a great example of this. It's organized by categories and features and allows you to see how recently a project was updated, as well as how popular it is. Working with your social media lead to make sure they're aware of these projects and amplifying the community member's reach is a great way to give back to the community as well (see Chapter 3).

- *Are you hoping to take a load off of your Customer Support team by providing a forum for your community to ask questions?* There are several good forum options out there. Discourse is a popular choice these days, as is Vanilla. Even Salesforce has gotten into the customer forum game recently.[8] Platforms like Influitive gamify the community, giving members tasks to complete and points to earn.

  The right forum can be a great way to take the daily pressure off of your support team and create a gathering place for your community at the same time. However, as with most things, a forum isn't a silver bullet. Forums can quickly turn into toxic environments if they don't have the proper care, nurturing, and information about setting expectations and providing stability I discussed earlier. Forums require constant moderation, which can be done by internal employees as well as external advocates (more on them shortly).

- *Are you wanting to build a place for community members to share ideas, ask for resources, and collaborate?* First, a word of caution. Unless you're involved in an open source project that already has a fairly large following, it's rare that this will blossom into the encouraging and supportive community gathering that you have in your mind (trust me, I've pictured this same scenario many a time). Unfortunately, more often than not, you're going to be

---

[8]https://www.salesforce.com/products/community-cloud/overview/

hard-pressed to keep the community conversations focused on the accomplishments and how they want to meet up with other community members in their area. The chances that this will devolve into an alternative support forum are far higher, and you'll be left trying to figure out whether to fold the group or continue it in a different fashion. If building a collaborative community gathering place is your goal, first look to see if there's a broader group that already exists (see the #EmailGeeks example from Chapter 5). Creating a specific channel in that already-existing platform is going to be far easier and will result in greater collaboration than trying to branch off on your own.

- *Are you needing a place to keep track of ongoing work and community feedback?* GitHub provides a surprisingly easy way to facilitate this with issues and pull requests. Bonus: you can have an asynchronous conversation with someone via comments to clarify what their needs are and how the company might be able to help, and it's all public for other community members to see and chime in with their feedback as well. Perhaps a community member will even jump in to submit a pull request that solves the problem.

- *Are you trying to create a platform for asynchronous conversation that can be archived for the sake of future community members, where you can float decisions and garner feedback from the community?* As old school as it sounds, an email list might be the best option for this. People can choose to dip in or out as their needs surface, and everything is archived for historical purposes. As a representative of the company, you can take votes, get feedback on particular issues, make announcements, distribute information, and facilitate back-and-forth conversations with your community members. Your community also benefits from the openness and searchability of the system—whether or not they're a part of the mailing list, they can search the archives to see if their question has been answered or if there's a conversation happening about something that applies to them.

Go with the Flow

Keep in mind that whatever platform you decide is best for your community, the community members will use the platform as they see fit. A word of advice—as long as they're within the guidelines of the Code of Conduct, don't fight them. How they're using it is obviously what's most useful, helpful, and beneficial to them. Instead of struggling to make it be exactly what you want, why not work with them? Learn why that particular process or workflow is most helpful to them. Understand what it is about the current experience that isn't working for them. Explore what changes you could make that would help make the current solution better.

As always, listening, problem solving, and facilitating a feedback loop are the top priorities of anyone involved in building a community. This means there are times when you'll have to set aside your ego and admit that your "baby"—the plan you facilitated—isn't the best solution for your community. It's now your job to roll up your sleeves and dig into finding a better solution.

Finally, if I haven't said it enough, going to find your community *where they are* is key. If they're using StackOverflow or Quora to ask questions, make sure you have alerts set up for those sites and that you make your presence there as welcoming and helpful as your own website. Are they on Twitter? Make sure you're aware of the popular hashtags and community-run accounts. Are they frequenting meetups? Plug into those meetups for an opportunity to connect with them 1:1 when you happen to be in the area.

Find what works for your community and stick to it—at least until it seems like that solution is no longer working. Then reevaluate your overarching goals, find another lever to pull that will tell the story from a slightly different angle, and give something else a try. As usual, flexibility is key.

Community Advocates

Once you find an online platform that works for your community, you'll often see a handful of people rising to the top—folks who are seemingly always online, or who jump at the opportunity to help the newer community members. Nurturing this group of people organically is the best way to create what is popularly known in marketing terms as an *influencer* or *ambassador* program. You'll notice I didn't start this chapter with "Create an ambassador program." These types of programs succeed most often when they're created out of an already-active community. In fact, unless you have a reliably engaged customer community first, your influencer program will fail. As Jenny Burcio,

Senior Program Manager at Docker and maintainer of the Docker Captains program, pointed out in her talk at SCaLE 2017, "Don't start an ambassador program if you don't already have the perfect ambassador in front of you."

An important thing to know at this juncture is that healthy communities aren't "owned" by any one person or organization. Sure, you may have been the one to grow and nurture this group, and most of the conversations may have to do with your company's product, but the success of the community is based on the community itself. If everyone decides to take their ball and go home, there's suddenly no one left to play with, and the community will die.

How do you keep that from happening? And relatedly, how do you encourage those top community members to continue on their independent missions to make the community a welcoming place? Online community strategist Shira Levine[9] has a model that she calls the "Shiramyd." It's similar to a lot of marketing funnels in today's ROI-driven society, but instead of driving acquisition, this applies to customer retention. Moving community members up the pyramid increases the stickiness of the group and mobilizes the community in a way that leads to growth.

The Shiramyd taps into the 80/20 rule—the belief that 20% of the people are responsible for 80% of the results. Some argue that this is now the 1% rule because of people's increased tendency to lurk.[10] I personally like the challenge of curating an active and diverse group of roughly 10% of my community members (head back to Chapter 1 if you need a refresher on why a diverse community is essential to your success). This 10% range allows you to stretch to find those individuals who are truly passionate about the problem your product solves in addition to scooping up the low-hanging fruit. Between those who are passionate about the product and those who are passionate about finding a solution (any solution) for the problem, you stand a good chance of receiving (and being able to use) unbiased, honest opinions that other developers will appreciate.

No matter the number you choose, the success of your community depends on reaching that top percentage of customers. The Shiramyd model not only helps us see who's on the rise in our community, it also encourages others to move up through the program and increase their engagement. Heather Whaling's Six Stages of Online Community Development,[11] shown in Figure 7-1, helps explain this a little bit more.

---

[9]Owner/founder of Fanchismo, frequent speaker at CMX Summit, and awesomely enthusiastic individual. She is @communitydrives on Twitter.

[10]https://en.wikipedia.org/wiki/1%25_rule_(Internet_culture)

[11]http://prtini.com/online-communities/

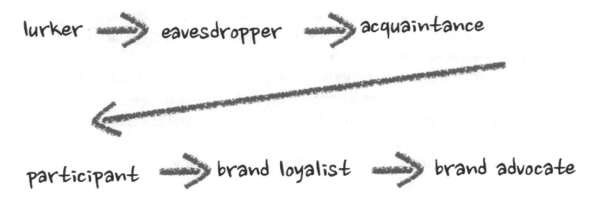

Figure 7-1. *The six stages of online community development*

In an accompanying article, she says the following:

". . . A person liking a Facebook page or following a brand on Twitter, Pinterest, or Instagram doesn't suddenly make them part of that community. Community isn't automatic. It takes work. But, as a brand, if you work at it and understand the stages of becoming a member of a community, you can lead people on a journey from passive lurker . . . to active participant . . . to brand advocate."

Similarly, Levine's Shiramyd (Figure 7-2) walks your audience up the pyramid from the general bucket of "people who could maybe someday be interested in using our product" through the sales process and to a solid place within your community of customers. Once you've successfully gotten them to this "customer" segmentation, the next step is to figure out what keeps the most engaged community members coming back:

- Once their questions are answered, why do they stick around to answer others? Make sure you're syndicating content down to keep them involved.

- What keeps them excited about your product and interested in what's next on the product road map? Keep them engaged and moving up the pyramid as they become more and more interested in the next phases of your development.

- What problems have you solved for them that inspire advocacy on your behalf? This is when you know you've hit gold with your 1% at the top of the Shiramyd—they become your external advocates, bringing back new customers and spreading the good word about your product to others in the greater community.

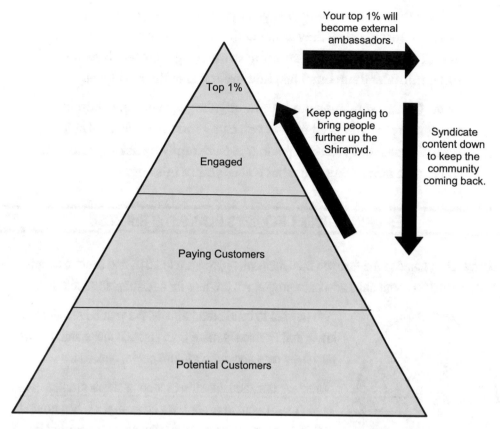

Figure 7-2. Shira Levine's "Shiramyd"

Once you figure out the answers to these questions, you can syndicate those actions down the pyramid, which encourages others to move upward. Levine uses the MEG (Maintain, Engage, Grow) model to keep this symbiotic relationship working:

- *Maintain*: Make sure you're encouraging your top community members. Are they happy? Are they continuing to be active in the community? Are there things you can do to amplify their voices or help them feel like they're being heard and supported? Be sure to maintain your relationship with them. The majority of your time and energy should be spent here, as the majority of your success comes from them as well.

- *Engage*: Be sure to actively engage anyone and everyone in your pyramid. Just because they aren't at the top level doesn't mean you should ignore them. Make sure you're meeting their needs as well and reminding them often just how great it is at the next level.

- *Grow*: Continue to grow the community. Engage with new potential community members whenever you can. Find the pockets of side communities that you have yet to tap. Constantly be asking who else you can be amplifying and what voices you're missing.

PEARSON STUDENT INSIDERS PLANS FOR SUCCESS

Lindsey Erlick founded the Pearson Student Insiders program in 2016 and exhorts people looking to build a community advocacy program to prepare for catastrophic success.[12]

"We needed to build brand affinity. We wanted students to know that Pearson is more than just textbooks and that we genuinely care about their future career success.

"When we first launched the Student Insiders program, we weren't sure what to expect. We knew that we had around 800,000 college students who used our products, but we weren't sure how many of them would be interested in this advocacy program, and we certainly didn't anticipate just how enthusiastic they would be.

"These days, I recommend that people prepare for every scenario, including success! One way that we did that was to front-load our content when we first started the program. We knew that we wouldn't have a problem going through it, and it kept us from having to scramble to pull content together down the road. Ensuring that there is always a reason for people to come back to the site means that your advocates stay energized and engaged, and showing them that you appreciate their feedback and engagement makes them feel valued and supported.

"The program isn't just about what the students can do for us—it's about what we can do for them. Our top priority is to put students at the center of everything that we do, and our

---

[12]Lindsey's talk from CMX Summit East in 2016: https://youtu.be/saTcOuAiOvc?t=5m54s

advocacy program helps us do just that. By getting to know our advocates better, we can create opportunities that benefit the Insiders and give them an additional reason to tell their friends and fellow students about the program. It's a symbiotic relationship at its best—we get to know our students better, which helps us improve our products, and they get access to professional development (for example, GRIT Assessment) and Insider-only invitations to online and on-the-ground events, in addition to real-world and resume-building experience as online brand advocates for Pearson."

Diversify

As you may have guessed from the Shiramyd and MEG models, creating a successful cohort of community advocates is no small feat. Even if you have a few folks who gravitate toward that position naturally, it takes encouragement and nurturing to keep them there—and wisdom to make sure that the group represents a good cross-section of your customer-base.

When you're looking at your group of community advocates, you'll want to make sure that both paid and free or open source customers are represented. As discussed in Chapter 1, this diversification is key to understanding the full spectrum your community covers. You'll also want to take a look at the spread of customers across your price ranges. This comes in handy when you're advocating on the group's behalf for a change or a feature request. If all of the members are lower-paying customers, you'll have a harder time advocating for a major product change since it doesn't affect the customers that keep your company up and running. But if you've got a solid representation from enterprise all the way down to free customers, you'll be able to show that it's a problem across the board, which gives you a solid argument for change.

Beyond diversifying the types of customers, you'll also want to do what you can to diversify your community as a whole. A lot has been said about diversity over the past few years in the tech industry as a whole, so I'll leave it at this: *diversity begets diversity*. If you're looking for diversity in your community, you'll want to start with diversity in your team. I'm not only talking about the obvious diversity markers of gender and race. Although those are crucial in order to be welcoming and inclusive in your community, with a focus on developers, you're also going to want diversity in programming languages, experience levels, and backgrounds, as well as writing, speaking, coding talents, and more.

Reto Meier said this best in his "Core Competencies of Developer Relations (DevRel)" blog post:[13]

> *Developers are more likely to trust people to whom they can relate, so to expand your reach you need a team that includes people with diverse backgrounds: languages, backgrounds, countries of origin, ethnicities, genders; as well as different programming languages, preferred IDEs, and industry experience.*
>
> *Presenting a diverse team as the public face of your engineering efforts may even help inspire a greater diversity in the industry—a win for everyone—so it's worth trying to create a team with even greater diversity than the company (and industry) that they represent.*

Build a Partnership

Now that you've got a diverse group of community advocates, the key is to keep them engaged and maintain good relationships with them. This is where your cruise director skills from Chapter 6 come into play. The relationships you're building with your community members aren't limited to the code in your product or the integration issues they may be running into. The better relationships you can build with them—*actual* relationships—the more likely they'll be to offer feedback, advocate for your product, and help out when the need arises. But this isn't just a one-way street. You'll find that building these friendships and being the bridge to other partnerships built within your community is incredibly rewarding and can often pay off in future endeavors.

---

[13]https://medium.com/google-developers/the-core-competencies-of-developer-relations-f3e1c04c0f5b

MOZILLA TECH SPEAKERS IS A SYMBIOTIC RELATIONSHIP

As we've established, creating a team of external advocates often greatly benefits the company. However, there are times when it greatly benefits the advocates as well. Mozilla's Tech Speakers is one such group. Program Co-Founder Havi Hoffman explains:

"Mozilla is a global community working to protect the Internet as a public resource. As part of our work, we think a great deal about supporting and inspiring a global community of volunteers. Early in 2015 I was asked to create a program that would engage a community of Mozilla advocates who were interested in doing more public speaking. We realized there were individuals around the world speaking about the work of Mozilla and the open web, and we had no way to support or extend the value of their activity and interests. The idea was to create a place to share resources as well as train our community advocates on the basics of public speaking in a group environment. Mozilla Tech Speakers was born as a result of that goal.

"We established 3 principles that define the program:

- *Open participation*: Working collaboratively and communicating openly in a decentralized environment, across time zones and cultures. There are definitely downsides to this model, but as long as they are managed properly, the upsides are huge: we extend our workforce, and volunteers extend their skills, access, and experience. Everyone benefits!

- *Psychological safety*: People thrive on teams where they are treated well. We've built a cohort of individuals that help each other. The Tech Speakers have created their own network effect: helping each other find job opportunities, connect with other community members, and advance each others' careers.

- *Minimum viable program design*: Flexibility, feedback, and constant tuning. We set up the first cohort with the intention of being flexible, responding to feedback, and iterating with each cohort. This allows us to meet the needs of the specific individuals in each program and quickly implement feedback as we go.

"These cohorts started out as a weekly safe space where people could give short talks and receive constructive feedback. These days we also offer master classes given by outside speakers such as Lara Hogan and record these sessions for the benefit of future cohorts. We also give tech briefings—talks that are designed for tech speakers but can also be viewed by others in the industry as a resource. Cohorts are now mentored by Tech Speakers alumni who run the initial group trainings, facilitating short presentations followed by group feedback. This has allowed us to scale beyond what my cofounder Dietrich Ayala and I could do on our own.

"After the training, these individuals are eligible to apply for funding to allow them to travel to speak at conferences and events that are relevant to Mozilla's product offerings and mission, and we provide a CFP calendar of these relevant events.

"I'm incredibly happy to say that we've not only seen the impact of these Tech Speakers reaching audiences that we wouldn't have been able to otherwise, but we've also seen a direct impact in the lives of the speakers who joined the program as students as well as those who are already employed as developers. A few Tech Speakers have gained employment as Developer Advocates or moved up in their careers as a direct result of being a part of the program. The former gives us a way to ramp up external advocacy and reach other areas of the tech industry. The latter allows us to move the industry forward and impact our community in a positive way. In both situations, we've provided incomparable value to the community as well as to Mozilla and our mission."

Communicate

How do you go about building these close-knit relationships? You start by introducing yourself, just like the beginning of any other friendship. Make sure people know who you are and that you appreciate their contributions. Amplify the work they're doing that relates back to your overall community. Offer to help out when they get stuck on a particular bit of code or need some wordsmithing help on an upcoming blog post. Make it clear that *they* are your priority, and that you always have their best interests at heart.

As discussed in Chapter 3, doing things like maintaining a private Twitter list of these community advocates so that you can quickly retweet or reply to their tweets can go a long way in building their confidence in your team. For those who are actively contributing content, this also shows that you want to give their personal brand a boost as a thank you for their efforts. This not only makes them feel included and valued, it gives you a picture of what motivates them—what topics they're interested in, what they spend their time on, and what issues they care about. You can use this information to spark future conversations as well as inform your decisions on how to compensate them for their help (more on that soon).

We'll talk more about the differences between your company's brand and your personal brand in Chapter 10, but something to keep in mind is that if you don't have control over your company's social media accounts (or even if you do), you can do some of these things from your own personal account. Given that you are a representative of your company, community members will often recognize it as one and the same. Keeping track of these community advocates as they progress in their career, celebrate birthdays or anniversaries, or achieve new heights in their personal lives is a nice way to connect with them on a personal level. Sending out a "happy birthday" tweet from your personal account could mean just as much (or more) than the company account recognizing their contribution to an open source tool.

In general, overcommunicating is rarely going to be frowned upon. Asking someone how the weather is where they're from or wishing everyone a "happy Friday" in your community forum is a way to show that your community gathering place is about more than just asking questions about your product—it's a place to actually connect with other people with similar interests and goals.

From releasing an informative changelog every week (or month) to hosting a "town hall" meeting once a month or "video office hours" on occasion, you can show the community that you're interested in getting to know them as well as the technology they're working on. The more you can connect with them on a personal level, the more they'll solidify themselves as a part of your community, and the more you'll find you care about the issues they bring to the table. It's a win-win for both the community and the community builder, and chances are, you'll see a bump in your personal brand awareness as well.

Prepare

No matter how much you plan ahead and prepare for every possible scenario, there will always be one you didn't anticipate. How do you handle incidents in the community that might warrant a response?

Some of these issues will be positive ones that need a reply or an official company stance. For instance, you may have a community member who, rather than waiting for you to build a client library for the language of their choice, has simply decided to build one of their own. That's fantastic, but at the same time, it's something that needs to be talked about internally in a timely manner. After all, is it owned by the community member? They are the maintainer and creator, after all, but then is it expected that the company will provide support for it? And if not, how do you communicate to your community that you won't be providing support for something that looks very much like an official client library?

Not all situations will be positive ones. For instance, how do you handle a Code of Conduct violation when the Community Manager or Head of Community is off the grid? Is anyone else on your team prepared to handle an antagonistic community member who may or may not have a valid complaint or issue?

Preparing for (or at least being aware of) any and every scenario you can think of from the beginning of each new program you launch can save you time and heartache in the long run, and let you be quick on your feet with curveballs that come your way. We've come full circle back to the role of our vision and mission statements—when new scenarios arise, run them past those litmus tests. Do they line up with the community we want to be in five or ten years? Do they support the overarching goals of the team? If not, respond appropriately by shifting your priorities, resetting expectations, and keeping a closer eye on those statements in the future.

Scale

As your community begins to grow, you'll find there are things you simply can't do because you're only one person. Even if you're lucky enough to have a larger team, trying to communicate with every community advocate one-on-one becomes an issue of time management at some point. Additionally, you'll find that you can't be in all of places you want to be (in person or online) or moderating all the channels in your forum as you once did.

RED HAT KNOWS HOW TO SCALE ITS COMMUNITY LEADS

When it comes to speaking at all the events and being in all the places, Red Hat Senior Manager, Community Leads Stormy Peters knows that the best way to grow your outreach is not to do it all yourselves. By empowering and paying for travel for community members, you can cover a lot more events, reach more potential users and community members, and energize your community all at the same time. Although it's easy to just send a community

---

manager to every event, it doesn't scale. One person can only cover one event at a time, and multiple events in a row become exhausting.

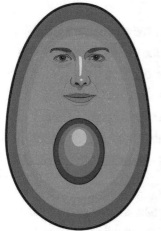

This particularly applies to a company like Red Hat, the world's leading provider of open source solutions. Although it has a comparatively large staff of community managers, it also covers a wide swath of topics, which means the pool of potential events is that much bigger.

"It's impossible to be everywhere at once, and it takes a lot of time," says Stormy. "When you're trying to attend all of the relevant conferences, you wind up traveling so much that you often don't have time to actually connect with your community.

"Additionally, people really want to hear from the individuals who wrote or designed the software—not just the person managing the community. While the community managers are often great speakers, sending the community members who are actively contributing to the code is exciting for both sides. The conference attendees get to meet the people who are making it all happen, and the community members get to experience the appreciation and excitement of talking to people who are using the software first-hand.

"Lastly, getting the engineers or community members out there advances their careers and is a great way to express your appreciation for them. Travel motivates a lot of people! You'll occasionally find people who are more than willing to work the conference circuit and speak about your product if you're able to cover their expenses and empower them to do so.

"All of these things work toward growing your community, since attendees are able to hear from the people who either wrote the code or have volunteered their time to work on the open source project. This in turn encourages other people to contribute to the projects and get involved in the process.

"A side benefit of amplifying your community's voice is that at times, you wind up finding a new community manager. Our RDO community lead, Rain Leander[14] started out in the community and was excited to go out and speak about the work she was doing on

---

[14]An amazing human being that I first met at CodeDaze 2016 and with whom I have since collaborated with on occasion in my consulting business; she is @rainleander on Twitter.

RDO. Shortly after, we wound up hiring her into the role! While this isn't a great example of growing your community, it definitely shows how amplifying your community's voice can accelerate their career path and benefit the company as well.

"It can be hard at times as a Community Manager to learn to let go and allow someone else to speak on your behalf, and that's understandable! As the face of the project, it can feel like you're putting your reputation on the line when someone else gives a talk about it. Additionally, there are times when the conference organizers will specifically request the Community Manager, because you're the known entity. In situations like this, the best response is to graciously accept the invitation, and then let the organizers know that you'll be bringing a co-presenter. In doing this, you facilitate the community member's entree into the public, allowing you to take a step back.

"At the end of the day, encouraging and enabling community members to speak about the project not only benefits you from a time-management and energy perspective, but it also serves to amplify the voices of the other people involved. This increases the diversity of viewpoints and backgrounds represented, which ultimately serves to grow the diversity of your project itself."

This is where the relationships you've built with the community advocates really start to pay off. After all, they're your customers. Who better to help represent your company at conferences or speak about the way your product helped them solve a major problem at their company? In our "show, don't tell" culture, these types of community accolades can be a huge help in moving your product forward in the technology market.

This can be a touchy subject, though. You don't want to take advantage of your community members, and you don't want to ruin your relationship with them that you've taken so long to build. There's also the issue of who manages those events, pieces of content, speaking engagements, and other items you're asking the community to help out with. You'll want to find people either on your own team or throughout the company whom you trust to maintain the same values and respect for those community advocates as you do.

By creating processes and documenting them clearly, you lessen the risk of someone stepping in and making a mess of your work. At the end of the day, you can't be the person who holds all the keys. If you are, you'll not only set yourself up for burnout, you'll set your team up for failure should anything happen to you. Spreading out the information—documenting the processes, maintaining a company-public doc with the community advocate's information, and explaining the value of this community advocacy program—all with the understanding that everyone interfaces with the community team before reaching out to these individuals, is essential to the health and happiness of your team.

The Question of Compensation

Part of the *maintain* piece of MEG is making sure that your community advocates are happy, which includes feeling appreciated for their work. That means making sure you aren't burning out your community advocates by asking them to do too much. The other piece is making sure they feel adequately compensated for what they've done.

Although "compensation" usually goes hand in hand with money, I'd steer clear of that in this circumstance, especially because it can complicate relationships with your international community members. Money can cheapen the exchange and make it feel like far more of a business interaction than a relationship. There are a few circumstances in which money changing hands does make sense—travel and lodging for someone who's helping out or speaking at a conference on your behalf, for instance. But generally, a handwritten note, personalized swag, a shoutout on the company Twitter account, or recognition at the company's yearly vendor conference will go a long way toward furthering your relationship with the community member.

SENDGRID'S OPEN SOURCE COMMUNITY

Elmer Thomas works as a developer experience engineer at SendGrid, a communication platform for transactional and marketing email that processes over 40 billion emails each month to drive engagement and business growth. Although SendGrid itself is a proprietary product, it maintains open source tools and SDKs to make it easier for developers to integrate. Elmer interacts with the open source community on a daily basis, managing their pull requests and issues and finding the best ways to solve their pain points.

"We do a personal 'intake' for each GitHub issue submitted by our community members, and there's a very intentional reason for this: we want to express gratitude for their contribution, but we also want to set expectations. Sometimes we'll simply need to clarify the issue and other times their request is

---

something that we know we won't be able to address for quite some time. But we've learned that if we take the time to engage with the community member and expand on the issue publicly, another community member might take the time to submit a pull request (PR) to solve that problem.

"Several years ago, we were faced with the huge project of updating all of our SDKs to support our v3 API. The current SDKs only supported the mail-sending endpoint of the API, and our task was to support all 230+ endpoints for seven different programming languages. We sketched out the project and realized it would take us about eight years to finish everything if we tried to do it all internally, so we turned to our community to give us feedback and help us make the updates.

"We quickly learned that we needed to reach out to people directly. We looked back at the data to see who our biggest contributors were—who was commenting the most, offering the most feedback and PRs, or most actively involved in the process? We specifically tagged them on the issues, letting them know that we valued their opinions and were looking for their help. With the resulting activity, new contributors started appearing out of the woodwork to help as well, which grew our community and gave us new people to work with on future projects.

"We treat those PRs like gold, because we look at that as an expression of a developer's love toward us. They're giving their time and choosing to spend their talents to further our product with no expectation of being compensated. As a result, we make sure to call them out publicly and thank them for their contributions when we merge the PRs. We also let them know that we value their opinions by asking for specific feedback around upcoming changes. And the occasional unexpected swag package doesn't hurt either! But overall, making sure that the community knows that we value them and their contributions is what keeps us able to move forward with these open source projects. We quite literally couldn't do it without them."

A simple acknowledgement of the work that they've done can speak volumes about how much you value their contributions. Keep in mind that these amplifications shouldn't be external only—you should be highlighting these accomplishments internally as well. Stakeholders throughout the company will see that the relationships you are building are valuable, and that money is being spent wisely.

This is also why you need to have an understanding throughout the company that the DevRel team, and only the DevRel team, makes these requests of the community advocates. The water can easily get muddied by warm handoffs that turn into requests from Sales or Marketing making their way directly to your community advocates instead of being filtered through you. There are a few issues that may pop up if others start making direct requests:

- As the community expert, you know the best person to write that article, work on that project, or help out at that event. There may be someone better to pass the task off to, but because the request wasn't made through the right channels, it's a lost opportunity.

- If a deal is struck with another department outside of your knowledge, you're no longer aware of the asks that have been made of your community advocates. You run the risk of overloading them as a result, or putting them in a position where they feel obligated to follow through regardless of their other commitments.

- Your community advocates have gotten accustomed to a particular system of work and compensation. If another department steps in and offers something different, the community advocate now knows there are other options available that can undermine the relationship you've been building with them.

Although these scenarios may not seem insurmountable, they add up quickly and slowly but surely chip away at the trust your DevRel team has earned. Once the community starts to lose confidence in the DevRel team's ability to successfully advocate on their behalf, the entire company can lose credibility with the greater developer community. Even just one or two of these situations can cause significant and sometimes irrevocable damage to the hard work that the DevRel team has put into these relationships (more on this in Chapter 9).

Whether you decide to compensate your community advocates with limited-access swag and social-media shoutouts, or you choose to use some of your budget to fly them out for an in-person superuser summit like Facebook,[15] the important thing is letting your community advocates know that they are appreciated. After all, without them, the success of your community, and therefore the success of your product, is at stake.

---

[15]https://techcrunch.com/2017/04/11/facebook-communities-summit/

A Stitch in Time Saves Nine

If, after reading through this, you don't think you have time to build out an advocacy program, I'd encourage you to think about it this way: investing in a community advocacy program will actually save you time and effort in the long run. It may be the only way to get work off your plate—using these enthusiastic community members to help you generate content, contribute case studies, and give regular feedback means you have time to amplify their voices and move other people up the Shiramyd, rather than spend all your time tracking down someone else to write the next piece of content.

CHAPTER 8

In-Person Events: The How, Why, and Where

Once you've figured out who your audience is and where they tend to congregate, the next logical question usually relates to events. Connecting with people online is important and a good way to observe trends, but meeting up in person allows you to get to know the actual people in your community on a different level. While talking on Twitter and even on video chat is a great first and second step, face-to-face interactions build on those online relationships in ways you can't predict otherwise.[1]

That said, as touched on in Chapter 4, in-person events can introduce some difficult challenges. From the question of "should we be sponsoring events, and if so, which ones?" to "how much is too much to spend on a conference sponsorship?" as well as how to document your "wins" at a conference and what the goals of attending, speaking at, or sponsoring an event should be—there's a lot to consider.

You might hear things like, "We don't have any money to sponsor any events, no matter how small the sponsorship," while someone else is saying "We should create our own conference," or "You need to be at the booth for the entire show." How do you wade through the confusion and start answering these questions?

---

[1]Pro tip: when facilitating a conference for your community, include their Slack or Twitter handles on their badges so they can easily identify their online friends and colleagues.

What Are You Trying to Accomplish?

Like most things, figuring out the right approach for events goes back to your key goals:

- Are you trying to increase your general brand awareness?

- Do you need feedback on the usability of your product?

- Is the company looking to expand into another geographical region or new audience segment?

It's possible to serve all of these needs with events, but chances are, you won't be able to serve all of them with the same event. It's also possible for you to spend all your time flying around the world attempting to solve these problems by attending, sponsoring, and speaking. But unless you're strategic about where you're going and why, as mentioned in Chapter 4, the only metric that upper management will see will be how many expense reports you've filled out.

Brand Awareness

Brand awareness is the most straightforward outcome from speaking at or sponsoring an event. Whether it's having time on stage or displaying your banner in the expo hall, having your logo in front of conference attendees can be the ever-important *first touch* and indicator of developer awareness discussed in Chapter 4.

But metrics around brand awareness are incredibly hard to track. This is where your trip reports, warm handoffs, and geographic maps of sign-ups via IP address come in handy. Taking a quick poll of the room before a talk helps get an idea of how many people are aware of your product, which gives you a good benchmark for the following year if you decide to speak or sponsor again.

Brand awareness can come in a variety of events. Speaking, sponsoring, helping to organize, or hosting an event at your headquarters are all ways of getting your company name out there, and not all of them cost a lot of money or time. Even simply attending an event can be a good way to meet the community. Host a coffee meetup one afternoon or take a group out to dinner one evening. Tweet that you're wearing a bright green shirt and will be giving swag away during the afternoon break (with a picture of said swag). You'll be surprised at how easily you'll be able to meet people and spread the word about your company.

Attending also gives you the advantage of scoping out a conference to see what other sponsors are there, how steady the booth traffic is, how technical the talks are, whether a product-specific talk might be a good fit for next year, and more. Bringing this information back to your company makes the conversation about whether you should sponsor the following year a lot easier.

Feedback

Whether you're trying to road-test your new *Getting Started* guide, figure out the best time-to-value proposition, or observe how developers are using your product, events are great places to get hands-on feedback from your potential customers.

Hackathons

If you're an API platform, the best place to get this hands-on feedback is at *hackathons*. Whether you choose to frequent only professional hackathons (ones that tend to pull in more full-time engineers) or college-level hackathons (often a 48-hour sprint over a weekend with little to no sleep for the attendees), you'll find yourself in the middle of an event where people are attempting to integrate with your platform as quickly and easily as possible.

This is where you'll want to pull out all the stops as far as your getting started materials go. Do you have an official *Getting Started* guide? Make it easy to find on your site. Or create a simple one-page handout that lists the relevant links (see Appendix C for an example of this). College or high school-level hackathons will actually give you better feedback most times, because the programmers at these events will get stuck on some of the basic areas of your API. Although this can seem like an inconvenience, it will force you to solidify your materials and explain things in a way that developers of any level will be able to understand.

However, before you pack your sleeping bag, you should know that hackathons aren't right for everyone. If your product is an enterprise-only offering that companies only start using once they've reached a certain number of customers, or if it's too complex for someone to integrate easily with a few other APIs in a span of a weekend, then hackathons probably aren't the best option for you.

If you do decide to take this route, plan to bring at least three technical people along for the weekend so they can take different shifts. Hackathons are typically round-the-clock events, and you don't want to wear out your staff or leave your booth unstaffed for more than a few hours each night.

There are three keys to engagement at a student hackathon:

- *Have an interesting or engaging challenge for the attendees to complete.* Most hackathons have sponsored prizes in addition to the grand prize categories. This could be a monetary prize, gift cards, some sort of fun technology (such as drones, robots, or LEGO sets) or something else entirely. The prizes are great, but the best challenges aren't determined by the best prizes. They'll get students over to your table, but you need to have a practical, easy-to-accomplish challenge that fits in well with the other sponsors in order for them to stick around.

- *Don't spend all of your time at the booth.* Walk around the event and observe attendees. Ask about the project they're working on (even if they're not using your API). Chances are, there's a mentoring opportunity or a hack you can show them to make a particular process easier. And in talking to them, you're inadvertently promoting your company. Elmer Thomas, Developer Experience Engineer at SendGrid (highlighted in a case study in Chapter 7) had this to say about SendGrid's presence at events in the early days of the company: "A lot of what we did early on was simply be ambassadors of the company by wearing our traditional blue hoodies at events and helping attendees in any way that we could. After a year or two of doing this, we started to hear various anecdotes from people who remembered us helping them on a tech problem unrelated to email. Years later, after they graduated from college or after changing jobs, their company was looking for an email provider, and that initial experience factored heavily into their decision."

- *Have great swag that will get picked up and used.* Think practical—branded pads of graph paper and pens for brainstorming sessions—as well as your standard swag such as stickers, pins, t-shirts, and so on. The more you can tailor your swag to hackathons, the more popular it will be. For instance, AWS handed out hooded inflatable neck pillows to winners of a trivia contest that they held at their table at a college hackathon. These were unique (I'd never seen them before and haven't seen them since) and practical, given that students could use them to take a quick cat nap and block out the bright gymnasium lights simultaneously.

But with the hundreds of hackathons that happen every year around the world, how do you know which ones to participate in? A good litmus test for college-level hackathons is whether they're involved in Major League Hacking (MLH)— the official student hackathon league, or as Tim Falls,[2] a long-time technical community builder calls it, the NCAA of hackathons. Every year, MLH helps power hundreds of student-run hackathons all over the world. MLH works closely with student organizers to mentor them and ensure the success of the hackathon, and as a sponsor, you know that when MLH is involved, you're going to have a good experience.

Another way to decide between hackathons is to look at the projects submitted at last year's event. How many projects were actually completed? How many used multiple APIs? Which projects won the overall prizes? This will give you a good idea of the quality of projects and the engagement of the attendees.

Conferences

If you're not sold on the hackathon mindset or don't have enough technical folks to staff one effectively, you can easily find feedback at conferences as well. Bring one of your coworkers from the product team along—having them onsite to hear what people think about your messaging and the use cases that they can think of off-the-cuff can inform the next iteration of your product road map.

If you're engaging with a new segment of your audience, make note of the questions they ask and the problems they're trying to solve. It may be that your product can solve that problem, but the messaging needs to be updated to reflect this particular part of the community. In Chapter 6 I talked about discovering SparkPost's "in" with the Ops crowd. We had to update our marketing message for this audience—we were no longer pitching our easy-to-use API but instead were showing that we could ease the stress and strain of maintaining your own email servers.

If your product isn't first to market, pay attention to what differences attendees point out between your product and your competitors. What product features catch their eye? What screenshots do they stop to take a closer look at? Which piece of paper collateral goes the fastest? Sometimes stepping into these conversations and asking more questions—what's their job title? what types of problems are they looking to solve?

---

[2]I've crossed paths with Tim several times over the years and have been energized by his work many times, from SendGrid to Keen and everywhere in between. His heart for the community and for the world is inspiring. He's @timfalls on Twitter.

what intrigues them about your product?—is helpful, and sometimes simply listening to conversations between colleagues can be enlightening.

Engage with the Community

There are times when the biggest metric you'll get out of an event is how many hands you shook and the number of people you introduced to each other. As a "technical cruise director", there are circumstances when this is the best outcome and not just a consolation prize. New events in a new location (potentially even with a new audience segment) give you an opportunity to make an incredible amount of introductions—new community members to more senior individuals, meetup organizers to potential speakers or sponsors, project leads to subject matter experts, and more.

As I've mentioned before, simply being around—listening to the community, engaging in conversation, and making introductions—can be an incredibly valuable use of your time. Depending on the conference, engaging with the community might be most easily accomplished at the booth where people know how to find you. Ideally, you'll have several team members with you, even at the small events, so that you can spend time at the booth meeting community members but also float between sessions and the hallway track. The connections that can be built at events can turn into lifelong friendships and valuable business relationships.

This is also another way in which you can use your platform to amplify the company's announcements. Let your community know you're going to be at particular events (whether speaking, sponsoring, or attending) by highlighting them on your website or posting about them on social media. You'll often have a presence in Slack teams or private Facebook groups that your colleagues aren't a part of, which gives you an opportunity to share the love and personalize the message. Asking who else is going to be there and then setting up a time to go out to dinner with these community leaders (and occasionally springing to get the bill for the table) can go a long way toward making your company name come to mind when a solution is needed.

Test the Waters

If you're just starting out with your events strategy, start small. Sponsor a conference or two and see how your strategies play out. Do you need to up your booth game? Does your swag need to be more enticing? Do your resource cards need to have a place to write contact information on the back (see Appendix D for my stand-by Developer Resource Card)? Does your on-site event team need to be better prepared for what to expect at the event (see Appendix E for an Event Playbook template)?

If you take your strategies for a test run with a local event that has a good reputation with the community, you're likely to get good feedback that you can apply to future events without breaking the bank. I've found over the years that most of my success at events came from the regional events—the local Ruby conferences or the volunteer-run DevOpsDays events—rather than the large convention-hall style conglomerates. It's too easy to get lost in a big expo hall with hundreds of other vendors who have flashier booth setups and bigger giveaway prizes. Although a regional event might have one-tenth the attendees, it's easier to actually engage with those attendees one-on-one because you're not getting as bombarded by people who are just hitting up the booths for the best swag and don't care about your product.

Maximize time, Minimize travel

Whatever your end goal with events, I encourage you to make the most of your time in one location and minimize the amount of time spent on planes and trains. Whether that means you combine several conferences into one trip or schedule speaking engagements at local meetups around a larger event, maximizing the amount of time you can spend in front of people gives you the most bang for your buck as far as travel costs go and minimizes the likelihood of burnout in your team.

I took one such trip several months before O'Reilly Media launched Velocity New York in 2013. We needed to spread the word about Velocity on the East Coast, as well as gauge people's interest in particular topic areas as we finalized the tracks. Over a span of three weeks, I spent time in Boston, Washington, D.C., New York City, and Philadelphia, attending conferences, sponsoring meetups, talking to community members over food and coffee, and in general getting an idea of the pulse of the East Coast as it related to DevOps and web performance.

Combining all these trips allowed me to spend more time engaging with the community than traveling back and forth. Using Amtrak, Airbnb, and local grocery markets helped minimize costs and allowed me to have some downtime in between cities, which helped me maintain the energy and stamina needed to continue talking to community members day after day.

TYPEFORM PLANS FOR WAVES OF DEVREL WORK

Getting in on the ground floor of a new Developer Relations (DevRel) team is a unique experience, as Andrea Revilla, Developer Relations Coordinator, and Eva Casado de Amezua, Developer Community Manager, will tell you. They work for Typeform—a platform that helps businesses get to know their customers through conversational data collection—and they're taking their time to build out a Developer Relations team that they can be truly happy with.

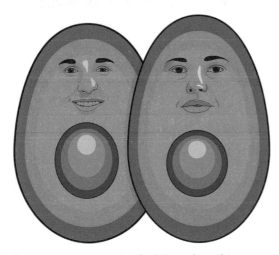

"We're in the planning and researching phases right now, both for the community that's forming around our API and for our Developer Relations team. Part of what we've been observing during this process is that the various types of Developer Relations work seem to come in waves. You have a couple of quarters per year that you should be really focused on product evangelism— attending and speaking at events, meeting with people and getting feedback, building brand awareness, etc. And then the other two quarters, you need to be at home, doing research, creating content, helping out on the coding side with sample applications and SDKs, and working on your community strategy.

"Acknowledging these waves of work helps to shape the goals for each quarter so that we know what to plan for and what we should (and shouldn't) expect of our team. We've also seen that it actively prevents burnout in our Developer Advocates. Knowing what their focus is each quarter helps them stay on track and have the amount of time that they need to accomplish each project. It also helps that they're not having to constantly switch gears. They know that they'll be traveling some quarters and home other quarters, but there is plenty of time to plan for all of those things without the stress of having to finish major projects in amidst conference talks and travel."

It should be noted that not all of your DevRel staff members will be enthused by this idea. Depending on their family situation and home life, it may make more sense for them to make shorter, more frequent trips. Those who are more introverted will likely need more time off in between conferences to recover from the experience. As I've touched on before, playing to the strengths of those on your team allows you to not only do what's best for your team members, but build up a reputation as a world-class DevRel team, which does wonders for your reputation in the developer community.

It will always be a balance to figure out how much travel is too much, and though it will depend on the individuals on your team, I feel strongly that there needs to be a general expectation. There will be exceptions to the rule (for example, individuals who choose a nomadic lifestyle for a time, or those who suddenly get an unusually large number of CFPs accepted during the fall conference season), but two things should be noted:

- *It is always okay to back out of a speaking engagement or sponsorship.*
  Conference organizers not only understand, but also often have a
  waiting list of speakers lined up precisely for this reason. Depending
  on the sponsorship contract, it can be a little tricky to cancel the
  entire sponsorship at times, but you can likely find someone to go
  in your place if necessary. If you can't find a colleague, ask your
  community. Who lives in the area and is often answering questions
  on your community forum? Who has given a few talks about how
  your product has changed the way their organization operates? The
  key is learning how to say no (more about this in Chapter 9 regarding
  how to prevent burnout) and then standing by your decision. There
  will always be another conference. There will also always be too
  many conferences. You will experience FOMO (fear of missing out)
  on a regular basis while in this role—it's just part of the job. Make
  sure the conferences you are choosing to speak at or sponsor are the
  best possible conferences with the information in front of you (more
  about that shortly) and then make a note of any conferences that you
  should check out next year.

- *I firmly believe that anything more than 50% travel is too much.* As
  community advocates and DevRel professionals, we're expected
  to be connecting with our community on a regular basis, but
  we're also expected to communicate that information back to our
  colleagues and contribute helpful content. In addition, don't let

the excitement of travel distract you from your online community. While engaging with your community face-to-face is indeed an important part of community building, you can't forget about the rest of your community online. Anything more than 50% travel actively keeps you from completing other tasks and often introduces unrealistic expectations that causes you to work overtime, writing content, answering questions, following up on threads, and trying to dig yourself out of the sinkhole that is your inbox. You're left in an impossible situation of either pushing back on deadlines with the reasoning that you're at an event or staying up late after an already-exhausting day to get the work done, neither of which is a good option. The former can cause your stakeholders to form biases against future events, and the latter is a recipe for subpar work that likely won't benefit your community or your coworkers.

Balance is key. Whether you choose to approach this as Typeform does in the earlier case study or find another way to ensure that your team isn't stretched too thin, it's a necessary part of managing a DevRel team.

Conferences, Conferences Everywhere

It used to be that "conference season" was fairly predictably between February and May, and then picked up again in September and October. These days, conference season is all year long, and the number of events is staggering. Expecting to be at all the events in your topic area is simply ludicrous—you'd run yourself (and your team) into the ground within two months simply trying to keep up with all the event logistics. So how do you go about choosing the right events to support?

Again, we return to your company goals as a touchstone for making all these decisions. If you're looking to foster brand awareness in a tangential community, look for the events that are a Venn diagram of your current audience as well as the new community you're trying to reach. Having the built-in recognition and comfort of your current community members allows you to make connections between the two groups and eases the transition. If you're looking into a new geographical area based on an increase in activity (traffic to your site, sign-ups, Twitter conversations, Stack Overflow user profiles, and so on), tap the community members who are based there to see which events they're most excited about and where they suggest you start.[3]

In both of these circumstances, organizing a community dinner or happy hour in conjunction with the event (either by formal invitation or word-of-mouth) can be enlightening for your understanding of the community as well as a way to endear yourself to them. For a few hundred dollars, you have an opportunity to connect with community members and get to know them on a personal level as well as have conversations about their professional needs, hopes, dreams, and pet peeves. These deeper conversations are often the ones that lead to genuine friendships tht last far longer than the current company listed on their resume.

So, start small with regional events. Research where the community is and make a point to be there. Support the smaller events even if they aren't as likely to result in MQLs (marketing qualified leads). Reach out to the local chapters of boot camps or diversity initiatives for an opportunity to give back like Jérôme Petazzoni did at Docker (see the case study in Chapter 6). These events are the most likely to result in mentorships and long-term relationships with conference organizers, speakers, and thought leaders in the making. Although these relationships are an exercise in the long game, they are also the ones that wind up cultivating trust for your product throughout the community.

The last key to deciding between events is to find ones that reflect your company values. Seek out the conferences that prioritize a diverse speaking lineup and an inclusive environment for their attendees. Support the events that are geared toward making technology a better industry as a whole. Contribute time and energy to the community-run functions that highlight women in tech or have a mission to take care of the next generation of developers.

---

[3]Note for smaller companies or startups with small sponsorship budgets: don't forget to ask for discounts. Most conferences are willing to negotiate on sponsorship fees, especially for first-time sponsors or new companies.

HEROKU'S CONFERENCE AND EVENT POLICY

Many companies are starting to recognize that they don't want to support conferences that don't have a Code of Conduct in place, but few have as direct and public a policy as Heroku. The Heroku platform makes it easy for developers to deliver, manage, and scale their applications from idea to URL in seconds. Developer Advocate Jonan Scheffler is a big part of making the Heroku experience as easy as possible and is dedicated to making it a comfortable and safe experience for the community as well.

"Heroku has had a Code of Conduct policy in place for our own events for many years now, and in 2010 we resolved that any events which we were going to support monetarily need to have a similar Code of Conduct. We have very specific expectations: the Code of Conduct must define unacceptable behavior such as harassment and discrimination, and it must have actionable steps as to how it will be handled if someone is in violation of the policy.

"If we do stumble across events that don't have a Code of Conduct in place, we often point them to a great template that the Ada Initiative worked on.[4] Honestly, though, while it may be a bit of confirmation bias, I don't often find conferences that I'm really excited about that *don't* have a Code of Conduct in place. Most 'can't miss' conferences for me these days seem to have their priorities straight, but that may be as a result of my looking for welcoming and inclusive conferences as well.

"These expectations reflect some of the core values at Heroku, and the policy was put in place when the company was much smaller. It's evolved as an expectation as we've grown, of course, but even now, as a part of the 12,000 person team that is Salesforce, the principle stays the same. We want to make sure that the events we're a part of, whether we're hosting or sponsoring, are a place where people can feel comfortable, safe, and included."

---

[4]http://geekfeminism.wikia.com/wiki/Conference_anti-harassment/Policy

Navigating the Maze of Meetups

Meetups are a dime a dozen these days, and choosing which ones to attend, speak at, and sponsor is one of the more difficult questions. Some that sound fantastic at face value have a terrible ratio of RSVPs to actual attendees, and others are horrible at marketing themselves but have fantastic content and a solid core group of passionate community members. You'll find some that are run like a monthly conference and others that, although not worth sponsoring, are the perfect opportunity to engage with your extended community over pizza and drinks.

Finding which meetups are worth your time is something of a trial by fire experience. Like most things community related, asking your community which meetups they frequent is a good starting place, as is looking at where the top thought leaders are speaking. If you choose to venture onto the Meetup.com website, looking for meetups that meet consistently and have a fair amount of attendees in addition to relevant talks is usually a good place to start.[5]

While it can be tempting to start your own meetup, it's likely that the better option is to foster your own community connections as a subset of another, already existent community. This is closely related to the "don't start from scratch" concept that I brought up in Chapter 6, but the nuance is key. Rather than starting your own product-specific meetup, start attending the relevant meetups in your area. Make it your goal to speak at a particular amount of local meetups for a quarter, and don't just sell your product—talk about the issues you're facing, the problems you're solving, the interesting bug you just found. Create content that's not only relevant to the audience but interesting and enticing and makes them want to know more about you as well as more about your company.

If you have the resources (people or monetary), reach out to meetups that aren't in your geographic area to see if you can provide speakers for their events or perhaps sponsor their Meetup.com membership fees. Talk to your top community members to see if they're willing to speak at meetups on your behalf, not as a sales pitch, but rather referencing how they used your product to solve an interesting problem that others might encounter.

---

[5]PJ Hagerty, founder of DevRelate and one of my cohosts on *Community Pulse*, created Meetup Land (`www.meetup.land`), which curates the top 20 meetups on Meetup.com for a particular topic.

Once you've found the reliable meetups in your area that are worthwhile to frequent, express your appreciation through monetary sponsorship, hosting the event at your offices if you have the space, helping them find speakers in your community, or simply by helping to amplify their voice through your corporate and personal social media accounts.

Again, although starting a meetup for your product can seem like a great way to build a presence in the greater developer community, I'd caution against it for a few reasons:[6]

- A meetup hosted by a company about its (usually proprietary) product is easily called out by developers as a sales tactic.

- Finding speakers for a monthly meetup whose theme is your proprietary product (unless you're a fully open source company) can be difficult. It can also drain not only company resources but any goodwill you've built up with the community.

- Even if you do have an open source product, limiting your meetup to customers and prospects limits your audience and keeps people from learning from others outside their immediate purview, which is often what people come to meetups to do.

- If there are already-established meetups talking about similar topics and bringing in a similar group of people to the one you're trying to start, you're actively detracting from the organic community efforts already happening in your audience segment.

In short, if you're looking to start a meetup that will bring your full community (potential customers, active prospects, and customers) together, you'll either want to find a broad topic that attracts a wide variety of people (for example, DevOps instead of Chef) or join up with another meetup that's already doing this. By openly supporting the community around you, you're actively building up your own brand.

---

[6]My cohosts and I explore this topic in Episode 20 of *Community Pulse*: `http://communitypulse.io/20-meetups/`

CHEF MEETUPS

If you take a look around for Chef-specific infrastructure meetups, you likely won't find them, and you might ask why. After all, Chef is an open source tool that caters to the larger DevOps crowd. Surely there would be enough people to keep a Chef-specific meetup running with attendees, sponsors, and speakers.

On the one hand, this seems like a missed opportunity. On the other hand, Nathen Harvey knows that by dipping into the already-established local DevOps meetups instead of creating new meetups, Chef gets to not only be highlighted as a sponsor but support the local community and truly be engaged with the people who are attending on a regular basis.

This way, Chef isn't responsible for finding consistent sponsors, meeting places, or speakers. On the flipside, it can step in to provide speakers either when there's a shortage or when there's an exciting announcement or a new conference talk that a local employee is working on.

It's all the best of the engagement opportunities without any of the concern from fellow attendees that Chef employees are only there to sell to them. It's a benefit to the community as well as to the local organizers, and that's a relationship that will be remembered, no matter what infrastructure product the organizers choose to use at their day job.

The Exception to the Rule

I have seen a handful of companies in San Francisco that organize and host successful meetups. They focus on broad topics such as Developer Success Engineering or Open Source Software, aiming to pull in a wide variety of attendees. By leveraging their network, they often pull in a variety of speakers for a panel or a series of short presentations. This allows them to not only represent their company alongside others in the industry but expand their marketing reach by drawing on the efforts of the other panelists involved. Embedding themselves in the community in this way can lead to broader awareness as well as an appreciation for the service they are providing.

NYLAS DEVELOPER EVENTS

From integrations with other APIs, to coproduced content or sample projects, to cohosted events, partnering up with other companies with a similar mindset is sometimes the easiest way to increase your brand awareness. The connections you make through engaging with the developer community are key to the success of these collaborative ventures.

Nylas produces email, calendar, and contacts APIs that power billions of messages across thousands of software applications. Although it doesn't have a business reason for fostering a specific community of Nylas customers, it recognizes that engaging with the developer community is important for two reasons: it helps build crucial brand awareness and encourages feedback from potential end users. As such, Tasia Potasinski, Head of Marketing, found a way to provide valuable content that would attract a developer audience: a quarterly meetup, dubbed Nylas Developer Events.

"With the help of the Nylas network, we were able to partner with other companies in the Bay Area, creating quarterly events that pulled in developers from all over San Francisco. We created panels focused on topics like Developer Success Engineering and How to Scale your API, which always featured one of our own developers as well as other panelists from companies big and small alike.

"Being able to partner with these other companies offered credibility to our brand for those who hadn't already heard of us. When we're represented side by side with panelists from companies like Slack and Twilio, it not only raises the bar of the event itself, it allows us to increase our credibility by sharing how Nylas has solved challenges that the attendees are facing. These opportunities are only possible as a result of the relationships we've built along the way. Whether it's calling up a professional contact to see if their company is willing to cohost the event or if they know someone who might be a good panelist, partnering up with our network proves to be beneficial for everyone involved.

"These events have not only increased our general brand awareness, they have also led to an increase in our hiring pipeline as well as more developers taking our API for a spin. They're often the highlight of the quarter for our employees as well, as it gives them a chance to show off some of the work that they've been doing and network with their developer colleagues."

This hearkens back to the #EmailGeeks community I mentioned in Chapter 5. There was a desire for an in-person meetup for technical folks to talk about email-related topics that dealt with more engineering-specific questions. Though the companies paying for the meetup fees and offering their office spaces for hosting the meeting might secretly be hoping for sales outcomes in addition to general brand awareness, at the end of the day, their name is getting out there because of their generosity and willingness to be a part of the community. You can't always assign ROI to an opportunity like this, which can make it difficult to sell to upper management at times, but this is a valuable long-term investment that shows the developer community that you are genuinely dedicated to them and their interests.

For those community professionals who are set on creating a meetup from scratch, there are two main components to be conscious of: finding a consistent venue and nurturing a backlog of speakers.

The venue issue can be solved fairly easily by finding a sponsor who's willing to give you a location on the same day of the week each month. Consistency is key for regular attendance as it makes it easier for planning purposes. Telling attendees that you meet on the third Thursday of the month, for instance, makes it possible for both the organizers and the attendees to predict potential conflicts.

Creating a backlog of speakers can be the most stressful part of organizing a meetup. Keep in mind that having one quality speaker per meetup is a perfectly acceptable standard to have. It's better to have a queue of people wanting to speak rather than working through the entire list in one night. If you find yourself without a speaker one month, get creative! Host a night of lightning talks—the tech industry's version of an open mic night. And make sure you have a talk or two in your back pocket in case a speaker backs out at the last minute.

Be sure that you encourage diversity in your speakers as well as in their topics. Meetups will often skew toward more intermediate to advanced topics, which is a logical progression, given that as a meetup grows, the community grows with it. However, this can cause issues for continuing to grow your meetup, as people may be hesitant to attend if the topics are always higher-level information. It also makes it harder to find speakers, because your pool of potential speakers is now limited to those who can speak to a higher-level audience. That makes it so that more junior developers don't feel like they can give a presentation, because they don't feel like they have that level of expertise. Offering lightning talks that cover more basic topics and can be complemented by the longer-form higher-level talks is a good way to get both groups involved.

FROM MEETUPS TO DEVREL AND BACK TO MEETUPS AGAIN

These days, Jason Yee is a technical evangelist and a frequent speaker at conferences all over the world, and it all started with a small Drupal meetup in Denver, Colorado.

"My introduction to the whole DevRel and community industry started when I was a developer attending the Denver/Boulder Drupal Users Group (DBUG).[7] I got involved for the same reasons that many developers do—I wanted to learn and get better at Drupal as well as get to know others in the industry. I got pulled into organizing the meetup by my friend Greg, who pushed me to give the opening comments one night when I asked him if we were going to get started sometime soon.

"I started speaking because of this meetup as well—as every meetup organizer knows, some months you simply get stuck and don't have a speaker, which means you need to be willing to get up on stage and talk about something interesting. It's 'the show must go on!' mentality—you figure out ways to get the community involved whenever possible, but sometimes there's a gap, and the responsibility falls to you to keep things going.

"The key to having speakers lined up for every month is being present. Instead of focusing on the logistics on the night of, make sure that you're actively visiting with and getting to know the attendees. Ask them what they're working on or how their most recent projects are coming along—their day job as well as side projects. Build the relationships that we as community professionals are so good at building, and then invite those people to speak at an upcoming event. It's pretty rare that someone will come up to you and volunteer the information that they're halfway through a project that might be really cool. It's all about connecting with the attendees and putting together the pieces of those stories as a result, and then telling them that it sounds like a great talk!

"One thing I learned is that you don't ask attendees if they want to talk—just tell them that you've worked them into the schedule for an event a month or two from now. It pushes them out of them comfort zone, but also lets them know that you believe they're capable of doing it! If they're truly uncomfortable with speaking, you can coach them and work with them to

---

[7]https://groups.drupal.org/colorado

create a short lightning talk instead of a full-length presentation, or have them co-present with another community member who's also familiar with the project and has a little more speaking experience.

"Lastly, diversity matters—not just in gender and background, but also in level of programming. You don't want to only have experts talking about advanced topics. Try to mix it up—as your community members level-up, ask them to reflect back and give a '5 Things I Wish I Knew Last Year' talk. As members move from novice to intermediate or intermediate to expert, they can teach those behind them. It's also inspiring for novice and intermediate attendees to see someone who's been at their level, now speaking to the group. And with some encouragement, those attendees will become your next speakers."

Speaking Engagements

Though the amount of time we all spend speaking at events may differ, part of being in Developer Relations is being in the spotlight. Whether it's just for a minute to give a quick sponsor pitch at the beginning of a meetup, a presentation to your sales team about the latest and greatest tools that your community is talking about, or a keynote in front of thousands of people, we all have to learn how to deal with the fear of public speaking.

Whether you wish you had paid more attention in your college speech class or feel fairly confident about your speaking abilities,[8] there's still a lot that goes into giving a talk at a conference, including finding the right event, researching the audience, figuring out the right topic for the right track, and then spending time to craft the best CFP you possibly can—and that's all before you know whether or not you'll be presenting that talk!

---

[8]If you're looking for good resources around public speaking, here are a few of my go-to's: Lara Hogan's book (and talk) on public speaking (http://larahogan.me/speaking/); Scott Berkun's advice on how to prep for and give a great Ignite talk, which applies to longer-form talks as well (http://scottberkun.com/2009/how-to-give-a-great-ignite-talk/); Christian Heilman's "what not to say" blogpost: https://christianheilmann.com/2016/07/06/things-not-to-say-on-stage-at-a-tech-event/

There are a fair amount of trainings and blog posts on writing a good CFP[9] so I won't spend much time here other than to remind you about something I've been talking about all along: know your audience. Although tools that allow you to take a shotgun approach to a CFP might be handy, they don't let you customize your proposal to fit a particular conference or audience. For instance, there may be any number of open source conferences out there, but some may speak to the latest developments in open source, whereas others address the community aspect, and still others talk about the processes and plans necessary to keep everything progressing in a clear and methodical manner.

Having a generic CFP that you shop around to a variety of conferences is fairly common, but make sure you research each conference, paying attention to the talks from previous years, the expected demographics of the audience for this year, and any new program tracks or topics that might be interesting focus areas.

When it comes to giving a presentation, again, make sure you've tailored your talk to your audience. Some CFPs require an outline of the talk, complete with time spent on each bullet point. I've found that when I use this tactic to build all of my talks, I not only have a stronger CFP but also a more focused talk. Outlining my main points allows me to firm up the topic and sets the tone for my slides at the same time. Another question to ask is: what's the "a-ha" moment you want someone to have during your talk? Knowing that will make your talk memorable and strengthen the focus.

Keep your slides simple. Use them to supplement your talk, adding a relevant (or goofy) image or highlighting a bullet point you're expounding on. By designing your slides with a level of simplicity, your audience can focus on your words rather than trying to read and listen at the same time. Richard Feynman explains why this is necessary in his book *What Do You Care what Other People Think?* (W. W. Norton, 2018). It boils down to this: people are capable of reading, listening, and comprehending, but not of all three at once. So, when we as speakers have a slide with a wall of text on the screen behind us, we're forcing our audience to choose whether they listen to us, read the screen, or understand the point that we're trying to make.

---

[9]I like this one in particular: `https://medium.com/devrel-life/the-art-of-the-conference-talk-proposal-3e97cd3bd33a`

As Melinda Seckington explained in her talk The Art of Slide Design at DevRelCon London 2017:

> *Your slides are not meant as notes or references for people after your talk. Your slides are meant for the audience that are there in the room with you. If you need to share something with people afterwards, use a format that actually makes sense for that . . . a blog post or a video of a talk . . . anything other than the slides that are meant for your audience. Make your audience the number one priority when you're making your slides.*

Next, don't use your time as a sales pitch unless it's a spot as a part of your sponsorship, and even then, make it interesting and informative for the audience you're speaking to. Instead of pitching your product, talk about how you solved an interesting problem or tracked down a particularly difficult bug. Walk through the technical aspects of a new feature, or how you used a different method to build out a product.

As in the corporate blog example mentioned in Chapter 3, giving technical talks that are interesting and insightful (even if they're not directly related to your product) will draw in developers who are interested in similar topics. That gives you an opportunity to build brand awareness as a company that does interesting work and employs intelligent people, which can lead to relationships and potential customers down the road.

One note for public speaking veterans: it may be tempting to whip together a talk at the last minute and not spend much time preparing for it, but attendees can often tell when that's what you've done. Even if you've spoken at dozens or perhaps hundreds of conferences, some of the attendees may have come to this conference to hear you specifically, which means your offhand comment about how you just finished your slides five minutes ago can be seen as inconsiderate. Of course, there may be occasions when you've got too many other things on your plate to put as much time into preparing for your talk as you would have liked to (it happens to all of us), but each and every speaking engagement should be treated as an honor.

Regardless of whether you're a veteran or it's your first time, crafting a coherent story is key to giving a good talk. Don't just throw slides together with bullet points and pictures—form a story arc with a beginning, middle, and end. Storylines will stick in the attendees' minds far longer than a list of tips and tricks; we are storytellers, after all.

As VM (Vicky) Brasseur says,[10] "This isn't just a presentation, it's a performance. And like any other performance, you have to know your lines; you have to know your placement; you have to know your blocking; you have to give a good performance to your audience or else they won't get good value out of it, and you will have wasted their time."

---

[10]PJ, Jason, and I interviewed VM (Vicky) Brasseur in a *Community Pulse* episode about how to submit the best CFPs and then give an awesome talk (`http://communitypulse.io/23-cfps/`). She is a phenomenal speaker, an open source legend, and an amazing human being. She is @vmbrasseur on Twitter.

CHAPTER 9

Dealing with Common Community Issues

I've now discussed how to establish your Developer Relations (DevRel) team as a valuable part of the company and chatted a bit about how to handle the day-to-day operations of the job. That should give you a good foundation for figuring out how Developer Relations will operate within your company and how to start pulling levers and telling stories. But there are a few other things you should be aware of before diving into your day-to-day role or going back to managing a Developer Relations team. These are akin to the monsters that live under the bed and grab your ankle while you're sleeping at night—they can sneak up on you when you least expect it, and it's best to always be prepared by checking under the bed before you go to sleep every night, lest they catch you off guard.

Burnout

The first of these monsters is burnout, and though *monster* might be too strong of a word for some of these issues, it's no exaggeration for this particular one. I'm not a doctor, but I do bring much of my own experience and resulting research to this particular conversation.[1]

Burnout is a prevalent phrase in tech these days, and the term can be used flippantly in casual conversation to describe everything from physical exhaustion (not getting enough sleep at night) to not having enough time in the day to finish your to-do list (having too many responsibilities at work).

---

[1] https://medium.com/@mary_grace/burnout-what-happens-when-you-take-on-too-much-ebd0be3ad1ad

M. Thengvall, *The Business Value of Developer Relations*, https://doi.org/10.1007/978-1-4842-3748-9_9

But true burnout[2] is a state of chronic stress and frustration at work that leads to physical and emotional exhaustion, feelings of cynicism and detachment, and a sense of ineffectiveness and lack of accomplishment. The problem with constant stress is that it impacts your perception of yourself as well as others. Burnout can also often increase the risk of depression or exacerbate depressive tendencies.

Although things have been getting better over the last few years, the technology industry as a whole tends to reward "hard workers" (often defined as people who are willing to get the work done regardless of how long it takes) and regard burnout as an excuse from someone who isn't capable of keeping up with the workload. There are a lot of resources about burnout in general,[3] but burnout in Developer Relations can be a much deeper and more prolonged issue.

The emotional exhaustion caused by chronic stress and frustration is only heightened by the tangible physical exhaustion caused by excessive travel and the sheer amount of time that we're required to be "on" at conferences. This combined with the number of various specialities we're often expected to maintain, the (sometimes unfair) metrics we have to deliver on, and the uncertainty around our goals and priorities can lead to a perfect breeding ground for burnout.

There's a commonly held notion[4] that most people don't last more than 18 months in these forward-facing, in-depth community building, advocacy-type roles. My hypothesis is that this has nothing to do with whether or not we love what we're doing, but that 18 months is as long as we can push ourselves at 180%, no-holds-barred, advocating for the company, community, product, and industry—basically for everyone but ourselves. That lifestyle is only sustainable for so long before it becomes soul-crushing instead of invigorating.

Most of us start out excited, passionate, and invested in this new career, but the limited resources available combined with the hardships I've covered elsewhere in the book can start to rob us of that excitement and energy. Nevertheless, we have a tendency to keep going rather than walk away. My theory is that we don't leave at the first sign of trouble because this isn't just a job to us—this is who we are. We're

---

[2]https://www.ncbi.nlm.nih.gov/pmc/articles/PMC4911781/

[3]Burnout.io has an amazing list of resources (https://burnout.io/en/latest/resources.html) as well as quotes from blog posts and talks that community members have given on the topic (https://burnout.io/en/latest/furtherReading.html).

[4]While this isn't a proven trend, it's been referenced in a number of blogposts from Developer Advocates and I've seen it ring mostly true in my own career as well as colleagues and friends.

community builders, both personally and professionally, and we feel too much loyalty to our communities to walk away. It often takes hitting rock bottom before we realize just how detrimental and debilitating the work has become.

April Wensel, founder of Compassionate Coding, makes this important distinction about the type of work that causes burnout: "What burns people out is not doing hard work, but rather feeling like their work doesn't matter."[5]

The crux of the matter is that most people know there will be basic, repetitive work that they won't enjoy. But when we're told that our time is best spent doing work that we're overqualified for rather than the work that we love and care deeply about, the message that sends is that the work we care most about isn't valuable to the company. Being told that the majority of your time is best spent on work that is far below your skill level is demoralizing, both because it's not what you enjoy doing and because it says that your manager doesn't see your true worth.

Unfortunately, this mismatch of expectations isn't all that uncommon in Developer Relations, especially if your manager doesn't understand the true value of your work or how to properly measure the value of the relationships and connections you're generating. This is where making sure that the upper management in your company is on board with your mission and goals comes into play. Having regular check-ins to make sure your immediate manager is aligned with your priorities is key, as is making sure that they're communicating the value of your work to the stakeholders throughout the company.

How to Prevent Burnout in Your Team

The number one way to prevent burnout is having clear and open communication from both management and team members. If you're a manager, you have the additional responsibility of not only taking care of yourself, but your team as well. Ultimately, it's up to each of those people to take care of themselves and be aware of what they're able to handle, but as a manager you're the one person who can make sure they aren't teetering on burnout because of the amount of work on their plate. But how do you keep an eye on these issues while not neglecting your own day-to-day work or—worse—micromanaging your team?

---

[5]https://medium.com/compassionate-coding/only-you-can-prevent-tech-burnout-be3f0504c627

Hold Bimonthly One-on-Ones with Each Member of Your Team

These meetings shouldn't be a time to check the status of day-to-day work or current projects. Rather, they should be a check-in about how your employee is feeling about their work. Questions like the following can get to the bottom of any potential issues before they become more serious and impact your employees:

- Is there too much on their plate?

- Are they in over their heads with their current tasks?

- Are there things they'd like to be working on to further their careers?

- What projects would they like to be involved in going forward?

- How do they feel about the current team structure?

- How do they feel about the company culture?

Asking these questions on a regular basis can make sure that nothing catches you off guard and can help your employees know they can express their feelings without repercussions, which leads to a more honest and open relationship.

When Mistakes Happen (and They Will), Hold Blameless Postmortems

Whole books have been written on this topic,[6] but the basic idea was expressed by John Lunney and Sue Lueder:

> *"For a postmortem to be truly blameless, it must focus on identifying the contributing causes of the incident without indicting any individual or team for bad or inappropriate behavior. A blamelessly written postmortem assumes that everyone involved in an incident had good intentions and did the right thing with the information they had. If a culture of finger pointing and shaming individuals or teams for doing the 'wrong' thing prevails, people will not bring issues to light for fear of punishment."[7]*

---

[6] *Accelerate*, by Nicole Forsgren, with Jez Humble & Gene Kim, is my go-to book for the concept of blameless postmortems, and other DevOps and Agile topics.

[7] https://landing.google.com/sre/book/chapters/postmortem-culture.html

Hold Regular Retrospectives

Even when you aren't in crisis mode, retrospectives can encourage a culture of open communication and alignment. As I touched on in Chapter 4, asking the following questions helps maintain a respectable level of trust, which empowers your team to pull levers, take risks, and try new things that might wind up being the key to the entire company's success:

- What's going well?

- What could we be doing better?

- What should we do differently going forward?

Additionally, this exercise helps you keep a pulse on what's actually happening in the day-to-day that you, as a manager, might not be aware of, so that you can help prevent burnout, additional stress, and problems that might pop up down the road.

Insist That Your Employees Take Time Off

Even as many companies turn to an "unlimited PTO" policy, more and more people are neglecting to take vacations.[8] There are many pros and cons to this type of a policy, but at the end of the day, it's the responsibility of both the individual employee and their manager to make sure they are well-rested enough to do their work. Some companies handle this by insisting that all employees take a minimum number of vacation days every year. Others require a two-week consecutive vacation.

However your company handles vacation policies and sick days, making sure you take the time you need in order to be your best self and do your best work is crucial. If you as a manager can keep track of your employees' time off and encourage them to take time off regularly, that not only allows you to empathize with their need for a vacation, it also relieves any fear or insecurity around being perceived as lazy or an underachiever. By advocating that your team take time off as necessary and actively encouraging them to do so when they haven't recently, it becomes clear to them that you prioritize their health over the day-to-day work. Managers who do this understand that if their employees don't take time off occasionally, they won't be able to contribute quality work.

---

[8]https://www.shrm.org/resourcesandtools/hr-topics/benefits/pages/unlimited-pto.aspx

Protect Them from Unnecessary Work

As a manager, you act as an umbrella for your team. It's up to you to protect them from stressors and keep them informed about the company-wide initiatives. It's also up to you to make sure they don't have too much work coming their way from other teams. Particularly at small companies and startups, it's fairly common for other employees to bypass the manager and just go straight to the employee with a request. Again, this is where your one-on-ones come in handy—they allow you to understand what work is on your employee's plate that you were unaware of and then help them push back and say no to work that doesn't line up with your goals.

It may be necessary on occasion to send out a company-wide email asking that anyone who has work for your team go through you instead of contacting your teammates directly. That allows you to distribute the workload evenly while meeting the needs of other departments. This can be valuable information as you evaluate your priorities for the next quarter and decide which issues to tackle next.

But be careful to what extreme you set these boundaries. Part of what sets Developer Relations apart is the fact that they can overlap with so many departments, and that teamwork is part of what makes your team so valuable. When you do feel the need to pull back from a particular project, make sure your work is clearly documented and leaves no question about what the next steps are or how someone else might pick up the project.

DEVELOPER RELATIONS AT GOOGLE: BALANCING SILOS VS. INFORMATION OVERLOAD

We've talked a fair amount about protecting your DevRel team from being inundated with information from other departments, or being pulled in different directions by unrelated projects. But in a company with as many products and technologies as Google has, creating a silo around your team has a completely different connotation. The IoT/Assistant DevRel team at Google focuses on Android Things and the Google Assistant, and as Developer Programs Engineer Nick Felker says, there are pros and cons to being protected from other sides of the business.

"On the one hand, I get to focus on the platforms that I care about, without getting overwhelmed by other product areas and their work. Being able to focus on what's important to me and my team is a huge win. Our manager has been great about making sure that we have the tools to be productive and keep us on track with our projects. If other product areas request our time, he's quick to step in and make sure that we're staying focused on our top priorities.

"The product focus is definitely a plus, since it helps us work on what we need to do, but at the same time, it's hard when a developer runs into a problem integrating with a particular product that isn't in my wheelhouse. I may not know who the right person is to pass them off to, because there are so many stakeholders.

"This is where good documentation and sample applications come into play—I'll find the right content and information to reference, rather than sending them off into the ether to try to connect the dots. As a result, we prioritize keeping our documentation up-to-date so that we can help the largest number of people without having to keep track of every single person on DevRel, which would be a full-time job in and of itself!"

Prioritize and Remove

In the almost inevitable circumstance where you wind up with too much work on your (or your team's) plate, there are a few questions that can help you prioritize the tasks as well as remove some from your to-do list. This section goes through these questions one by one.

What Is It That Only I Can Do?

Asking this question allows you to push back on work that either isn't a priority for the DevRel team or is something that could be picked up by another team with a little bit of time or training. By making sure that the work you're doing is something that no one else can do, you're increasing your value and narrowing the scope of your to-do list. This not only helps you in the moment, it also gives you a way to recognize work that could be delegated in the future.

Which of These Items Actively Further My Goals?

As I said in Chapter 4 with relation to Libby Boxes, it's important to make sure that you can directly trace your everyday actions and deliverables back to the overarching company goals you're trying to push forward. Another way to ask this question is: "Am I being driven by the urgent work or the important work?" The Eisenhower Method helps to divide your time into "Urgent" and "Important" boxes using the parameters of deadlines and responsibility.

Items that fall into the Important/Urgent quadrant are tasks that you should do immediately (for example, crises or deadlines). Items that are important but not urgent are given a deadline and are done by you in the future (such as planning and strategy items or personal recreation and health). Things that aren't important but are urgent are delegated to someone else (for example, meetings that are necessary but not ones you have to actively contribute to, or potential distractions like Slack or unexpected and unimportant phone calls). Finally, things that are neither important nor urgent are dropped completely (busy work).

Work that is both important and urgent will typically take precedence over the quarterly goals, but this should be an anomaly, not a regular occurence. By removing everything from your to-do list that doesn't push the team goal toward completion, you ensure that the work you're doing is important and helpful to the rest of the team, and ultimately to the company.

What Work Has to Be A+ and What Simply Has to Be Completed?

A common theme for many DevRel professionals is perfectionism borne out of a desire to be helpful, exacerbated by our people-pleasing tendencies. Tim Urban's Yearning Hierarchy[9] prioritization model comes in handy here. He uses a bookshelf as an analogy for prioritizing projects:

- *The Nonnegotiable Bowl*: This bowl sits on top of the bookshelf, protected and guarded, but also front-of-mind and visually prominent.

- *Top Shelf*: Which ones are the top priorities that I'm choosing to pursue at 110%?

- *Middle Shelf*: What projects are important to avoid completely failing at?

- *Bottom Shelf*: These are the projects that it'd be nice to work on, but only if there's time.

- *Trash Can*: What is easy to fall into but should be resisted at all costs?

---

[9]The blog post is about careers, but if you scroll about halfway through the article, you'll get to the bookshelf image I'm referring to: https://waitbutwhy.com/2018/04/picking-career.html. Or you can find just the image at https://28oa9i1t08037ue3m1l0i861-wpengine.netdna-ssl.com/wp-content/uploads/2018/04/yearning-hierarchy-2.png.

To look at it another way, the items in the Nonnegotiable Bowl and on the Top Shelf must be A+ work, whereas the Middle Shelf can be B- or C work, and the Bottom Shelf is extra credit. This is key to remember when figuring out who your stakeholders are, as discussed in Chapters 1 and 2. You don't have enough time in the day to make all your work A+ work. By prioritizing the stakeholders in the company, you're also able to prioritize the work you're being asked to do.

Your Nonnegotiable Bowl should be the tasks necessary to keep your team happy and healthy. That's it. Although work that contributes to the overall company goals is of course necessary and often urgent, if you're not taking care of your team, they won't be able to do the work. By prioritizing them, you'll give them the confidence to do good work and trust you as their manager to help them prioritize that work and protect them from being overloaded.

The Top Shelf should be the quarterly goals that have been agreed upon by you, your team, and your management. This is work that needs to be done and done well. Deadlines need to be met, and the work needs to represent the best work your team can produce. This is your time to shine!

The Middle and Bottom Shelves contain work that is being passed off to your team by stakeholders throughout the company. These shelves require prioritization in and of themselves. Which stakeholders have the biggest influence or impact on your team? Which ones, though helpful allies, don't have influence over your budget or how your team is perceived throughout the company? Tasks delegated from the former should be on the Middle Shelf—work that should be completed but doesn't necessarily have to be A+ quality. Tasks delegated by the latter go into the "if you have time" category, and those expectations need to be communicated to the stakeholder upfront.

Encourage Documentation and the Sharing of Information

Finally, just as openness and transparency are crucial to maintaining awareness of your team's well being, openly sharing information about the status of projects as well as documenting processes around community building, submitting CFPs, writing technical blogposts, creating sample applications, and so on are essential parts of preventing burnout.

Although this concept may raise concerns about being easily replaced, the opposite should be true—by documenting the work you're doing, others can see more clearly the amount of work you're doing and what an expert you are in these particular areas. In doing so, you become even more valuable to the company, while freeing yourself up to take a well-deserved vacation, because someone else can step in to handle your work while you're offline.

The *bus factor* principle comes into play here as well. I mentioned this briefly in Chapter 3 in relation to the value of a company voice/stylesheet document in case a particular employee is suddenly out of commission. Also known as a *lottery factor*, this concept dives into the consequences of losing a key expert with no notice due to a tragedy (hit by a bus) or a sudden exit (wins the lottery) from the company.

The more you can document the work your team is doing, the better you'll be able to support their need for time off following an intense week of conferences or an unexpected personal issue, and the more comfortable they'll be with asking for the time.

How to Recover from Burnout

The best answer to handling burnout is prevention, but there may come a day when you realize too late that you're already in the middle of it and need to find a way out.

Tell Your Manager

Don't wait to feel better. Don't try to be strong. Don't try to hold off until your project is complete. Do not pass Go. Do not collect $200. Go straight to your manager and be honest with them.

The sooner you let your manager know there's too much on your plate, the sooner they can help you evaluate the immediate priorities and make necessary changes. Ask for their help evaluating what is urgent versus what is important and find ways to delegate or delete the rest.

Take Time Off

As soon as possible, take time off. Whether it's a day or a week or a month, find a way to disconnect from your work email, Slack, Twitter accounts, and everything else and notify your teammates that you'll be unavailable for a set period of time. This is another place where documentation comes into play. If your current projects and everyday tasks are documented, others can step in to handle them while you take the time you need to recover.

Taking time off is important on a day-to-day basis as well. From taking a sick day instead of simply working from home while attempting to recover from an illness to scheduling vacations as discussed earlier, taking time off to recharge is integral to staying healthy in the long run, both mentally and physically.

One last note about taking days off: mental health is slowly losing its "taboo" status, but many people still view taking a "mental health day" as an evasion of responsibility or an excuse to take a day off from work when the weather is nice. Yet mental health is just as important a consideration as physical health, and should be taken just as seriously. Here's how I view it: if I'm feeling incapable of working that day, whether due to illness, migraine, or burnout, I should call in sick. By pushing myself to work regardless of my limitations, I prolong the recovery period and actively sabotage my productivity, setting myself (and potentially my team) up for failure.

Put Your Oxygen Mask On First

Given the typical frequency of travel among DevRel teams, I'm sure you all have the various safety phrases—or songs, thank you, Virgin America[10]—memorized by now. There's a line in every safety speech that instructs you to put your own oxygen mask on first before helping those around you. This isn't because airlines want children or people with disabilities to go without oxygen for longer—it's because if we aren't getting oxygen, we can't be expected to help others.

The typical Developer Relations professional is expected to be "on"—interacting with attendees at conferences or community members online—fairly often, and sometimes at back-to-back events. Putting our own oxygen mask on first is essential, whether that means setting aside time just for yourself, saying no to personal or professional obligations, or ordering room service in your pajamas after a long conference day. Otherwise, you're going to be short-selling your community and, more importantly, lining yourself up for burnout.

Learn to Take a Step Back

As community professionals, we get used to being online at all times, solving problems for our community, or up late at conferences, networking and connecting people at events. But it's not healthy to do this on a regular basis. Even though it's easy to get pulled

---

[10]https://www.youtube.com/watch?v=DtyfiPIHsIg

into answering just one more question online or engaging in just one more conversation in person, we must learn our limitations and set boundaries. There's no end to the work that we *could* do, but there is an end to the work that we need to do at that moment.

Kathryn Barrett,[11] a former colleague of mine at O'Reilly Media, used to set her instant message status as "Saving lives here!" as a reminder to herself (and the rest of us) that although our work was important and influential, nothing tragic would happen if we stepped away from our computers and took a day off. An email might be a day later than planned, or website copy might be updated slightly later than originally intended, but life would go on. In short, we can take time off, and we must if we're going to continue doing our best work and being our best selves for the community we're serving.

Limit Your Involvement

As a manager, being an umbrella for the team means protecting them from work that isn't appropriate, but there will be times when you or your team is asked to handle things that don't fall under your purview. It's important to keep in mind that just because someone else wants to pass work off to you, you aren't necessarily responsible to see that work through. Use your manager as a barrier—telling others you need to check in with them first, or that they've asked you to not take on additional work at this time.

Be cautious when accepting access to certain systems or programs. For instance, I have never had access to a support ticketing system. While I'm sure it could have been helpful on occasion to follow up with a particular community member or other, there is an entire team with the responsibility to field those issues. I would collaborate with that team on occasion when a community member asked about the status of a ticket, or provided additional information, but I made sure to set a boundary for our involvement so that we couldn't be called on to help out with support tickets. Likewise, I actively made sure I wasn't involved in sales calls, because the Sales team had technical people for exactly that purpose. I made sure to answer questions and helped field any concerns that the sales team might have regarding a particular prospect, but again, by setting that boundary, I made it clear what my involvement would (and wouldn't) be.

The Developer Relations team often has a unique skill set that can benefit many different departments, as covered in Chapter 5, but we're not responsible for fixing issues for all the other departments, no matter how helpful we'd like to be. This seems like a

---

[11]Technical writer extraordinaire and one of the earliest supporters in my career; she's @kathrynb on Twitter.

somewhat selfish viewpoint, but if we're constantly called upon to help everyone else, we're less likely to get our own work accomplished, which only serves to diminish our perceived value for the company. If we give colleagues the impression that we're the only ones who can help, we're essentially teaching them to take advantage of us, rather than allowing them to reach out to the people who can help them the most, or teaching them how to fish.

Take a Look at the Forest

When your day-to-day tasks keep you in the weeds, there may be times when you lose sight of the big picture. Taking a step back, not only from your computer but from your work, can put things in perspective and allow you to be more effective, more efficient, and more motivated to do your work on a regular basis. It can also lead to great ideas for leading and growing your community as you take the time to see the forest as well as the trees.

J. Paul Reed[12] came up with the idea of a "four-hour decompress" a few years ago, borne out of a personal business retreat that he took. He made a commitment to fight off burnout by engaging in this four-hour decompress every week, using it as a time to reflect, evaluate, and recenter his goals and ideas before tackling another work week.

In his blog post on the topic[13] he describes the process and intent behind this exercise. I've adopted this as a semi-regular practice as well. Here's what it looks like for me:

- During the first hour, I deliberately disconnect from my normal day-to-day work. I usually wrap up the last few things that are hanging over my head and then go for a run or a nice walk with my dog to get my brain disconnected from work-related tasks. My phone and computer also go on Do Not Disturb at this point—I want to make sure I'm not going to be interrupted.

- I then find a place where I can comfortably relax and spread out. Whether that's a coffee shop, the library, a picnic bench at the park, or the hotel pool or an outdoor seating area when I'm traveling, I'm looking for a place where I can settle in for a little while.

---

[12]Founder of Release Engineering Approaches. He's been a business mentor of mine since I spun up Persea Consulting and a friend for many more years than that. He is @jpaulreed on Twitter.

[13]https://medium.com/@jpaulreed/dodging-burnout-4-hours-at-a-time-965f1921e6a2

- During the second and third hours, I find something that is constructive to work on, but isn't directly related to my everyday work. Sometimes this means digging into articles about community building that I've been meaning to read or making progress on the latest business or work-related book I've picked up. Other times I might be whiteboarding the latest topic I've been thinking about—drawing connections between my day-to-day work and the big-picture observations I'm making about the industry.

- As I wind down in the fourth hour, I'll journal a little bit about what I've read or learned—sometimes publicly in the form of a blog post and sometimes in my own notebook. I'll reflect on how I'm feeling about my work, think about next steps I need to take, reprioritize my workload, or take stock of my own feelings of burnout.

Taking this time to deliberately disconnect from my "normal" work is a way for me to do a personal retrospective. What's going well? What could I be doing better? And what should I be doing differently going forward? Just as it's important for a team to explore these questions, it's important for me to ask them of myself as well. Without this big-picture view of my work, I run the risk of getting too far down the path of burnout, or too far away from my personal mission and goals without realizing it.

Whether you're a teammate or team manager, this four-hour decompress can help you see the problem areas in your community strategy, help you keep a pulse on what's happening in the Developer Relations industry, and allow you to provide insights into your own work as well as your community.

Imposter Syndrome

Imposter syndrome, similar to burnout, has become an overarching term for feeling like you're not up to the task at hand, but have to "fake it till you make it." But imposter syndrome goes one step beyond this. People start to doubt their accomplishments and have a persistent, often internalized fear of being exposed as a fraud. That can easily lead to overwork and burnout caused by an incessant need to prove themselves or measure up to those around them.

The Ada Initiative defines imposter syndrome as "a common reaction to doing publicly visible and publicly criticized work like that done in open technology and culture; it's a feeling that you haven't earned and aren't qualified for the status you or your work have and a fear of failing publicly and being discovered to be an impostor. It is very prevalent among women in the space, many of whom have been socialized to value other's opinion of their work above their own, and to do things 'by the book'."[14]

You Don't Have to Be Good at Everything

One of the biggest examples of imposter syndrome in Developer Relations is feeling as if we're imposters because we don't know enough about a particular topic. Although we're often viewed as experts in our fields, there are times when we're asked questions that we don't know the answer to, or have to give a talk on a topic we aren't completely comfortable with. We often forget that it's not only okay to say, "I don't know," but that these admissions often lead to opportunities to connect community members with other individuals, whether colleagues or other community members. As I've said throughout the book, one of the most valuable aspects of Developer Relations is the ability to listen, observe, and identify trends within the community. It's not our job to know all the answers, but to amplify the questions and get the conversation started—then sit back and take note of what happens next.

Unrealistic job descriptions are another thing that can cause imposter syndrome in DevRel. From speaking at conferences to producing regular content to maintaining a social media presence and staying up-to-date with the latest developments in the tech industry as well as your particular programming language, it's simply too much to expect of one person. In addition, in your spare time you're expected to foster relationships with your community members. While you may actually do all of these items at one time or another, it can be frustrating, confusing, and humbling to see a job description that lists all those things. The list of expectations is too much for anyone attempting to maintain a healthy work/life balance, but far too often we watch a "rock star" Developer Advocate land the role and seemingly excel.

Most recruiters are starting to understand that asking for a rock star is a misnomer,[15] but the word is still pervasive enough in the tech industry that it feels at times as if a company is asking us to fill a role that should be handled by an entire team instead of

---

[14]https://adainitiative.org/continue-our-work/impostor-syndrome-training/

[15]https://www.forbes.com/sites/lizryan/2015/06/29/im-so-over-we-need-a-rock-star/
  #3f4ddf050c1f

just one person. As discussed in Chapter 5, when you're starting to build your Developer Relations team, you need to pick and choose which initiatives to get started with and, as a result, which skills to hire for. One person can't handle every single aspect of Developer Relations that you so often see at bigger companies such as Google and Microsoft, and it's not a fair position to put your new hire in.

The Generation Gap

A common description of imposter syndrome is the feeling of not belonging in a particular profession or among particular people. One thing to keep in mind about this is that although open source community building has been around in some form or another since the mid-1970s, the nuances of the Developer Relations industry are still relatively new. Many of us stumbled into this profession in one way or another—I have a journalism and PR background; others have theater backgrounds; still others are engineers who enjoyed interacting with community members in addition to writing code. We're all still figuring this out piece by piece, brick by brick, and its fluid nature lends itself to confusion and uncertainty at times.

There isn't a "by the book" way to do Developer Relations. Even writing this book has been an exercise in research, conversations, trials, and setting up general guidelines rather than rules. Stopping to clarify statements, admitting we don't have the answers, and asking for help are all keys to being successful at our job. Additionally, as Kelsey Hightower said in an episode of *Community Pulse*,[16] part of the fun is the risk. If we aren't pursuing the unknown, Developer Relations loses some of the intrigue that sets it apart from other departments.

It's possible that there will be a generation gap in a few years, once there are additional resources and some of the basic processes have been widely adopted. There are job openings for "DevRel interns" these days, and it's becoming more common for someone to ask for mentorship when they're initially entering the field, which wasn't a possibility even in the mid-2010s, when there were fewer of us in the industry. But in the meantime, learning to take things one interaction at a time and being willing to admit we don't have all the answers will help us learn, grow, and continue to make connections both within our company and within the industry.

---

[16]http://communitypulse.io/24-imposter-syndrome

How to Fight Off Imposter Syndrome

Simply acknowledging that imposter syndrome is a "thing" is a good start that will help you move on to acknowledge other things, like what you've accomplished lately, and the fact that you actually know far more about a particular topic than you thought you did. Valerie Young, author of *The Secret Thoughts of Successful Women: Why Capable People Suffer from the Impostor Syndrome and How to Thrive in Spite of It* (Crown Business, 2011), establishes five categories that people suffering from imposter syndrome typically fall into. This section breaks them down.

The Perfectionist

Perfectionists have a tendency to set high goals for themselves (whether or not the goals are attainable). If they fail to meet the goal, they experience self-doubt and worry about not measuring up to the standards that others expect of them. Even if they achieve the goal, they often won't celebrate it, because they always feel like they could have done better. They often fight this off by overworking themselves, which can lead to burnout. This vicious cycle of perfectionism, work overload, and burnout is incredibly difficult to escape and requires a reset of priorities as well as expectations.

Celebrating achievements, whether you feel like it was your best work or not, is one way to fight off this form of imposter syndrome. Acknowledging completed projects is essential in avoiding both imposter syndrome and burnout.

Accepting B- or C work is another way to push back imposter syndrome. Give yourself grace to know that not all of your work is going to be perfect, and it doesn't all need to be! Being able to complete a project and know that it's good enough and doesn't need to be A+ quality is a liberating feeling that can help protect against burnout as well.

The Superwoman/Man

This category of imposter syndrome refers to individuals who push themselves to measure up to those around them and often work long hours as a result, volunteering for projects they know will garner respect from those around them. They tend to be addicted to the validation that comes from completing work, rather than the work itself. Although celebrating achievements is a healthy habit, actively seeking out this affirmation is a dangerous pattern to find yourself in, because when you don't receive that external praise, you feel as if your work didn't measure up.

By cultivating your own confidence in your work rather than depending on the validation of others to know that you've done well, you'll be able to recognize a healthier work/life balance and begin to appreciate the work you've completed. You may need to reset expectations with your colleagues if you're no longer taking additional work that isn't related to your goals or those of your stakeholders, which can be difficult but is worthwhile in the long run.

The Natural Genius

Some people are used to success—they got straight A's in school or grew up with the reputation of being smart. When faced with new challenges or situations where they don't immediately succeed, they have a hard time acknowledging that they don't know the answer, because it contradicts their identity as the "genius" in the room.

Moving past this category of imposter syndrome requires you to see yourself as a work in progress. Rather than beating yourself up or refusing to accept help when you lack skills in a particular area, acknowledge that there's always room for improvement and create specific, actionable steps that you can take to develop those skills over time.

The Rugged Individualist

As mentioned, admitting that you don't know everything isn't a sign of weakness, but it's often viewed as one, which can lead to imposter syndrome. Rugged individualists are people who insist on being independent and never want to admit a lack of knowledge for fear of being revealed as a phony.

There's an important balance here, because DevRel requires you to know a fair amount of information about a lot of different topics. In the realm of T-shaped skills[17] DevRel teams are often far stronger on the horizontal bar (collaboration with other areas) than they are on the vertical (depth in any one skill). In other words, you have a broad frame of reference that expands into many different topics and departments, but you don't spend enough time in any one topic area to grow into a specific vertical.

Again, admitting that you don't know something about a particular topic is not only okay, it allows you to stretch, grow, and learn more, often endearing you to those around you, rather than coming across as a know-it-all or someone who's hard to approach.

---

[17]https://en.wikipedia.org/wiki/T-shaped_skills

The Expert

This last category of imposter syndrome includes people who are viewed as experts within their company or community but who don't necessarily view themselves as experts. This is related to the rugged individualists and rock stars mentioned earlier. People who fall into this category are terrified of being exposed as inexperienced or unknowledgeable, in part because they've been told so many times that they're rock stars and examples to follow within the community, and they don't want to let everyone down.

Putting people on pedestals hurts everyone involved. It increases the expectations for the people on the pedestal and turns them into heroes, when they're no different than the people around them. But it also actively keeps them from admitting their faults and flaws, because they don't want to be "debunked."

There's no shame in asking for help when you need it. Additionally, striving to build up your skill set to keep up with the changing times is valuable professionally but can also be a form of procrastination. At some point in time, you'll need to put that knowledge into action. Getting involved in a mentoring program can be a great way to remind yourself that you are knowledgeable about particular topics. Sharing what you know not only benefits others and builds them up, it helps remind you that you not only belong in this space but can transfer valuable skills to others.

As you may notice, burnout and imposter syndrome are closely linked. When you feel like you aren't qualified, you force yourself to work harder to prove yourself. That can lead to unnecessary overwork as well as a feeling of isolation—no one else could possibly understand what you're going through, and admitting your feelings to anyone would require revealing that you're a fraud. In reality, almost everyone has felt like an imposter at one time or another, including Kate Winslett, Seth Godin, Maya Angelou, Tom Hanks, Sheryl Sandberg, and Neil Gaiman, among others.

As a manager or stakeholder in your company, you play a direct role in ensuring that your staff doesn't fall prey to imposter syndrome. Encouraging them to ask questions, explore, and admit when they're making an educated guess based on incomplete knowledge allows them to feel comfortable taking risks. Giving members of the Developer Relations team a place at the table when discussing next steps for the product road map or making changes that will directly impact the community and then listening closely to what they have to say lets them know you value their opinions. As experts in the community, their feedback should be a valuable part of the decision-making process, but all too often it's given retroactively, after the launch of a new feature or a pricing change, because they weren't involved from the beginning. Including the Developer Relations team in these conversations not only reinforces your employee's confidence in their expertise, it increases the community's trust in your product, because they know their feedback is being heard.

Battling Distrust

Being successful in Developer Relations requires a large amount of trust from the developer community. That may seem obvious, but it's not a straightforward endeavor. Although Sales, Marketing, and even Engineering can at times get away with making changes to the product road map, slightly overselling the capability of the service or being too overbearing with their outreach, developers look to the Developer Relations team to cut through the noise and deliver the truth.

Ashley McNamara, Senior Developer Advocate at Microsoft, said the following in a post about Developer Advocacy:[18]

> *To be a Developer Advocate means lending a helping hand when people need it most, or meeting someone halfway when a product is missing the mark. To be put in a position where you can facilitate this dialogue takes trust. A Developer Advocate's job is to embolden this trust by being clear, highlighting things that might have otherwise gone unnoticed, and paving roads where there are none, [which] means being a true advocate for your community. . . . Sometimes that means you may have to upset people inside your own organization, and you can't be afraid of that.*

This trust, or social capital, is hard to earn and easy to lose. Like a bank account, every good interaction you have with a developer makes a deposit into this social capital account, and every bad interaction withdraws from it. Unfortunately, as we saw in Chapter 3, it doesn't take much for a company to fall from grace in the eyes of the developer community, and bad interactions make for good stories. In short, every good interaction is a small deposit, but every bad one is a huge withdrawal. I cover this a little bit more in Chapter 10 when I talk about building your personal brand, but in short, it's incredibly important to show developers by your actions—not just your words—that you (and your team) are a resource they can trust.

---

[18]https://medium.com/@ashleymcnamara/what-is-developer-advocacy-3a92442b627c

The difficulty comes when your words are no longer backed up by your company. You can pass community feedback along to various teams, but if you don't have a seat at the table when decisions are made, you ultimately don't have control over what the final decisions are. How you handle the resulting conversations with community members can make or break both your company's reputation and your personal brand. In some cases, you'll be able to explain that even though you communicated the feedback, the company decided to go in a different direction for specific business reasons (note that you'll earn more credibility with the community member if you're able to disclose what those business reasons are). Spend that capital wisely, though. If you have to use that defense too many times, developers will begin to understand that the company's "business reasons" matter more than their customer community.

HOW TWITTER REGAINED THE TRUST OF THE DEVELOPER COMMUNITY

As Andy Piper, global head of Developer Advocacy at Twitter, says, "Credibility is hard won, and easily lost." Years ago, Twitter—an online news and social networking service—made a few changes to the API that weren't so popular with developers. They are far from the only business that has suffered from losing the trust of the developer crowd, but what happens when the changes you're making are necessary for the greater good of the user base, even if it means taking away some privileges? Andy explains how he's approached the issue:

"Over the years, the landscape has changed. The need to protect the users is greater than ever before, which means that we may not be able to let developers do things that they used to be able to do. For example, we recently announced that you can't post to multiple accounts at the same time, as people were using it to troll other users.

"In many ways, it's been the natural evolution of a product and a platform, and people are simply upset that they can't do the things that used to be available to them for free. Those are the conversations that are important to have in the open, and then marrying that with the internal aspects of it—helping your colleagues understand why it's important to be open and honest with the community and have these conversations in public in order to combat the distrust. If we just made unilateral changes and never explained why, it leaves an information vacuum.

"So we've spent the past few years on airplanes, traveling to conferences and speaking at events; we've engaged in one-on-one honest conversations with people in public forums; we strive to be humble and honest, always saying sorry when we screw up, and empathizing with our community's reactions to our choices. In addition to all of these things, we've learned that thanking our community is key, as is consistency in our messaging and in the way that we relate to them.

"While I may not have the traditional 'metrics' to show that the community is beginning to trust us again, I have some measures of success that tell me we're heading in the right direction. There are a few key people who, when I joined Twitter, had no respect or trust for the company, and are now allies. Our Twitter Developer Communities have grown all over the world, and we now have regular meetups on six continents. And our forums have an engaged set of community members as well.

"In short, by being passionate, patient, and authentic, you can engage developers and have open and honest conversations about your platforms. By expressing your desire to hear what people have to say and following through with actions, you have an opportunity to regain the trust of your community and rebuild those relationships."

Trust is also an issue when your product is open source but the only contributors are your internal engineers. How can you convince the community that you welcome their contributions if you haven't received any? Just like most of us are hesitant to visit a restaurant that doesn't have any reviews on Yelp or stay at an Airbnb that doesn't have information left by previous travelers, finding your very first contributor can sometimes be a tough sell. This is where your network comes into play. What community members do you know who might be interested in the product you're building? How can you leverage their network to bring in your initial contributors? If you start with community members who already trust you, you'll be able to build up your credibility with the rest of the pertinent community.

In reality, building up that trust takes time. Developer Relations isn't the magic bullet to ingratiating yourself to the developer community, even though that's how many companies approach it. The way to build that trust is the same way you learn about the community, form your team goals, and contribute value back to the company: first listen, observe, and identify trends within your developer segment. Get to know the key stakeholders and learn what their key problem areas are. Then, once you've invested time and energy getting to know them, start making them aware of ways that they can help give back to your product as well as to the rest of the community. It's when companies try to skip those first two steps that they run into trouble, but if we approach it from a relationship-building standpoint, it makes sense why we benefit by following these process. Convincing a community member to care about your product before getting to know them and proving that you have their best interests at heart is a near impossible feat. But if you take the time to invest in them, they're often more than willing to return the favor.

CHAPTER 10

Building Your Personal Brand

It's important to remember that as a Developer Relations (DevRel) professional, your personal brand is just as important as your company brand. There are two key things to remember about this: on the one hand, as a public face of your company, your personal views reflect on your company, but on the other hand, you can use your platform to amplify the good that your company is doing for the community.

Views Are (Not Only) My Own

Everything you do in the public setting, whether online or in person, can directly reflect on your company. Although I understand the intent behind the disclaimers people include in their Twitter profiles that say "Views are my own and not a representation of $COMPANY," these statements don't absolve you of responsibility for what you're saying when you're the public face of a company—or mean the employer can't fire you for something inappropriate you say online. At the end of the day, your opinions, thoughts, and retweets do in fact reflect on your company, because as Chapters 2 and 3 point out, you are the bridge between your company and the community. This may not seem fair, but it's the reality we live with as Developer Relations professionals, and it's something you'll need to come to terms with if you haven't already.

Some individuals handle this by having a public Twitter account they use to interact with the community and retweet company tweets or promote relevant developer content, and also maintaining a private Twitter account reserved for close friends and family members. Others reserve Facebook for close friends and family, using Twitter as their primary public-facing feed. There are many ways to approach this public-versus-private challenge, but here's my rule of thumb: if I wouldn't feel comfortable tweeting

© Mary Thengvall 2018
M. Thengvall, *The Business Value of Developer Relations*, https://doi.org/10.1007/978-1-4842-3748-9_10

something from the company account, I shouldn't tweet it from my personal account either.

That said, of course I do put a personal spin on my Twitter account. You'll often see pictures of my dog Ember and my partner Jeremy, missives about community-related issues, or my latest writing adventures.[1] But in general, I keep politics, personal issues, and community gossip off of my public-facing accounts. As you begin to build your personal brand as a part of community building (via speaking at conferences, engaging in conversations, and being a more prominent part of a particular community), you may suddenly find yourself with an unexpected platform. I'd encourage you to use that platform to promote things like diversity and inclusion, amplifying the voices of others for the betterment of the community as a whole.

Amplify the Good

There may be an occasion where you as the community manager have to diffuse a situation that may have nothing to do with your specific role, but nevertheless needs to be addressed. As you grow in your role in the community and become the "face" of your company, you are in a unique position to tackle difficult situations. Here is where being an individual versus a company mouthpiece can become a unique but rewarding challenge. You may be able to step in and diffuse a difficult situation with a community member who, though passionate, may be causing more harm than good. You can send a message directly to a developer who might be frustrated with how the company is handling an interaction (after letting your social media manager that you'll be handling this one personally). You can divert attention away from bashing competitors and bring people back together under the umbrella of solving problems for the industry.

Likewise, when faced with opportunities to amplify community members, you can put a unique spin on things and call attention to moments that deserve a little bit of extra attention. You can quote a company tweet and put a personal touch on a thank you to a community member who has really stepped up in the last few months. You can acknowledge new community members or connect core maintainers with newbies in an effort to further establish their expertise.

---

[1]For example, the Twitter moment about this book: `https://twitter.com/i/moments/` `983238008429133825`

As discussed in Chapter 3, your ability to capitalize on your personal network and bring those people into the fold of your company's community is a key way you can contribute value to company efforts simply through being a "technical cruise director." By the same token, make sure you're not only interacting with these folks on your personal account. If you don't connect them with other people at your company or other community members, those community members won't have any connection to the product or the community when you eventually leave the company.

This key here is balance. Some DevRel professionals get hired because of their "rock star" status in a particular developer community. Though that position is a valuable one to hold, you need to be careful to protect your network from coworkers who see you as an easy way to get access to that group of people, while simultaneously making sure you're still fulfilling your role at the company to be the cruise director and connect members of the community with your colleagues. This can be a difficult line to walk, particularly when your company likely wants to take advantage of the fact that you have a platform with which you can promote your work. You have to make sure you're still contributing valuable content to your community instead of blindly agreeing with whatever the company is saying.

Putting your own spin on things is key to balancing this properly. Instead of just retweeting a company tweet, quote it and explain why it's important to you and your niche of the community, why you enjoyed reading (or writing) about the topic, or your personal connection to the piece—a community member's contribution perhaps, or the behind-the-scenes point of view you can offer. By adding your own voice to the content, you not only amplify the company voice, you also lend credibility to it. Find the ways that the product has impacted your personal projects, your favorite use case, or a particular hackathon app that tickles your fancy. By having a connection to the things you're talking about with your community, whether online or in person, the elevator pitch won't seem rote—it will be personal, and your audience will see that.

There will be times when Marketing or Sales asks you for your personal list of community contacts from a particular niche, and you'll need to decide how to handle that request. There are circumstances where a warm handoff (referenced in Chapters 4 and 6) is completely appropriate here. Other times, you'll want to be the one to manage the entirety of that relationship rather than handing it off to someone else in the company. You'll largely be relying on your gut for that distinction: which of your colleagues is asking? Who are they asking for an introduction to? Does this colleague truly understand the importance of community or do they just see the dollar signs for the particular deal they're trying to close with that community member's company?

If you're confident that the introduction is a good one for both the company and the community member, move forward with a simple email, explaining who the colleague is and why they were seeking the connection. If you decide you need to handle the relationship, first do a quick gut check to make sure it's not an issue of micromanagement or imposter syndrome rearing its ugly head (see Chapter 9 for a refresher course on those). If you're still sure that it's best for you to handle the relationship (for example, the individual is an important, but sensitive, thought leader in the community, and you don't want to run any risk of ruining the relationship), schedule a meeting with the stakeholder who requested the introduction. Explain the situation with empathy and understanding, and ask how you can help. Make sure you understand the full situation as well as the desired outcome before you approach the community member, and then call in a favor with them to accomplish the task before you.

Similar to the social capital bank accounts described in Chapter 9, these bigger favors are ones that you'll want to make sure are worth your while. You have a limited number of times that you can cash in on these favors with the community before they decide you're simply a shill for the company and don't have their best interests at heart (see Chapter 7 for more on having the community front-of-mind at all times).

Foster Your Own Community

In case you aren't already convinced, let me be blunt: fostering your own community benefits both you and the company you work for. When a company hires you, they also "hire" your network, and it's part of your role to leverage that network to promote your company. Whether that means pulling in a favor to speak at a new conference that happens to be a great fit for a recent product released or lesson learned, asking your friends to beta-test a new feature, or posting a company tweet in one of your many Slack teams, strategically taking advantage of the places you frequent and the relationships you've built as a "cruise director" through the years reinforces the value you bring to the table.

As mentioned in Chapter 3, this requires you to maintain your own community connections at the same time that you're exploring new areas for your company. Make sure you're keeping up with communities from previous companies, as well as folks from conferences, programming languages, and networking events. It should be noted that *keeping up with* is a spectrum—it can mean everything from following each other on

Twitter to maintaining a loose presence in various Slack teams to occasionally attending meetups that the community frequents.

While at O'Reilly Media, I worked primarily with the DevOps and Web Performance community, which fell under our "Velocity" practice area. I also dabbled in the maker and hardware space, often helping out with Maker Faires around the country. Chef was a logical progression in the DevOps space, but I kept up with my Web Performance community as well, returning to the SFHTML5 meetup on occasion and engaging on Twitter with some of the authors and conference speakers I had gotten to know. When I moved to SparkPost, those connections were suddenly relevant in my day-to-day role as we worked on improving our client libraries for our API and frequented front-end developer conferences. The overlap between Makers and the open source world also increased, allowing me to reconnect with contacts from years past in order to get feedback on how to launch new open source projects. And DevOps made an appearance again as well, as I mentioned in a Chapter 6 case study, and I called upon a few of my closest contacts in order to pick their brains on managing their own email servers so that we could better serve that audience.

These days, my entire business is built on relationships. Contacts from years gone by are reaching out to see whether I can help their company improve their community strategy. Fellow community builders are contributing their stories and helping promote this book as well as my newsletter[2] in addition to learning and growing together in our craft. And I got reacquainted with my DevOps crowd through the promotion of and CFP for REdeploy.[3]

I've known dozens of Developer Relations professionals who have found their next gig through their network, never having applied via official channels, simply because they actively surrounded themselves with movers and shakers in their communities. By making themselves valuable to their community, they not only served the community better by making more introductions, turning community members onto new opportunities for blogging and speaking, or amplifying the voices of other individuals also providing resources for this space, they also actively proved their value back to their company.

---

[2]*DevRel Weekly* is a weekly newsletter full of relevant articles, job postings, and events that shows up in your inbox every Thursday, curated by yours truly (`https://devrelweekly.com`).

[3]REdeploy is a conference that explores the intersection of and interactions between resilient code, teams, and people. Coproduced by J. Paul Reed and me, the inaugural conference took place in August 2018 (`https://re-deploy.io`).

As I touched on in Chapter 2, by being helpful and engaging beyond the specific resources your company is providing to the community, you show the community that you have their best interests at heart. This endears you to them, which in turn lends your company credibility as well. These interactions are what stoke the fire of "I know someone who works there . . . it's a good company!" that I've referred to previously. Regardless of the community member's knowledge of your actual product, they have good associations to it based on their interactions with you and therefore (sometimes unconsciously) become an advocate not only for you, but for your employer as well.

Be Authentic

The key to these interactions and to building up relationships like the ones I referenced above, which will last far beyond this particular job, is authenticity. That may seem to be at odds with the initial assertion in this chapter that you need to be careful what you say in public spaces, but I believe there are ways to be authentically you while still representing a company.

Let Your Personality Shine

If you take the time to look at some of the technology thought leaders on Twitter, it's clear that they aren't afraid to be themselves. They talk about their animals, their hobbies, and their families, as well as what they had to eat that day, how they set a personal record at a race last weekend, where they're going on vacation, and more.

Some people have embraced gifs with a passion,[4] while others have mastered the art of bitmojis. Some are open and honest about the ins and outs of their entire day, while others tend to pick and choose the moments when they'll let you see behind the curtain. In other words, there's no "right" or "wrong" way to interact with your community online, so long as your humor is appropriate and the communication are welcome.

---

[4]Some of us have needed a teacher to perfect our gif game—shout out to Gareth Greenaway, Software Developer at Saltstack, for helping me improve mine. He's @garethg on Twitter—come for the gifs, stay for the content.

Share about topics that inspire you. Ask people for their opinions on particular matters. Tag people who you think might be interested in similar topics or who could benefit from an article. Write from the heart and be authentic in your sharing—you'll find that others will appreciate your authenticity and reciprocate with their own.

CASE STUDY: TAOS'S TIARAS

Sometimes building your own personal brand comes as a direct result of building your company brand. This was particularly true for Julie Gunderson, Community Manager at Taos, a comprehensive technology solutions provider delivering critical services to help customers modernize the delivery and management of their applications.

"At my first Southern California Linux Expo conference (SCaLE) in 2015, I wanted to do something that would set Taos apart from other companies. While brainstorming ideas, I recalled numerous conversations around diversity and inclusion at previous events I had attended, which are topics that I am passionate about as well. Out of that passion came the idea for the DevOps Princess, as well as handing out princess tiaras at SCaLE.

"Upon arriving at the conference, I ran into Jill Rouleau, who loved the idea and volunteered to drive me to purchase the tiaras. We brought 30 tiaras back, and I began talking to people about what it means to be a DevOps Princess—someone who is truly inclusive and supportive of others and strives to make the world better (regardless of their gender). Anyone can be a DevOps Princess.

"As I started to hand them out to community members, people started wearing them around the conference, and word began to spread. The real game changer came when EmberDog posted a tweet asking if he could be the DevOps Princess mascot.[5] Soon after, a handful of other community members tweeted about the tiaras,[6] and I got a phone call from my manager who was excited by the number of tweets Taos was seeing as a direct result of the handful of tiaras I had brought to the conference.

---

[5]https://twitter.com/ember_dog/status/569246196759277569
[6]See https://twitter.com/mary_grace/status/569316539989516289. Fun note: I actually still have my tiara!

"Eventually, the tiaras became a personal brand as well as a company brand. I gave a talk at Ignite Velocity about what it meant to be a DevOps Princess, Taos sponsored DevOpsDays Silicon Valley and gave each of the speakers a limited-edition tiara, and people began approaching me at other conferences asking if I had tiaras. People recognized the tiaras as Taos swag and they knew that I was the one who had started it. This gave me a greater platform to talk about my passion for diversity and inclusion in the tech industry and highlight the fact that many of the leaders at Taos are women.

"The tiaras opened doors for me, from connecting with industry thought leaders after giving talks about them at a conference, to pivoting my entire career trajectory to focus more on community building. By creating this brand, I became recognizable and stood out from the crowd. To this day, people wear their tiaras to events and excitedly show them to me.

"It takes a community to build brand awareness, and this case was no different. The success of my brand was due to SCaLE attendees being supportive, my company trusting me to take a risk, and community members tweeting about it to spread the word. This experience has shown that it's worth taking the risk to pursue an unconventional idea. You never know the impact it might have, for both your personal brand as well as your company's."

Don't Overdo It

We've talked a lot about balance between your personal brand and your company's brand in this chapter. There's one more thing that should be noted: personality is great, but be cautious about overdoing it. People want to get to know who you are outside of work, but oversharing with regard to your personal life, be it religious or political leanings, personal projects, or what you're eating for dinner every night, can have an impact on your brand, which can sometimes lead to trouble with your company.

As mentioned, your views are not only your own. As the public face of a company, you have to be even more careful to not paint your company in a bad light based on the personal information you're sharing online. Many people choose to have private Twitter accounts as a result, restricting their public account solely to work-related announcements. Others choose to use Facebook for personal announcements and relationships.

Keep in mind that there's a cost-benefit analysis that goes into every public-facing blog post, conference talk, and yes, social media post. For instance, if you've got opinions about politics (who doesn't?) and use your social media platforms to enact social change, it may limit your job opportunities, but could simultaneously gain you more respect for being outspoken and honest with your opinions.

Lastly, when something that you're involved in succeeds, let others sing your praises. Posting announcements or promoting speaking engagements is to be expected and is generally accepted, but there's a fine line between making sure people are aware of the efforts you're making and coming across as arrogant. My general rule of thumb is to post an announcement, then retweet people's responses to it as they trickle in. That way I'm actively amplifying the community's voice (especially when it's offering a different perspective than my own) but allowing others to boost my personal brand.

Practice Empathy

As you begin to interact with community members from around the world, don't forget to practice empathy. A solution that worked well for someone else might not work for the next person, and they might also be having a rough day. It stands to reason that you're going to run into people who are occasionally grumpy, or even genuinely angry, at something that you (or your company) has said or done.

Practicing empathy, listening before responding, and doing your best to fully understand the situation and where they're coming from are all key pieces to responding appropriately. Often, giving them the space to vent is all that's really necessary. If someone is passionate enough to publicly express their frustration in a way that isn't generally appropriate, that can be a good indication that something awesome is hiding underneath all that frustration. It's our job to dig in and figure out what the pain point is, and whenever possible, find a solution. Taking the time to listen and then respond in a kind, compassionate way may be exactly what you need to do to turn them from a naysayer to one of your best advocates.

Use Your Platform

As you refine the topics you're passionate about, explore new trends in the industry, and invest more heavily in particular parts of your community, your platform (whether online or in person) should begin to reflect these topics as well. But don't box yourself in. If another topic emerges that catches your interest or seems to be a problem area for your community, pursue it, engage with it, and do what you can to drive influence in that area.

For instance, in addition to community building and Developer Relations, I speak often about burnout. It's a relevant topic for community builders and developers alike and is an issue that runs rampant in the tech industry as a whole. By leveraging my network, I found an organization called Prompt,[7] which encourages conversation around mental health issues at tech conferences and meetups, and I now have opportunities to speak about burnout all over the world.

Using your platform may look similar to this: speaking at local conferences about non-technical topics that you're passionate about, offering workshop tickets to underprivileged people as Jérôme did at Docker (see Chapter 6 for his case study), or talking about and facilitating conversations around difficult topics like equal pay or sexual harassment on Twitter. The unique ways in which you choose to use your platform set you apart from others in the industry. Suddenly, you're not only a Developer Advocate at $COMPANY—you're a great resource for information on the Go community, or an advocate for open source projects, or the go-to person for articles about the latest productivity tools for engineering teams.

As Aja Hammerly said in a blog post about personal branding,[8] "we are all developing our personal brand even if we aren't doing it deliberately." We who are lucky enough to be entrenched in the Developer Relations industry must choose to do this intentionally, for the betterment of ourselves, our community, and our company. Figure out what works for you by pulling levers, listening to the community, gathering feedback, and pulling another lever—just like you test out metrics or figure out the next step on your mall map. Find the story that works well for you. Find one that is authentic and genuinely you, and that allows you to be your best self.

---

[7]http://mhprompt.org

[8]https://www.thagomizer.com/blog/2017/11/30/personal-brand.html

APPENDIX A

Trip Reports

Trip reports (referenced in Chapters 3, 4, and 8) serve as a gut check and a way to analyze how the trip was as a whole instead of just an overall "it was effective" or "it was a waste of time." The exact information you should include will depend on the goals of your company, but here are a few items that should translate well across all industries:

- Types of people in attendance

- Geographic demographics

- Types of developers (front end/back end, specific language preferences, and so on)

- Job titles (managers, individual contributors, C-suite or VPs)

- Sponsor interactions (did people spend a good amount of time in the expo hall?)

- Caliber of talks (sessions as well as keynotes)

- Overarching themes from the sessions or hallway track

- General impression of the conference

These reports encompass both qualitative analysis of a (sometimes significant) investment as well as warm handoffs (referenced in Chapters 4, 5, 6, and 8). They include information about where you've been, what events you attended, a general summary of the events and their value, a list of popular topics that came up in various conversations, and a list of important contacts you made while on the trip. This last piece is often a bulleted list of its own, naming individuals you met throughout the trip and listing the various people within the company you'll be connecting them to (Marketing, Sales, Business Development, Product, and so forth), as well as explaining why this individual is someone important to follow up with. These reasons could range from "this person

© Mary Thengvall 2018
M. Thengvall, *The Business Value of Developer Relations*, https://doi.org/10.1007/978-1-4842-3748-9

is the foremost expert on topic X" to "this individual runs an amazing meetup that we should sponsor in the future."

Trip reports make it easier to take "anecdotal" evidence and turn it into metrics:

"I've heard about this new topic from five of the thought leaders in our community in the past two weeks; we should explore that particular topic more."

Sample Trip Report

Trip: Name of Event / Trip / Occasion

Date(s)

Location

Why You Went
A quick summary of why this event and/or trip was particularly important. For example, many of my trips to the East Coast while at O'Reilly Media revolved around our preparations for our first Velocity New York. Many connections that I made while at local events turned into potential speakers, program committee members, or authors.

General Observations/Themes
Theme 1

- Why is this theme important/relevant to company initiatives?
- How is this information useful to the company as we continue to move forward toward X, Y, Z goals?
- How do these observations line up with what we're seeing elsewhere? Is it possible that this information is geographically specific?
- What follow-up questions can we ask other community members to verify this information?

Theme 2 . . .

Event Name

General attendance stats and information about the event.

Details about the schedule:

- How was the day broken up?
- What were some of the popular sessions?
- Were there tracks, and if so, what were they?

Special events:

- What seemed to go over well with the attendees?
- What additional events could we include at our future conferences/events?

Tags/Social Media

Social media intel:

- Were attendees active on Twitter, and if so, what was the hashtag?
- What were the popular topics on Twitter?

People/Companies/Projects Worth Noting

Person's name (@twitter handle), title, company:

- Description of who they are and why the interaction was important
- Name of internal person to whom you'll make an intro (if relevant)

Company name (@twitter handle), sponsor level (if applicable):

- Company tagline and brief description of what they do
- What's the next step?
  - Potential partnership?
  - Potential conference sponsorship?
  - Potential competition?
- Name of internal person to whom you'll make an intro (if relevant)

Project name (@twitter handle), tagline:

- Brief description of who created it and what it is (book? tool? community forum?)
- Why is it important/relevant for the company?
- Name of internal person to whom you'll make an intro (if relevant)

Event Scorecard

Event Scorecards (mentioned in Chapters 4 and 8) go hand-in-hand with Trip Reports. This was a tool that the DevRel team at SparkPost used to measure the success of each event that we sponsored. We found that if we only used the subjective measure of "Was it a good experience?" to judge whether or not we should sponsor the event the following year, we were likely to give a biased response based on whether or not we personally had a good experience rather than whether it was objectively a good event for the company.

Although we did have a Good Experience (y/n) column for our gut impression of the event in our Event Scorecard, there are also columns for number of partnerships formed, whether or not an employee spoke at the event, how heavy the foot traffic was at the booth, how much feedback we got (both about our competition and about SparkPost), and more. These quantifiable data points helped us balance the "Did this event go well? y/n" question that was traditionally asked at the end of every event. The data points also ensured that "number of sales opportunities" wasn't the only number used to judge the success of an event, because not all of the events that we sponsored as a DevRel team were prone to lead generation (see Chapter 8 for more on that topic).

There were a number of times when I felt that an event had gone extraordinarily well, but when we ran the numbers in the Event Scorecard, it turned out to have been only mediocre. Alternately, there were a few volunteer-run events that were incredibly difficult to handle from a logistics standpoint but wound up being really valuable from both a lead-generation and relationship-building standpoint. In both cases, running the numbers allowed us to take a step back from our emotions and evaluate the conference from an objective standpoint.

We not only recorded all the numbers, we also assigned a percentage score to each particular item, which allowed us to both keep track of the relevant items and figure out an overall score between 1–100 for each event. This helped us determine whether we'd sponsor the event the following year.

© Mary Thengvall 2018
M. Thengvall, *The Business Value of Developer Relations*, https://doi.org/10.1007/978-1-4842-3748-9

It's important to note that not all items were scored—or rather, some of them were scored at 0%. That's because for line items such as number of leads and number of attendees, the number could drastically swing the score in favor of the conference simply by being a large event. Rather, we tracked the number of leads divided by number of total attendees, which gave us a percentage of attendees scanned.

Each of the questions was scored on either a yes/no measure or a high/medium/low measure. The yes/no questions were obviously more objective, but both provided valuable information. The total possible points for each category is listed immediately under the category title, followed by the sample answer, which is followed by the resulting score.

For instance, the number of leads divided by the number of attendees is scored high/medium/low. In the sample scorecard linked at the end of this appendix, the resulting percentage is 28.22%, which means the booth staff scanned 28% of the approximate number of attendees present at the conference. I've scored that as high according to the percentages outlined in the scorecard—high is anything over 25%, medium is between 10–25%, and low is less than 10%. Your percentages may vary based on your goals or experience. Therefore, because Leads/Attendees can earn up to 8 points, and this was a high-scoring event for this parameter, it receives the full 8 points.

Likewise, for the Relationships Built metric, the scoring system is high/medium/low, but the way it's determined is more subjective. This is intentional. It may be that your team only makes two connections to follow up on while on site at the conference, but those may be with the CEO of a key company that you've been trying to reach and a local community leader who's an influencer in the specific developer audience you're pursuing. The *number* is low, but the *value* is high. Likewise, you might make 30 different connections that are worth following up on, but only 3 of those are useful in the long run, resulting in future connections or increased visibility in a particular community. The highest score that can be achieved for this metric is 15, so the appropriate scores are either 5 (low), 10 (medium), or 15 (high) total points.

You can view the sample Event Scorecard at `http://bit.ly/event-scorecard` and at `www.marythengvall.com/devrelbook`.

APPENDIX C

Hackathon One-Page Handout

As referenced in Chapter 8, having a simple one-page document to hand out to hackathon attendees is a helpful and informative way for people to engage with your API in the 24–48-hour timeframe of the event. This handout should have basic information about how to use your API, as well as common use cases. Ideally, these examples will lead to attendees coming up with innovative ways that they can integrate your API into their project.

We called it the Hackathon Handout at SparkPost. This version is from Q2 2016 and might contain information that is out of date or no longer applicable, but can serve as a basic template for how to create your own.

We also had our *Getting Started* guide[1] that allowed attendees to get up and running quickly, which is essential given the time constraints. Although it's often preferable to point people to a collection of sample apps and use cases on your website, physical printouts are helpful for attendees to pick up at hackathons as they're going from one sponsor to the next at the beginning of the weekend. Ensuring that they have a page to refer back to when they get back to their work station means there's a higher chance they'll use your API for their project.

---

[1]https://www.sparkpost.com/docs/getting-started/getting-started-sparkpost

© Mary Thengvall 2018

M. Thengvall, *The Business Value of Developer Relations*, https://doi.org/10.1007/978-1-4842-3748-9

Build Something Awesome

with Email Delivery and Analytics Made for Developers

Snapchat, Messenger, FaceTime, and Kik are all great, but **email is still the king of communication**. Email is universal, has zero barriers to adoption, and it's an open standard, no matter your users' platforms.

Whether it's automated emails to verify a password, personalized messages to your user list, or a sophisticated triggered onboarding program, SparkPost provides the tools necessary to track your users' reactions and to keep them engaged.

HERE ARE A JUST FEW WAYS YOU CAN USE SPARKPOST IN YOUR APP:

Transactional Emails

- Sign-up Form
- Password Recovery
- Notifications & Reminders
- Purchase Receipts

Inbound Relay

- Auto-Replies
- Raffle
- Voting System
- Proxying
- Double-Blind Messaging

Data and Analytics

- Email Delivery Reporting Dashboards
- Drive Engagement
- Recipient List Maintenance

What will you build?

Let us know @SparkPostDev or developers@sparkpost.com

Find more information about how to use SparkPost, as well as today's challenges, prizes, judging criteria, and more at **developers.sparkpost.com/hackathons**

Need help? Join us in our #hackathons Slack channel: **slack.sparkpost.com**

APPENDIX D

Developer Resource Card

Having a resource card specifically for developers (mentioned in Chapter 8) is key when you're sponsoring a technical conference. Like most things geared toward developers, however, it needs to be clear of marketing lingo and sales tactics. Create something that's a useful resource for developers whether they're already a customer or simply browsing. First, include a paragraph or two explaining why your product is important and relevant, and what problems you're solving for your particular developer community. Then provide a list of references that give developers access to other relevant resources available on your site. From GitHub repos to Twitter handles and links to your developer forum, this gives you an opportunity to showcase all the ways your company is providing a good experience for your developer audience.

By leaving the back of the card relatively plain you have an opportunity to personalize the card onsite, drastically lowering the chance that the attendee will simply throw the card away at the end of the conference. Circle a particular resource on the front, write your contact info on the back, or jot down an additional link or information on how they can find a certain blogpost or documentation article. By taking 30 seconds to make a note on the card, you not only show the developer that you're willing to go the extra mile to provide helpful resources, but you cement your interaction in their mind, which is essential at any conference where attendees are interacting with dozens of different sponsors.

© Mary Thengvall 2018
M. Thengvall, *The Business Value of Developer Relations*, https://doi.org/10.1007/978-1-4842-3748-9

Here are a few Developer Resource Cards I've used over the years. These cards might contain information that is out of date or no longer applicable, but can serve as a basic template as you create your own.

Chef Developer Resource Card

chef.io

learn.chef.io

docs.chef.io

Email info@chef.io

Twitter @Chef

Download Chef
downloads.chef.io

Chef Training chef.io/training

YouTube youtube.com/getchef

Community Site
learn.chef.io/community

Community Slack
community-slack.chef.io

SparkPost Developer Resource Card

SPARKP*O*ST

Email. We've Got It Down.

You know your app needs to send email, but we know your secret (email's not something you want to have to deal with), so **let us handle it for you**.

SparkPost does what you need—triggered message generation, personalization, sending, webhooks and inbound relay, and performance tracking—with none of the baggage.

Send via REST API or SMTP, integrate in the languages you love with our client libraries, and benefit from comprehensive real-time analytics. **Together, let's build something awesome**.

SparkPost Developer Hub:
developers.sparkpost.com

Community Slack Channel:
slack.sparkpost.com

Documentation and Help:
support.sparkpost.com

API Docs:
developers.sparkpost.com/api

Tools:
sparkpo.st/devtools

Client Libraries:
github.com/SparkPost

Stack Overflow:
stackoverflow.com/tags/sparkpost

Twitter:
@sparkpost

Email:
developers@sparkpost.com

RESOURCES

APPENDIX E

Sample Event Process and Playbook

Having a playbook that your team follows for each and every event (mentioned in Chapter 8) is key to showing up at a conference, meetup, or hackathon prepared for all possible circumstances. There are a lot of moving parts when it comes to events, and it's possible that not all of them will be taken care of by your team. Having a checklist of items not only keeps everyone on the same page, it also ensures that everything happens in a timely manner. These playbooks, used in combination with a collaborative to-do list,[1] allow everyone who's responsible for a piece of the event puzzle to stay up-to-date with what's finished, what needs to happen next, and who's responsible for each piece.

Like most things suggested in this book, these playbooks need to be personalized for your company. There are likely tasks that won't apply to you as well as others that are unique to your company and haven't been included here.[2]

Event Process Template

This document outlines the process for event goals, selection, and preparation.

---

[1]Asana is my go-to, though Trello, Evernote, and JIRA are all options as well. You can find other suggestions by searching for tools that follow the agile methodology.

[2]If you'd like to copy this template to create your own internal documents, feel free to copy the file: `http://bit.ly/event-process`

© Mary Thengvall 2018
M. Thengvall, *The Business Value of Developer Relations*, https://doi.org/10.1007/978-1-4842-3748-9

Event Goals

There are three types of events: conferences, hackathons, and meetups. There are overall goals as well as goals specific to each event type.[3] The goals below are suggested based on a company goal of increased brand awareness.

Overall Goals (in Order of Priority)

- Increased brand awareness in the developer and API communities

- Direct feedback on the COMPANY product

- Position COMPANY as a thought leader in the developer and API communities

- Generate new prospects for Sales to follow up with

Conferences

- Per 1,000 attendees:

  - 10 relationships built (individuals to follow up with for potential partnerships, feedback, or future warm handoffs)

  - 100 leads (business cards, badges scanned, raffle entries, and so on)

  - 10 leads passed directly to sales

- Social media:

  - Follow 40 new Twitter accounts

  - Gain 10 new followers

---

[3]The goals you set for each event will depend on your overall company goals. Are you sponsoring events to get more awareness? Your goal may be geared toward how many people watched your demo or interacted with you at the booth. Are you trying to build out a community of customers? A good metric to track might be how many sign-ups you got for your beta-testing program. See the Libby Boxes exercise included in Chapter 4 for more on how to determine the correct goals for your team.

Hackathons

- Per 1,000 attendees:

    - 5 action items with regard to content/edits

    - 3 apps/companies to follow up with afterward for potential partnerships or warm handoffs

    - 20 resumes

    - 75 leads (raffle entries)

- Social media:

    - Follow 20 new Twitter accounts

    - Gain 20 new followers

Meetups

- Per 100 attendees:

    - 2 relationships built (individuals to follow up with for potential partnerships, feedback, or future warm handoffs)

    - 20 leads (raffle entries)

- Social media:

    - Gain 2 new followers

Event Selection

Identify Event (1–2 Quarters Prior)

Aim to vet half again as many events as you'd like to sponsor each quarter. You'll want to figure out the answers to these questions to narrow down the available events:

- *Audience*: Is your audience front-end or back-end developers? Is there an overlap? Is your product a tool for the DevOps community?

- *Programming language*: What language is your API built with? Which client libraries or SDKs are your customers using the most?

- *Geographic region*: Where are you seeing the most traffic to your website? Where are most of your customers based? What new regions are you trying to break into?

- *Size of event*: Are you trying to get feedback, raise awareness, or engage with the community? Each of these goals is best met with different sizes of events.[4]

Research Event (1–2 Quarters Prior)

- Reach out to event organizers for sponsorship info

- Decide on the best sponsorship package

  - Hackathons requirements (BUDGET RANGE):[5]

    - Table at event

    - Logo on T-shirts

    - Demo/tech talk is a bonus

  - Conferences requirements (BUDGET RANGE):

    - Table at event[6] (can be negotiable, but is more difficult)

  - Meetup requirements (BUDGET RANGE):

    - Lightning talk

    - Opportunity to engage with the attendees, either before or after the meetup

---

[4]See Chapter 8 for more information.

[5]Typically, I care less about the recruiting opportunities at hackathons (students tend to give companies their resumes regardless of whether there's a recruiter there or not) and more about the demos. It's usually possible to negotiate for the requirements listed above in exchange for removing the recruiting package.

[6]This is the only requirement for a conference sponsorship to be valuable. Sponsoring events without a booth or table is more difficult because there's nowhere for you to meet up with attendees. That being said, as mentioned in Chapter 8, there are ways to meet your community members while onsite even if you don't have a booth.

Seek Event Approval (8+ Weeks Prior)

- Email STAKEHOLDERS[7]

  - Basic info about the event

    - What are the dates?

    - Where is it being held?

    - How long has it been running?

    - How many attendees do they anticipate?

  - Why are we interested in this particular event?

  - Sponsorship package info:

    - Cost

    - What the sponsorship includes

  - Number of COMPANY attendees[8]

    - *Hackathons*: 3+ technical people depending on length of hackathon (a 24-hour hackathon can usually be handled by three people rotating through; 36-hour hackathon is better with three or four if possible; 48-hour needs four or five people)

    - *Conferences*: Three or four people (for example, Developer Relations teammate, engineer, technical account manager/ solutions engineer, Business Development and/or Sales) so that people can take breaks, engage in conversations, take a look around the expo hall, attend sessions to get a pulse on the topics, and so on.

    - *Meetups*: One or two people (either two Developer Relations teammates or one Developer Relations teammate and one engineer)

---

[7]These are the individuals who will make decisions about whether or not you can sponsor this event. It might be the head of Marketing if that's where your events budget lives, or it might be the head of your department in addition to your teammates.

[8]More information about this breakdown is included in Chapter 8.

- Once approved by STAKEHOLDERS, email the organizers, confirming the sponsorship package

- Send invoice over to ACCOUNTING (EMAIL) and include the approval email from STAKEHOLDERS for reference

- Create folder in SHARED FILE SERVICE and upload invoice and contract.

- Update your internal events sponsorship spreadsheet.[9]

  - Fill in sponsorship information on the YEAR Possible Events tab

  - Copy the information over to the appropriate Quarter tab

  - Create a tab for this particular event to track expenses and contacts

    - Name the tab: EVENT (MONTH DATE(S))

    - Place the tab in chronological order within the appropriate quarter

  - Add targeted metrics

- Create a collaborative to-do list[10]

  - Name the to-do list EVENT - LOCATION (MONTH DATE(S))

- Add to your public list of events where your company will be present

---

[9]The following four steps relate to this specific template: http://bit.ly/sponsorship-spreadsheet

[10]Asana is my go-to, though Trello, Evernote, and JIRA are all options as well. You can find other suggestions by searching for tools that follow the agile methodology. The best way to create this to-do list is to have a pre-saved template that you simply copy each time. That way, you only need to change the dates and update who the responsible party is rather than build it from scratch each time.

Event Preparation

Tracking Links and Discount Codes (6–8 Weeks Prior)

- Ask TEAMMATE to create any necessary tracking links or discount codes for the event

  - Links for promotional materials specific to the event (for example, swag bag cards)

  - Discount codes or a specific link for tracking sign-ups

  - Tracking links to be used in follow-up emails to any contacts made at the event

Collateral (6-8 Weeks Prior)

- Decide on collateral

  - Booth

    - What supplies will you need at the booth (tablecloth, monitor, laptop, power strip, pop-up banners)?

  - Swag

    - What swag do you have in inventory and how much is appropriate to bring given the number of attendees? Using a "swag bucket" calculator is helpful here as it simplifies the decision-making process, providing a standard amount of swag allocated to each event depending on the number of attendees.[11]

    - Check your swag inventory to make sure there is enough swag for your event and make a public note of what you intend to use for the event either in the swag cupboard or an inventory spreadsheet.

    - Leave a note in the to-do list as well so that when it comes time to gather supplies for the event, you know what to pack.

---

[11]For a swag bucket template, see http://bit.ly/swag-buckets

- Giveaway/Prize

    - What's the best fit for this audience? An IoT device? An electronics hacking kit? An Amazon gift card?

    - Decide on the raffle prize and add the cost to the appropriate event tab in your spreadsheet.

    - Add the prize to the list of items that you'll need to ship for the event.

- Order swag if necessary

- Submit request for applicable images to Design

    - Blog post and social media

    - Conference advertisements (sometimes included in event sponsorships)

    - Booth graphics (sometimes included in event sponsorships)

    - Giveaway signage

Social

- Gather the event info so that the social media team can craft tweets around the event (6 weeks prior)

    - Hashtag for event

    - City

    - Dates

    - Level of sponsorship

    - COMPANY speakers and relevant talks (if any)

    - Schedule for expo hall

    - Raffle/giveaways

    - COMPANY attendees

- Pre-event blog post if applicable (2 weeks prior)

- Twitter

- Follow the event's Twitter account and hashtag, and retweet or reply to applicable content

- Schedule several tweets in advance of the event using the proper hashtag

  - Publicize the sponsorship and mention who will be attending

  - Call out any community members who are involved/speaking

  - Promote the conference in general

- Schedule tweets throughout the event

  - Promote the giveaway

  - Ask people to visit the booth

  - Remind people of the applicable speaking slots

Logistics

- Book travel if necessary (6 weeks prior)

- Ship booth and all swag (3 weeks prior)

  - Pull swag

  - Add shipping costs to the event tab in the Events Spreadsheet

- Create a booth schedule with shifts (2 weeks prior)

- Meet with team who is attending/working the conference to fill them in on the process and expectations (1 week prior)[12]

Communication with Community Members

- Pre-event mailing (at least 1 month prior)

  - Include information about the conference and any speaking engagements in company newsletters or relevant communications with customers prior to the event

---

[12]Send an email with all of the basic information and then have a follow-up meeting to answer any questions. The more touch-points you have, the more prepared your team will be. You can find a sample email template at http://bit.ly/booth-staff-email

- Post-event mailing (prep 2 weeks prior to event; send 1 week after event)

    - Thank people for stopping by the booth

    - Include links to any demos that were being shown at the booth

    - Include information about slides or video content available from a speaking engagement (if applicable)

    - Use tracking links to invite people to sign up for an account, join your community, or fill out a form for more information

Plan to Connect with Community Members

- Look at the sponsors and speakers lists (1 month prior)

    - Work with your Sales team to find out which of the sponsoring companies are prospects. You'll want to introduce yourself while onsite if possible. Your job isn't to sell, but by making relationships with employees at a prospect company, you have a good chance of making a warm handoff to Sales down the road.

    - Note any community members or customers that are speaking. Try to connect with those individuals while at the event and attend their talk if at all possible. Showing them support and meeting them in person deepens the community bond.

- Plan a community dinner or meetup

    - Whether you wind up paying for the whole dinner or not, it's a good opportunity to meet up with community members and spend time with them away from the event.

Event Execution

There are three types of events: conferences, hackathons, and meetups. Each event will have a playbook with a day-of event checklist.

Large Event Playbook (Hackathons and Conferences)
Arriving On Site

- The first morning of the event (or the afternoon/evening before, depending on the event schedule), meet up with the full team to reinforce objectives and talk through the plan for the conference.

    - This meeting is not optional for employees working the booth. Put it on the calendar in advance of the conference so that they can plan to attend.

    - Items to cover:

        - Do we have a talk/workshop/demo? If yes, what time and where? How many people should be there to help, and whom?

        - What swag we'll be handing out and how quickly we want to do so (T-shirts could be for Day 1 and socks for Day 2; if we're limited on stickers or other swag, make sure we portion them out, and so on).

        - Know our elevator pitch, as well as common questions we might hear.

        - Know any interesting sponsors, including any of our partners. This is especially important for hackathons—what APIs could easily be used in conjunction with COMPANY?

        - Are any of our community members speaking/attending?

        - Expectations from team members during the event:

            - Times they're expected to be at the booth. This should be communicated beforehand as well.

            - Collecting lead data, whether through business cards, lead scanners, or simply writing down contact info.

                - If we know of any specific target leads/partners/contacts who will be at the event, that will be communicated ahead of time.

- While at the booth, be focused on the community. Engage with them, make conversation, draw people in. If you need to step away to do some work or take a call, that's fine, but please don't do so at the booth.

- Dress code

- We should not have any other work responsibilities while at the event except in case of an emergency. If your manager expects you to be keeping up with other tasks while onsite, please communicate that ahead of time so it can be handled.

- Flex time

  - *For conferences*: If the expo hall is open longer than a normal workday, have employees talk to their manager about taking at least one day of flex time to recover from the event.

  - *For hackathons*: If it's not a local event where you can run shifts of different employees every two or three hours, have all employees talk to their manager about taking at least one day of flex time to recover from the event. If held on a weekend, employees should take at least one day of flex time for each day worked.

- Scope out the event space—where's the expo hall? Where's our booth located? How long does it take to get here from home/hotel? What's the registration situation like? If we're giving a talk, where is it located?

- Check in and get badges.

Setup

Technical Setup

- If you're anticipating sign-ups onsite at the event (for example, at a hackathon), be sure to whitelist the IP address so attendees will be able to sign up for accounts.

- Find your IP address[13] at the event location and take note of it for tracking purposes later.

- When the event is over, be sure to remove the IP address from your whitelist.

- Make sure we have all of the proper cables/cords/power adapters for the monitor and presenting laptop, as well as other devices if applicable (for example, iPad for scanning leads).

  - Laptop

  - Monitor power cable

  - Connector cables

  - iPad power cable (if necessary)

- Plug laptop into monitor and double-check all connections and cables to ensure everything is working.

- Find out what the wifi information is and whether there's a separate connection for sponsors.

- If we're giving a talk, find out what equipment is already in the room and what we need to bring in.

Booth Setup

- Scope out the booth area and decide where you'll display and store the swag.

- Ask about security and who will be in the room after you're finished setting up to determine whether swag should be left out or if you'll need to arrive early the next morning to lay it out instead.

- Set up any banners or pop-ups first, as these take the most space to assemble.

- Obtain lead retrieval system if necessary. Make sure you understand how to collect leads and how to retrieve the leads after the show, as well as have the appropriate charging cables.

---

[13]https://whatismyipaddress.com is a handy resource. Or simply Google "What is my IP address?"

- Organize swag in such a way that it's easily accessible throughout the day.

- Log into the laptop and open these browser tabs:

  - DEVELOPER SITE

  - GITHUB / GITLAB REPOS

  - USER INTERFACE OR DASHBOARD

  - CUSTOMER PAGE

  - PRICING PAGE

  - Any other specific links relevant to the topic of the conference (for example, specific tools that are applicable to the topics at the conference)

- Download the Chrome extensions Keep Awake (https://chrome.google.com/webstore/detail/keep-awake/bijihlabcfdnabacffofojgmehjdielb?hl=en) and Revolver - Tabs (https://chrome.google.com/webstore/detail/revolver-tabs/dlknooajieciikpedpldejhhijacnbda?hl=en). These will allow you to rotate through tabs as well as prevent the computer from falling asleep.

- If there is a place to stash packing materials or extra containers during the event, fantastic. If not, try to put it behind the booth so it's unobtrusive and out of the way.

- Once everything is set up, take a group picture in front of the booth to tweet using the conference hashtag. Take a picture of the swag as well to show people what you've brought.

- Each night, be sure to stow the laptop, giveaway prize, and badge scanner in safe places where they can't "walk away" when someone isn't looking. If there isn't an easy place to stash things that feel safe, take them back to your room at the end of the day.

During the Event

- Arrive at the booth 20–30 minutes prior to the expo hall opening to set up the laptop and put out any additional swag/giveaways.

- Make sure the laptop is plugged in and turned on, with tabs rotating and Keep Awake turned on.

- Keep swag stocked at all times (with aforementioned portioning in mind).

- Be conversational and welcoming to the community.

- Tweet about the event while on the ground—especially if you're speaking—and don't forget to use the conference hashtag. Include pictures!

- Make sure to document your conversations, both the content of an exceptional conversation as well as the contact info. If there's a lead scanner available at the conference, scan their badge before they walk away from the booth. If there isn't, ask for a business card or resume, or write their contact info down so we can send them resources after the show.

- Take breaks! Things tend to be slower during sessions, so take the time to wander the expo hall, enjoy some fresh air, get something to drink, grab a snack, attend a session, check email, and so on.

Tech Talk (Hackathons)

- Touch base with the organizers—will they be announcing each tech talk? If so, would they like us to remind them five or ten minutes before ours begins?

- Arrive at tech talk room 15 minutes prior to our scheduled time. Set up if possible, or be prepared to set up as soon as the previous speaker is done with their presentation.

- Have one or two teammates on hand to answer questions and walk around the room to observe and assist.

- Make sure you have teammates back at the booth to cover questions while you're in the tech talk. Also make sure you head back to the booth right after the talk, bringing traffic with you if at all possible.

Teardown

- Pack everything back up into as few boxes as possible. Disassemble the booth/banner and carefully pack it back up.

- If you've been provided with a return shipping label, carefully place this on the box(es), making sure to cover up/remove any previous labels with barcodes.

- Check with the sponsor coordinator to see if they'll be shipping things out from the site, or if we can leave it with the convention center. If not, call UPS (or appropriate carrier) to arrange a pickup at your location.

Meetup Playbook

Pre-Event

Slides, Advertisements, and Collateral

- If you have a short intro at the beginning of the meetup, pull together a handful of fun, image-heavy slides that tell attendees briefly who you are, why you're there, and why you chose to sponsor this particular meetup.

- Whenever possible, host a raffle or giveaway, or hand out discount codes or tracking links in order to gather attendee information.

Arriving Onsite

- Arrive 15–20 minutes early to set up a banner, spread out stickers and resource cards, meet the organizers, and so on.

- If any coworkers are attending, have them arrive early as well to get oriented and to go over any goals and expectations from the meetup.

During the Event

- Once everything is set up, take a picture to tweet using the conference hashtag. Take a picture of the swag as well to show people what we've brought.

- Be conversational and welcoming.

- Tweet about the event while on the ground—especially if we're speaking—and don't forget to use the hashtag or tag the meetup account. Include pictures!

- Make sure to document your conversations—both the content of an exceptional conversation as well as the contact info. Be sure to ask for a business card, or at least their email address. Jot down a few notes after your conversation so you don't forget what you were talking about.

Teardown and Aftermath

- Disassemble the banner and carefully repack it.

- Follow up with intros and/or direct emails to the folks you met at the meetup to make sure those connections stay fresh.

- Go through the Twitter stream from the meetup—the meetup Twitter account, the event hashtag, and the meetup organizers—and follow people talking about the meetup. Take part in relevant conversations and post any pictures that didn't make it up during the event.

Event Follow-up

- Blog post (if applicable) (1 week after)
  - Recap any lessons learned, discuss talks given by teammates or community members, and highlight particularly great things that happened at the event.

- Retrospective with team (1 week after)

  - What went well?

  - What could have gone better?

  - What were our expected versus actual measures?

  - Would we do the event again?

- Using the information from the retrospective, fill in the Event Scorecard (Appendix B).

- Turn in any leads to Marketing and Sales.

- Update the Events spreadsheet with final cost of event as well as number of leads. If you know of accounts created onsite (from hackathons), also fill in number of accounts.

- Send follow-up email to people you met at the event.

- Update the website and remove the event.

- Remove the IP address from your whitelist.

- Share photos taken at the event internally.

Index

A

Algolia, 50
Ambassador program, 130
Anecdotes *vs.* facts, 56–58
The Art of Community, 110
Avocados, 44–45, 63
Awareness Acquisition Activation
      Retention Revenue Referral
      Product (AAARRRP), 62

B

Battling distrust, 186–191
Benevolent dictator, 113
Blameless postmortems, 172
Brand awareness, 148
Burnout
    balancing silos *vs.* information
      overload, Google, 174–175
    chronic stress and frustration, 170
    Compassionate Coding, 171
    emotional exhaustion, 170
    employees take time off, 173
    physical exhaustion, 169
    prioritization of work, 176–177
      encourage documentation and
        information sharing, 177–178
      goals, 175
      stakeholders, 177
      to-do list, 175

recover
    four-hour decompress, 181–182
    involvement, 180–181
    online conversation, 180
    oxygen mask, 179
    take time off, 178
    talk to manager, 178
relationships and connections, 171
retrospectives, 173
unnecessary work, 174
Bus factor principle, 178

C

Changelog, 127, 139
Chef software
    fostering, 115–117
    meetups, 161
    open source community, 115–117
    Supermarket, 128
Chop wood and carry water (proverb),
    111–112
CMX Hub, 123–124
CodeNewbies community, 118
Code of Conduct policy, 9, 80, 115,
    125–126, 130, 140, 158
Community
    builder, 80
    collaboration, 129
    creating from scratch, 107–109

© Mary Thengvall 2018
M. Thengvall, *The Business Value of Developer Relations*, https://doi.org/10.1007/978-1-4842-3748-9

Printed in the United States
By Bookmasters